(Continued on Page 366)

Smart Advice with a Smile
The Murphy's Laws Computer Book Series

Let's face it. Most computer books just don't feature the "can't put it down" excitement of an Ian Fleming spy novel or the heart-palpitating romance of Danielle Steele. But they don't have to put you to sleep, either. **The Murphy's Laws Computer Book Series** gives you the answers you need and keeps you entertained at the same time.

Written with wit and filled with useful information, **The Murphy's Laws Computer Book Series** *helps everyone*, even the most reluctant computer users, get the best of their computer and computing. In the series, there are books on word processing, spreadsheets, PCs, and operating systems—and even more books are planned. Every book in the series promises to give you the information you need on the software you use without boring you into oblivion.

Always smart, never stuffy. Every computer user will want to use **The Murphy's Laws Computer Book Series** whenever there are questions about the computer.

Look for **The Murphy's Laws Computer Book Series** at your favorite bookstore.

For a complete catalog of our publications:

SYBEX Inc.
2021 Challenger Drive, Alameda, CA 94501
Tel: (510) 523-8233/(800) 227-2346 Telex: 336311
Fax: (510) 523-2373

 SYBEX is committed to using natural resources wisely to preserve and improve our environment. As a leader in the computer book publishing industry, we are aware that over 40% of America's solid waste is paper. This is why we have been printing the text of books like this one on recycled paper since 1982.

This year our use of recycled paper will result in the saving of more than 15,300 trees. We will lower air pollution effluents by 54,000 pounds, save 6,300,000 gallons of water, and reduce landfill by 2,700 cubic yards.

In choosing a SYBEX book you are not only making a choice for the best in skills and information, you are also choosing to enhance the quality of life for all of us.

Murphy's Laws of Word for Windows

Murphy's Laws of

WORD
for Windows™

Christian Crumlish

SYBEX®   San Francisco   Paris   Düsseldorf   Soest

Acquisitions Editor: David Clark
Developmental Editor: Sharon Crawford
Editor: Guy Hart-Davis
Technical Editor: Maurie A. Duggan
Production Editor: Carolina Montilla
Book Designer: Claudia Smelser
Production Artist: Suzanne Albertson
Screen Graphics: Cuong Le
Typesetter: Ann Dunn
Proofreaders/Production Assistants: David Silva, Elisabeth Dahl
Indexer: Matthew Spence
Cover Designer: Ingalls + Associates
Illustrator: Robert Kopecky
Screen reproductions produced with Collage Plus.
Collage Plus is a trademark of Inner Media Inc.
SYBEX is a registered trademark of SYBEX Inc.

To S.B.N.

Acknowledgments

I'D LIKE TO thank R.S. Langer, Dianne King, and Barbara Gordon for their support. David Clark, acquisitions editor, never fails to help me out with advice or answers to my questions. To Sharon Crawford, my developmental editor, goes credit for the Murphy's Laws concept and blame if the idea flops. Her no-nonsense advice and encouragement have helped to make this book better. Guy Hart-Davis, the Text Butcher (aka my editor), has held me to high standards and contributed not inconsiderably to the humor and tone of this book. If you detect a rather sort of British ring to some of my remarks, you can chalk those ones up to him.

My technical editor, Maurie Duggan, has kept me honest, correcting my errors and the hidden assumptions that, unexposed, could leave readers frustrated and confused. I am grateful to Claudia Smelser, whose light, engaging design meshes perfectly with this book's editorial approach, and Robert Kopecky, whose illustrations capture exactly how I'm sure most of us feel sitting in front of a computer. My thanks also to a crack production team—Carolina Montilla, the production editor, Suzanne Albertson, the artist, Ann Dunn, the typesetter, and David Silva and Elisabeth Dahl, the proofreaders. Lastly, I'd like to thank Matthew Spence, whose index helps make this book so easy to use.

Thanks to all the people who have suggested laws or volunteered mishaps and screw-ups they've encountered.

My leap into full-time writing, in the middle of the worst economy here in California since the Depression, has been made easier and less intimidating by the outpouring of support and encouragement from my friends and family. I'd also like to thank James Brady for his kind words about my first SYBEX book. And I'd like to thank my agent, Bill Gladstone.

Hanging in there all along through the ups and downs, the peaks and crashes, has been Briggs, my friend, my partner, my business advisor, my favorite writer.

Contents at a Glance

Table of Contents

Part 2 Take a Look at the Big Picture

Part 3   **Be a Professional, or Just Look Like One**

9 ☞ **THE WONDERFUL WORLD OF DESKTOP PUBLISHING   135**

Part 4 Adapt Word to Your Workplace

16 ☞ CUSTOMIZE WORD TO SUIT YOUR NEEDS   265

17 ☞ PRINTING PROBLEMS AND SOLUTIONS   281

Introduction

Murphy's Law: Anything that can go wrong, will go wrong

NO, MURPHY'S LAW was not invented for the computer, but it might as well have been. Computers—these supposedly labor-saving devices that have spread like mushrooms from offices to schools and now even into homes—make you pay for any gains in productivity or efficiency with headaches, frustration, and grief. Has anyone ever tried to convince you that computers would make your life easier? Did you smack them? Why not?

If you have to use a computer, you know that half the time they cause more trouble than they're worth. Word for Windows can do all kinds of things a typewriter can't do, but typewriters never make two hours of your work vanish from the face of the earth forever.

Who Are You?

You're a regular person. You sometimes have to use a computer, like it or not, but you're not looking for a degree in computer science. The computer is a tool for you, or a nuisance, but not a way of life. You don't think like a geek, and you like your explanations in plain English, without a lot of double-talk or padding.

What's the Big Idea?

Most computer books and manuals, like the documentation that comes with your software, tell you how things are supposed to work, what happens when things go right. Not this one. I know that things go wrong twice as often as they go right, so this book tells you what can go wrong, and how to make things work right.

I assume you don't want to learn any electrical engineering or programming before you can print out a memo (which is just as well, because I'm a writer, not an electrical engineer or a programmer). So this book just answers your questions, solves your problems, and then gets out of your face so you can get on with your life.

I'll explain things in context, with practical examples and some tips and advice thrown in. I'll point out shortcuts and always tell you the quickest and easiest way to get results. When something about the program is lame, I'll tell you it straight out so you don't get suckered into wasting your time.

What's not in this book? Boring long passages you can't avoid reading, condescending explanations that make you feel dumb, examples you have to type in, and things you don't need to know.

Have It Your Way

I know that if you've got time to read a book through, you're going to read something fun, not a computer book. So this book is set up to be used as a reference. Topics are self-contained, so you don't have to look all over the book for a crucial piece of an explanation and you don't have to go back and read the entire chapter up to the point you're interested in. The table of contents, the Mega-Index™, and even the inside covers should help you find your way into the book. Then just read what you need.

The book has 20 chapters and they're grouped together into six parts. (But don't take the parts too seriously. They're really just an excuse for cartoons.) Here's a blow-by-blow account.

Part I: All You Really Need to Know about Word for Windows

If all you want to do is scratch the surface, here are the bare necessities of Word. This part will tell you how to do all the normal things you'll be doing all the time, and none of the weird things you might never do. Even Chapter 1 will take you a long way.

Part II: Take a Look at the Big Picture

How to plan and organize your documents.

Part III: Be a Professional, or Just Look Like One

You paid for this program (or someone did). Take advantage of it to make your documents shine like professional publications.

Part IV: Adapt Word to Your Workplace

If you use Word on the job, or at school, here are some special things you may need to know.

Part V: Show Your Computer Who's Boss (Your Computer Is)

This machine's supposed to be so smart. Make it work for you.

Part VI: In Case of Emergency, Break Glass

If something can go wrong, it will go wrong. If something does go wrong, read Chapter 20, *Disaster Recovery*.

Those Little Guys in the Margin

You'll see little pictures in the margin to identify different types of notes and explanations. These are to help you read only what you need. The icons (that's computerese for "pictures") I use in this book are as follows:

 This guy alerts you when I want to give you some advice, tell you a shortcut, or plug another part of the book that you might find relevant.

 This guy will warn you to take it easy and proceed with caution when there's something you could do to screw yourself up if you're not careful.

 This guy will warn you when there's something you could do easily that you'll really regret and that it might not be so easy to recover from.

 This guy will alert you when I'm going to explain something technical that you don't really need to know. Read these notes only if you wonder why something works the way it does or has the name it has.

These Boxes Contain Information That Might Come in Handy but Is Usually Just Technobabble

I'll use the icons above to let you know what kind of information is in the box. Sometimes it will be something interesting or something you'll want to know, but most of the time you can skip right past it if you're not interested.

What the 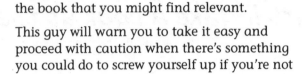, Boldface, and Italics Mean

I'll use ⟫→ to indicate a menu name and menu choice, so File ⟫→ Save means select the Save command on the File menu. Generally, words in **boldface** are for you to type in, and words in *italics* are terms you may be unfamiliar with or text to look for on the screens.

You Know What Happens When You Assume?

I assume you know a little about Windows and how to operate Windows programs. Mainly, that means you should understand how to click, drag, and double-click with your mouse (you do have a mouse, don't you?), how to select a command off a menu, and how to make selections in a dialog box and click OK.

I'm also going to assume that you already have Word installed on your machine. If not, try asking someone to install it for you. Actually, it's not very difficult even if you have to do it yourself. Basically, you run Windows, put the first disk in drive A, select File ➼ Run in the Program Manager, and type:

```
a:setup
```

and click OK. Then follow the instructions and accept all of the Setup program's suggestions unless you have a good reason not to. If it gets any hairier than that, ask someone who knows your computer to take you through the installation.

Keep Me Honest

I can't write a book about Murphy's Laws of Word without realizing that, inevitably, things will go wrong. If you find anything incorrect or misleading in this book, write to me:

Christian Crumlish
c/o SYBEX Inc.
2021 Challenger Drive
Alameda, CA 94501

I'll fix whatever's wrong in the next edition of this book and even thank you in the acknowledgments.

So What Are You Waiting For?

Time's a-wasting. Jump on in.

PART 1

Partridge's Law: No feature added to your program in the last two years is worth learning

This part covers the bare essentials of Word. First, we'll go over the everyday jobs of writing, saving, and printing. Then you'll see how to move around your document. Next, you'll find out how to fix your mistakes and revise your documents and how to get Word to check your spelling. Then we'll cover how you can spruce your documents up and make them more presentable. Finally, I'll show you how to make the Word screen a comfortable environment to work with.

All You Really Need to Know about Word for Windows

Chapter 1

ALL YOU REALLY REALLY NEED TO KNOW ABOUT WORD FOR WINDOWS

Najarian's Rule of Percentages: 90% of people use 10% of a program 90% of the time

SKIP THIS CHAPTER if you want. After all, it's just the basics. If you already know your way around Word, you probably won't learn much new here. On the other hand, it might not hurt you to review what you probably already know. Look, at least skim it! Sorry. It's okay. I don't take it personally.

What Have We Here?

Let's start by making sure we're both looking at (and talking about) the same thing. Take a quick inventory. You should have an IBM-type PC (as opposed to a Mac) that consists of the following parts:

- ☞ a keyboard

- ☞ a screen

- ☞ a box, with one or more disk drives outside, and a hard disk and more inside

- ☞ a mouse—if you don't have one, put down the book and go get one—Word for Windows is a real pain without a mouse

Synonyms for the Wonkily Inclined

The box is sometimes called a *CPU* because it contains a CPU, or Central Processing Unit—sounds official, doesn't it? You could consider the CPU the actual computer and everything else "peripheral" devices. The screen may be referred to as a *monitor*, as it allows you to monitor what you and the computer are saying to one another.

You should also have Windows and Word for Windows installed on your machine. All set? Good.

Turn On, Tune In, Drop By

If your computer is on and the screen is showing something (anything), then you can skip ahead. If the computer's off (no lights on anywhere, no humming, no high-pitched whine—well, maybe a high-pitched whine if you've got kids), then turn it on! There should be an on-off switch on the box. It might be marked 1 and 0 (that's binary-computer-nerd-talk for "on" and "off").

Make sure there are no disks in any disk drives before you turn the computer on. (It's all right if they're hanging out of the drives, as long as they're not pushed all the way in with the little "door" or latch closed.)

If the screen is blank even after you've turned on the computer, you'll probably have to turn on the screen as well. It may have a switch across the bottom front or conveniently located in the back where you can barely reach it. If the screen is on and still blank, press any key on the keyboard. If that does nothing, your screen is broken. No, really, play with brightness and contrast knobs. Still nothing? It's broken.

Enough with the Preliminaries!

To start Word, type

    WIN WINWORD

at the DOS prompt and press the Enter key.

What's the DOS Prompt? For That Matter, What's DOS? (Believe Me, It's Boring)

And sort of a waste of time, because once you start Windows, you can forget all about DOS. DOS (pronounced *doss*) is what's running on your machine when nothing else is running. DOS stands for Disk Operating System. Without it, your computer would never know you exist.

The DOS prompt is a sign on the screen that DOS is ready for you to tell it something. Here are some possible DOS prompts:

    C:>
    A:>
    C:\>
    C:\
    >
    C:\MUSIC\WESTERN\FOLK\INSTRMTL\PERFORMR\DULCIMER\>

It doesn't really matter what it says if you're about to run Windows programs. Now forget about all this. Just type what I told you to.

Then go get some coffee or something, because it usually takes Windows and Word a few minutes to get their act together. Now skip ahead to *What Are You Looking At?* unless there's a problem.

If WIN WINWORD Doesn't WinWork for You

Then start off with just Windows. Type WIN at the DOS prompt and press Enter. If Windows starts running automatically when you turn on your machine, you can also continue from here.

Icon, Icon, Who's Got the Icon?

Pull down the Window menu in the Program Manager and look for the Word for Windows group. If it's there, select it. If it's not, select Windows Applications or just plain Applications. The Word icon should be in one of these groups. It's this one:

When you've located the Word for Windows icon, double-click it and Word will begin. Time to warm up that cup of coffee.

What Are You Looking At?

Your screen should look like Figure 1.1. I'm pointing out some of the things you'll be using, but don't worry about the names of screen doohickeys or exactly what everything does. At least, don't start worrying until you have to do something with them.

Word will tend to look the same as it did the last time it was run. So if the previous user removed elements from the screen or ran Word in a window instead of full screen, what you see will differ from what I'm showing here. That's fine, so stay cool.

FIGURE 1.1:
You should be looking at a screen something like this, but don't panic if you're not. Read on.

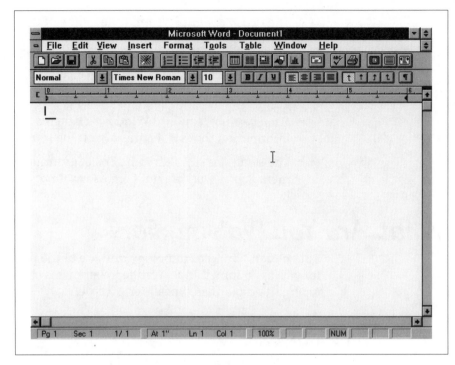

Word for Windows tries to give you as much space to type in as possible, but it's hemmed in a bit on three sides by the graphical elements pointed out above. You judge how useful they are.

☞ The *title bar* is a standard Windows feature that gives the name of the program and/or the document you're working on.

☞ The *menu bar* is another familiar Windows feature. It allows you to choose commands off menus.

☞ The *Toolbar* is a set of "buttons" you can click as shortcuts to Word commands. Not all Word commands are available on the Toolbar.

☞ The *chocolate bar* is a feature that's unavailable so far (it still has a few bugs in it).

☞ The *ribbon* contains shortcuts for some of the most common text formatting commands. Because typewriters had ribbons, it's called a ribbon, even though that makes no sense at all.

☞ The *ruler* is used mainly for page formatting. It's called a ruler because it looks like a ruler, what with the inch marks and all.

☞ *Scroll bars* are standard Windows elements that allow you to get to information that's not currently on the screen.

☞ The *status line* supplies some basic information about the document you're working on, such as what page you're on.

What Are You Waiting For?

But enough boring terminology and use of the passive voice. It's time for you to do something! Word for Windows is a tool for writing, for typing. It's a glorified typewriter. So type!

Don't look back

There are only two things in the typing area of the screen before you start typing, a vertical line and a horizontal line. (Okay, and maybe the mouse pointer too. Don't be smart.) The vertical line is the *insertion point*. It shows where the next thing you type is going to appear. The other line marks the end of your document. Both of them move along as you type.

To correct as you type, use the Backspace key—the leftward-pointing arrow above the Enter key. Pressing it once erases the character to the left of the insertion point.

Let Word handle line breaks

When you get near the end of a line, don't hit Enter as you would with a typewriter. Just keep typing. The words will "wrap" to the next line. Only use Enter for starting a new paragraph (or for forcing a new line).

The overrated Tab key

When you press Tab, a tab "character" is inserted, just like any other character. It looks like several spaces, but it's just one character. If you backspace over it or delete it, it will be eaten in one gulp, not five or eight or whatever bites.

How to insert characters that ain't on the keyboard

If you want to use a character or symbol that does not appear on the keyboard, such as ™ or ¥, pull down the Insert menu and select Symbol. You'll see a dialog box like the one shown in Figure 1.2.

FIGURE 1.2:

The Symbol dialog box. Here's where you find all the weird characters your keyboard doesn't have.

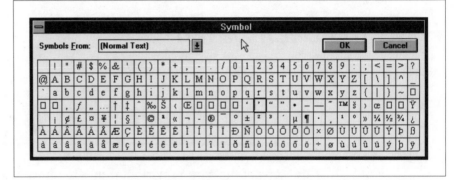

If you click on a character and hold down the mouse button, you'll see it magnified. If it's the one you want, leave it highlighted and click OK. You can also just double-click any character. If you don't see what you want, click the down arrow next to the Symbols From box, and choose a different set of symbols to look at. If you can't find anything you like, click Cancel. You can't always get what you want, you know.

I know it's "the first day of the rest of my life," but what's today's DATE?

If you don't know today's date but you trust your computer's internal clock, pull down the Insert menu and select Date and Time. A little dialog box will appear and offer you many choices of date or time formats. Click on the format you like and then click OK. The date (or time, if you insist) will go into the document at the insertion point.

Some Useful Technobabble about Dates, Field Codes, and Unlinking

If you insert a date rather than type it, it exists as something Word calls a *field code*. Don't worry about that too much. It means the date will be updated when you print your document. You can update an old date yourself by putting the insertion point anywhere in the date and pressing F9, the Update Field key. If you don't want the date to change after you first insert it, put the insertion point on the date and press Ctrl-Shift-F9, the Unlink Field key.

Have You Been Saved?

Save your work regularly! I'll say that again:

This is one of the most important things to remember about computers. If you don't learn to do this from me telling you, you're sure to learn the hard way. You'll be up late at night finishing the report that means your whole future and there will be a brownout and you won't have saved for the last four hours and all your work will be down the drain and you'll lose your job and end up penniless on a park bench. Mark my words.

Read This for Disaster Insurance or I'll Say I Told You So

You can have the computer make a secret copy of your document and up-date it regularly. Then when disaster strikes, you just run Word again and it will automatically bring the last update of the secret copy back to life. To set up Autosave (that's what it's called), pull down the Tools menu and select Options. Choose Save from the Category box at the left. Then check off Automatic Save Every, change the number of minutes between saves, if you want, and then click OK. Warning: This does not substitute for regular saving. It will only help you if Word ends abruptly. If you quit Word the nor-mal way, the autosave copy of your document is erased. So I repeat: Save Your Work Regularly!

If worst comes to worst, read Chapter 20, *Disaster Recovery.*

The first time you save, you'll have to give your document a name, and if you're smart, you'll make note of where you're saving it, so you can find it again in the future.

The First Time You Save

To save a document, click the Save button on the Toolbar (the one with a little picture of a disk on it, third from the left). This one here:

The Save button is a shortcut for the Save command on the File menu. From the keyboard, hit Shift-F12.

If this is the first time you're saving this particular file, you'll get a dialog box with Save As at the top.

Type a name for your file, eight letters or fewer. Word will add a .doc extension to it unless you type an extension of your own, but don't try to be cute. Your file will be easier to find later if it ends in .doc like all other Word documents, because .doc files are the ones Word shows unless you tell it different.

Then a box with Summary Info at the top will appear with your name (or the name of the legitimate owner of the program) in the Author box. You can just click OK, or put information in this box and then click OK.

If you find the Summary Info box a waste of time, as I do, you can prevent it from showing up. Select Tools ➥ Options, and then in the box that appears, click Save in the Category box at the left side (or press S). Then uncheck Prompt for Summary Info and click OK.

Save the file in a different directory

Just under Directories: in the dialog box is the directory your document will be saved in if you change nothing. In Figure 1.3, it's the main *Winword*

FIGURE 1.3:
The Save As dialog box. This controls where Word hides your precious documents, so pay attention.

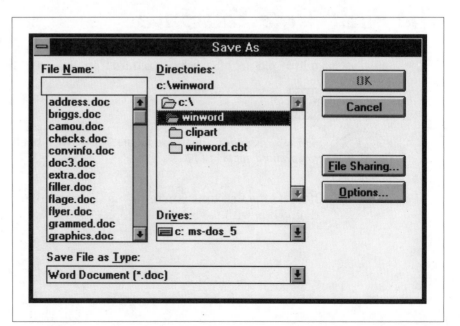

directory on the C:\ drive. If you want to save the document some-where else, click on a different directory name in the list box below. If the directory you want does not appear, you're going to have to find your way around the directory tree. (Just click any directory in the list box to see its subdirectories.)

If you put your doc in a special directory, make a point of remembering it's there or you'll have trouble finding it later.

Save the file on a different drive

To change the drive you're saving your document on, click the box under Drives: and then choose a new drive from the list that appears. I'll explain more on this a little further up ahead, under *Make a copy on a disk.*

Change nothing

If you change nothing, your document will be saved in the same direc-tory Word itself is in. This is okay, but eventually you'll be better off set-ting up a special directory for documents to keep them separate from other kinds of files. (You can do this in Windows or DOS.)

Make a Copy of Your Document

To save a document with a new name or in a new location after the first time you've saved it, you have to choose Save As on the File menu.

Make a copy to avoid retyping

If you want to reuse something you've already written, or make changes to a copy of a document without destroying the original, just select File ➻ Save As and then type a new file name and click OK. Then go ahead and make any changes you want. The original file will still be around *and* you'll have a fresh new copy to mangle any way you like.

Make a copy on a disk

You can save a document to a disk by specifying the A or B drive in the Save As dialog box. Make sure there is a disk in the drive first or Word won't let you select the drive. Why would you want to save a document to a disk? In case your computer blows up, for one thing, or so you can carry your document to someone else's computer.

What's the Difference between a Disk, a Diskette, a Floppy Disk, a Hard Disk, a Disk Drive, a Hard Drive, and Software?

These words proliferate just to annoy you. When I mention a *disk*, I'm talking about either of two types of removable, squarish disk that you can put into a slot in your computer. One type is bendable (floppy), but DON'T bend it! The other type is made of hard plastic. These types of disks are also sometimes called *floppy disks* or *diskettes*.

One problem is that the *hard disk* inside your computer can also just be called a disk. If there's ever any possibility of confusion, I'll make it perfectly clear what type of disk I mean.

Diskette comes from the fact that all removable disks are now smaller than the original type (which was 8" to a side). They were also called *floppies* or floppy disks in contrast to the hard disks, which are rigid. Those words are obsolete now, with the rise of the hard, plastic Macintosh-type disk.

The slot you put a disk in is called a *disk drive,* or just *drive.* The hard disk has a disk drive also, the *hard disk drive,* or more usually, just the *hard drive.* So why so much use of the words hard and soft? You have to keep in mind that, traditionally, programmers have been geeky males. But the distinction has come to mean unchangeable versus changeable. *Hardware* is the equipment you get. It's fixed. *Software* is the program (such as Word) that you run on your equipment. It can be changed. All clear now?

Scary Error Messages Are Sometimes Exaggerated

Say you save your document to a disk in the A drive. Then you take that disk to another computer, say, to print out. After a while you return to your machine and there's an awful error message in a big ugly dialog box on the screen. Something like *Unrecoverable Disk Error* or *System Error: Error Reading Drive A.* Don't panic! Word is overreacting to the fact that you've taken the disk out of the drive. For some reason, it checked and found nothing there. Just put the disk back in the drive and click OK or press Enter. Then save the file again to the hard disk. To avoid heart-attack scares, get in the habit of saving a file back on the hard disk after you save a copy to a disk, or just closing the document and then opening it again from the hard disk.

The Second Time You Save (and Thereafter)

Saving is easy after the first time. Every ten minutes or so, or whenever the spirit strikes you, select File ➠ Save, just like the first time. Only this time no dialog box will appear. The save happens very quickly and a character count appears in the Status bar and hangs around there till you do something.

Every time I take a break from writing or get up to water the dog, I click the Save button without even thinking. Try to get into a habit like that.

Print It Out—The Whole Point, After All

Word only works as well as a typewriter if you've got a printer or access to one. You can type all day, format beautifully, and if you can't get output, you might as well have been tracing your words in the air.

There is a very quick and easy way of printing if your printer is set up correctly. Just click the Print button in the Toolbar, the fourth one from the right with the tiny picture of a laser printer on it:

Your document prints with no back talk and no grief. That's all there is to it. If you have problems or want to do something tricky, check out Chapter 17, *Printing Problems and Solutions*.

Dazed and Confused? You Need Help!

I know, I know. We all feel this way sometimes. Nothing's working the way it's supposed to. It happens. If you run into a problem, in general, I encourage you first to flip through this book for the answer to your question. If, heaven forbid, the solution is not between these pages, your next recourse should be the Help feature.

To get into Help, pull down the Help menu and select Help Index. This puts a new window up in front of the Word screen. Your best bet is to select the Alphabetic Listing option (the options are green if you have a color monitor). This will take you to a list of topics and possibly lead to the answer to your problems. The Help system allows you to jump from entry to entry and is heavily cross-referenced.

If you click on the visible part of the Word screen, the Help window will disappear, but it will still be open, "behind" Word. Press Alt-Tab to bring it back. When you're done with Help, choose File ➨ Exit to leave it.

If Help is no help, you need to find a local guru to look at what ails you.

It's Never Too Late to Change Your Mind (Well, Hardly Ever)

Oops! What have I done? These are words we never like to hear from our own lips. Eventually, though, you're bound to do something you regret. Maybe you'll delete a huge passage you spent hours crafting, or alphabetize your dissertation. It's been known to happen. The first rule of thumb to remember is Don't Panic! Don't do anything rash. It's those first minutes after a disaster that can set the results in cement. If things get really bad, refer to Chapter 20, *Disaster Recovery*.

The beauty of Undo is that it gives you an option you never have in real life, to change your mind after the fact, to unring the bell, as it were.

Undos and don'ts

You can undo typing, deletions, and most menu commands. Just click the Undo button—the seventh one from the left, the one that's supposed to show a pencil eraser erasing. Doesn't look quite like one, does it?

You are transported back in time to moments before your mistake. (Unless you've just done something that can't be undone, in which case Word will beep and nothing will happen.)

The button is a shortcut for the first option on the Edit menu. The option will say something like Undo Edit Clear, or Undo Typing, or whatever else you just did. If you've just done something that can't be undone, the option will be unavailable (grayed out).

You can only undo the most recent action. This is another reason to save your work regularly. Then, if it's too late to undo some terrible mistake, you can always go back to the last saved version of your document.

Undo that undo that you do so well

You even get to change your mind again. If you undo something by mistake, the first option on the Edit menu becomes Undo Undo. Choose it and your document will revert to the way it was before you undid what you did. You can change your mind this way, back and forth, till the cows come home.

Exit Pursued by a Bear

When you gotta go, you gotta go. But when you're finished typing (okay, "word processing"), don't just turn off the computer. First, exit Word. To do so, pull down the File menu and choose Exit. If you have any unsaved changes Word will ask you if you want to save them. Choose Yes to save changes and quit, No to quit without saving changes, Cancel to change your mind and stay in Word, or Help to get a boring explanation of what I just told you.

The quickest shortcut for exiting is to double-click the control box in the upper-left corner of the screen. Don't worry—Word will still prompt you to save any unsaved changes. Yes, there is a command that'll dump you out of Word (and Windows) and unceremoniously junk all your new work, but I'm not going to teach it to you.

Why close without exiting or exit without saving?

You may notice that there's a Close option on the File menu. This allows you to close the document you're working on (and save it if you haven't yet), and remain in Word. Why would you want to do this? No real reason besides getting it out of your face, unless you've opened up nine Word documents and you want to open another one. Nine's the max, so you have to close one first. And why does Word give you the option of exiting without saving your work? Well, maybe you've mangled your doc and you were happier with the last draft, or maybe you were just writing some notes or other drivel that you now have no need for. Just be careful not to say No unless you really mean it.

Pick Up Where You Left Off

You've quit, you've saved, you've walked away from it all, and now you're back. How do you pick up where you left off? It's easy. Run Word again and pull down the File menu. The last four items at the bottom of the menu will be the last four documents you worked on. Select the one you want and you're in business.

If you share your computer with others who have opened their own documents in the meantime (selfish creeps) or if you yourself have worked on four or more other documents in the meantime, then it's not quite so amazingly easy to reopen the doc you want, but it's still pretty easy.

Click the Open button (the second one from the left, showing an opened file folder). This button is a shortcut for the Open command on the File menu.

The Open dialog box shown in Figure 1.4 will appear.

FIGURE 1.4:

The Open dialog box—the gateway to all your documents

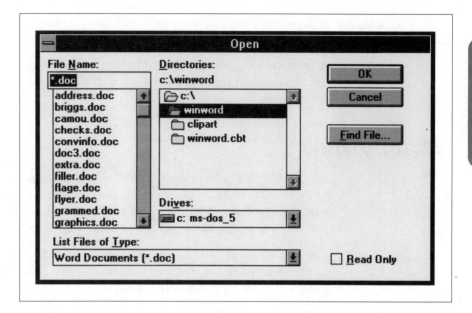

You may notice that it looks an awful lot like the Save As dialog box. Under File Name, there's *.doc and then a list of Word documents. Yours should be there unless you saved it to a different directory or disk drive. If you did so, then you made a point of remembering where you saved it, just like I told you, right? Switch to that same directory or drive and your document will appear in the list to the left.

Double-click the document name to open it (or click the name and then click OK if you're a purist).

By the way, the * is a "wildcard." It stands for *any* file name. Just ignore it.

Open Word and a Doc at the Same Time—for Hotshots Only

From Windows, run the File Manager and bring up the directory your document is in. Its name should appear in the file list for that directory. Double-click on the file name and Word will start and open up that doc for you. Then take a bow.

Save Your Changes

After you've reopened a document and done some work on it, remember to save your changes. Do this exactly the same way you did it before.

Start Anew

As I mentioned before, Word allows you to open nine documents at once. In fact, you can tile them all so each one is in a tiny little useless window. But I didn't tell you how to start a new document, only how to start typing on the blank screen or open a document you already saved.

The quickest and easiest way to start a new document is to click the New Document button in the Toolbar, the first one on the left, with a picture of a blank piece of paper on it:

The typing area will go blank again, but the title bar will now say Document2 or Document3 or … you get the idea. This doesn't close any documents. Any open documents are still there and accessible via the Windows menu.

Chapter 2

CAN'T GET THERE FROM HERE

Green's Law of Scrolling: The words you're looking for have just scrolled off the screen

---

AT FIRST YOU probably won't even think about how to get around a document. It's really a non-issue if you're just writing short memos. Then you'll figure out that the arrow keys move you up, down, left, or right and you'll use them for everything. If that's good enough for you, don't bother with this chapter, at least not yet. If you're ready to absorb some shortcuts, however, read on.

You Have the Technology

The keys you use to move around are all grouped together. If you have the fancy-schmanciest kind of keyboard, they're between the alphabet keys and the number keypad, with the arrow keys arranged in an upside-down T at the bottom and Insert, Delete, Home, End, PageUp, and PageDown, lumped together at the top.

Insert and Delete aren't used to move around. They're just there apparently to screw you up, so when you try to get to the end of a line you delete a character by mistake, for instance. That happens to me all the time. If this happens to you, remember Undo (Chapter 1).

I can't believe I have to hit the up arrow 300 times to get to the beginning of my document!

You don't. Of course, you can always hold down an arrow key and get it to start repeating, but there are better ways. To get to the top of your document, just press Ctrl-Home. To get to the end, press Ctrl-End. Don't bother memorizing that.

What if I just want to get to the top of the screen?

That's easy too. Just press Ctrl-PageUp to get to the beginning of the first line of the screen. Press Ctrl-PageDown to get to the end of the last line on the screen.

What about getting to the end of a line?

Press End. Now there's an easy one to remember. Press Home to get to the beginning of a line.

Take three baby steps! Mother, may I? Yes, you may!

As I said, the arrow keys move you "just one" in each direction. That means one character to the left or right, or one line up or down. If you're in a hurry, you can hold down Ctrl before pressing an arrow key and take slightly bigger steps. Ctrl-← moves you left one *word*. Ctrl-→ moves you right one word. Ctrl-↑ moves you up one *paragraph*. Ctrl-↓ moves you down one paragraph. It sort of makes sense, doesn't it? Word considers any group of characters between two paragraph marks (or between a paragraph mark and the start of a document) to be a paragraph.

The first time you hit Ctrl-←, it'll just take you to the beginning of the word you're in, unless you're already at the beginning. After that, it will jump a whole word at a time. Likewise, the first time you hit Ctrl-↑, it'll just take you to the beginning of the paragraph you're in, unless you're already at the beginning.

Giant steps are what you take ...

If you want to skim through a document looking for something, you'll probably use PageUp and PageDown. They move you up or down a whole screenful at a time. It's the fastest way to move and still make sure you see everything.

All the movement keys in one place

These are the movement keys:

TO MOVE THE INSERTION POINT...	PRESS...
Top of document	Ctrl-Home
End of document	Ctrl-End
Top of the screen	Ctrl-PageUp
Bottom of the screen	Ctrl-PageDown
Beginning of a line	Home
End of a line	End
One character to the left	←
One character to the right	→
One word to the left	Ctrl-←
One word to the right	Ctrl-→
One line up	↑

TO MOVE THE INSERTION POINT...	PRESS...
One line down	$\downarrow$
One paragraph up	Ctrl-$\uparrow$
One paragraph down	Ctrl-$\downarrow$
Up one screen	PageUp
Down one screen	PageDown

Standard Windows Scroll Bars

The scroll bars across the right side and bottom of the screen work like any other Windows scroll bars. That is, you can click the arrow at either end of a scroll bar to shift the view of the screen just a little bit, click on the scroll box and drag it along the scroll bar to roughly the right position, or click in the scroll bar itself to move the view one screenful (and the scroll box a corresponding amount).

The insertion point will scroll off the screen with the text if you jump around using scroll bars, but you can then press any arrow key to bring it to the current screen.

Go Directly To...

If you know the page number you want to check out, you can get to it directly with Go To on the Edit menu. It will bring up the Go To dialog box shown in Figure 2.1.

Just type the page number and press Enter, and you're there.

Find a Needle in a Haystack

And if you forget where you used a certain phrase somewhere in your document, you can look for the specific words you have in mind, with Edit ➻ Find. This brings up the Find dialog box shown in Figure 2.2.

Just type the word or words that you're looking for and press Enter or click Find Next. Word will jump you to and highlight the next instance of that word (or words). If it's the one you want, click Cancel. If it's not,

FIGURE 2.1:
The Go To dialog box offers quick access to distant parts of your documents.

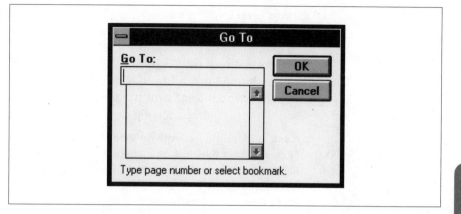

Some Other Quick Ways to Go To Where You're Going To

Here's two even shorter shortcuts for going to a specific page.

☞ Double-click the status bar (the strip across the bottom of the screen). This brings up the Go To dialog box. Type the page number and press Enter.

☞ Press F5. The words Go To: appear in the status bar, followed by an insertion point. Type the page number and press Enter.

FIGURE 2.2:
The Find dialog box. Use it to find anything—even the pun in punishment.

you can keep looking by clicking Find Next (or pressing Enter) again. If Word reaches the end of the document, it will ask you if you want to keep looking from the beginning. It's up to you. If it searches the whole document without finding what you're looking for, it will tell you that the "search text" is not found. Click OK and then click Cancel, or retype the "search text" and try again.

If you're looking for something that you think is earlier in your document, not later, you don't have to look all the way to the end and then start over from the beginning. You can click Up in the "Direction" box before clicking Find Next. Just remember you did that, because it will stay set to Up and you'll have to click Down later if you want to switch it back.

Don't Get Too Smart for Your Own Good

You may have noticed all kinds of other options on the Find dialog box. I'll explain some of them in Chapter 3 when I tell you how to edit with something called Replace (which works like Find but also lets you change whatever you find automatically).

How to Be Two Places at Once, and Other Mysteries

If you ever get tired of jumping back and forth between two places in a document, I have a solution. Split the screen. At the top of the vertical scroll bar (along the right side of the screen) is a little black line. Click it and drag it to about the middle of the screen, or just double-click it.

This action splits your screen, dividing your document. Look at the vertical scroll bar now; you'll see that there are two little ones that you can scroll separately. Just scroll one part of the screen to the other location.

When you're done, you can double-click the little black line again or drag it back to the top (or bottom) of the scroll bar. If you need to see more of one part of your document, you can click the little black line and drag it to a new location.

Chapter 3

SIMPLE EDITING AND CORRECTIONS

Nadeau's Law of Editing: Each successive draft of your document gets worse than the one before

EVERYBODY MAKES MISTAKES. There's no shame in admitting it. With Word you don't have to be a touch-typist or even a good speller because you can always go back and fix your mistakes. And not just mistakes. Any important document deserves several passes and the opportunity to make changes and improvements.

If you see yourself make a typo, you'll probably double back and fix it, but if you're typing a rough draft, you might as well just type and let your mind flow freely, and then later, when you're in a critical mood, come back and make changes and improvements.

Edit as You Go with the Keys Next to Your Right Hand

I never learned "real" typing. I have a fairly fast, glorified hunt-and-peck typing style. This means I'm constantly making little mistakes and fixing them as I go. If you just typed "hte" when you meant "the" or "lopp" instead of "loop" *and you noticed it right away,* then you can just back up and make the change, with Backspace. If you see a mistake a few lines back and you want to fix it so you don't miss it later, then you can get there with arrow keys and make the correction with either Backspace or Delete, or maybe Overtype.

The keys used for these on-the-go corrections—Backspace, Delete, and Insert—are all clustered together above and to the right of the Enter key.

What's the difference between Backspace and Delete?

Backspace erases the character to the left of the insertion point. Delete erases the character to the right of the insertion point. So Backspace is a natural for corrections on the fly. If you have to position the insertion point before making changes, it's your call whether to put it at the beginning of the offending text and use Delete, or to put it at the end and use Backspace. You'll get a sense of what's most comfortable for you.

What's Overtype and what's it for?

With your eyes on the right side of the status line, hit Insert. Notice the letters OVR appear there. They indicate that you are in overtype mode, which means that if you start typing (don't!), you'll type over whatever characters are there to the right of the insertion point. Hit Insert again and the indicator disappears, meaning you are back in Insert mode, the normal mode for Word.

Don't let all this talk of "modes" get you down. It's just the computer-geek way of saying that some rules apply to how the program works. When you change from one mode to another, different rules apply.

When you move the insertion point to the middle of a line and start typing, everything to the right gets pushed along to make room for the new material. With overtype, which most people and most other programs refer to as "typeover," what you type replaces what was already there. Use this feature sparingly.

Don't forget to turn overtype off when you're done with it. Check the indicator if you're not sure. There's nothing more annoying than typing-over when you meant to insert. If it happens, even Undo won't help you much.

Return to the Scene of the Crime

I recommend that you do your serious editing separate from your writing. Writing is creative and needs to flow. Editing is analytical and critical and tends to choke off creativity. Just type away and then return later to what you've written to clean it up, fix mistakes, and make improvements.

If you have to edit more than a character or two here or there, you need to know how to select text with Word. Let's run through that quickly.

Selection Tips

You'll notice that most talk of editing starts with selecting something or doing something to the selection. If you're unsure about how to make a selection or would like to know some alternatives and shortcuts, this section is for you. Otherwise, skip ahead.

You can select text starting anywhere and ending anywhere, or you can select specific words, sentences, lines, paragraphs, etc. Most of the time you'll do it with the mouse.

Select Anything

There are four basic ways to select any portion of text:

☞ Click the mouse and drag

☞ Click and Shift-click

☞ Shift-arrow keys

☞ Hit F8 repeatedly

You can always click at one end of your target selection and drag the mouse to the other end. Even if the selection you want runs off the screen, just keep dragging and the screen will scroll. (It might scroll too far, though, so be careful). Figure 3.1 shows a typical selection in progress.

FIGURE 3.1:

Click and drag to select part of your document. Your selection will be highlighted.

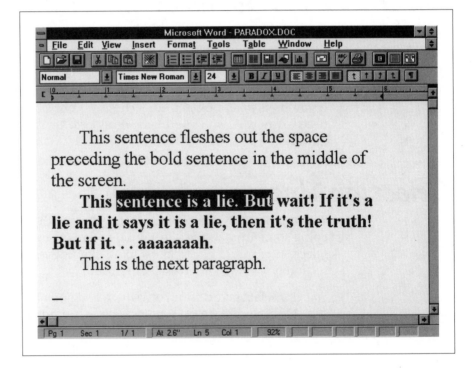

You can also click at one end of a target and then hold down Shift and click at the other end, because Shift "anchors" a selection at the location of the insertion point.

For that same reason, at any point, if you hold down Shift and then move the insertion point with the arrow keys, a selection will appear between the anchored point and the new location of the insertion point.

Select a word

To select a single word, double-click anywhere in the word. If there is a space after the word, it will be selected as well.

Select a line

To select a line of text (regardless of whether it ends with a paragraph break), click in the left margin area just left of the line you want.

Select a sentence

Hold down Ctrl and click anywhere in the sentence. The selection will include the space at the end of the sentence, if there is one.

Select a paragraph

To select an entire paragraph, double-click in the margin to the left of the paragraph. The selection will also include the (usually invisible) paragraph marker at the end of the paragraph.

Select everything

To select your entire document, hold down Ctrl and click anywhere in the left margin. You can also pull down the Edit menu and choose Select All.

Extend a selection

I have one last useful selection tip for you. The F8 key allows you to make any kind of selection without using the mouse (in case you like to keep your hands on the keyboard). If you press F8, EXT will appear in the status line and a selection will be anchored at the insertion point. You can then use arrow keys to select just as you would with Shift, or hit F8 again. (If you get stuck in extend mode, hit Esc to turn it off, and then hit an arrow key to deselect the selection.)

If you hit F8 a second time, the word nearest the insertion point will be selected. Again, you can use arrow keys to fine-tune the selection.

If you hit F8 a third time, the entire sentence will be selected. Ditto for the arrow keys.

If you hit F8 a fourth time, the entire paragraph will be selected. (Yes, the arrow keys ...)

If you hit F8 a fifth time, the entire document will be selected. (Arrow keys.)

If you hit F8 a sixth time, nothing will happen, except Word will beep at you.

If you hit F8 a seventh time, you obviously have nothing better to do. Take up a hobby.

Natural deselection

If you select something by mistake, or for any other reason want to "deselect" a selection, just press one of the arrow keys. If you press ← or →, the insertion point will end up at the beginning or end of the deselected selection. The ↑ and ↓ keys work as normal.

Delete a selection

To delete selected text, just press Delete. This is a quick way to get rid of a whole chunk of stuff. Just select it all and hit Delete. If you change your mind right away, you can undo it.

Type over a selection

If you plan to replace selected text with something new, you can just start typing. The first thing you type will replace the entire selection, and then as you continue to type (assuming you're not in overtype mode) the new text will insert itself where the selection used to be.

Move It, Buddy (or Copy It)

But you don't select text just to delete it. And you don't select text just to deselect it, unless you're some kind of a nut. Usually, you select it so you can move it somewhere, or copy it to save on original thinking. In Word, you can move text as easy as clicking and dragging.

When copying or moving a selection, watch out that the space at the end—if any—doesn't get doubled up with a space at the destination.

Drag and Drop—At Last, Something Worthwhile

Once you've selected text, you may notice that the mouse pointer changes if you move it over the selection. Normally, the mouse pointer is something called an I-beam. When it's over a selection, though, it turns into a little white arrow pointing up and to the left. When it's like that, you can drag the selection and drop it in a new location.

The quick move

Just click the mouse on selected text (and hold down the button) and the pointer will change once again. This time, in addition to the arrow, a little gray box and a dotted insertion point will appear, like this.

Editing

Drag that dotted insertion point to wherever you want to move the selection to, and release the mouse button. Like magic, it disappears at the old location and reappears at the new location.

This works best when you're dragging to a new location that's currently on screen. If you drag the selection to the edge of the screen, it will scroll like crazy and it will be hard to stop it precisely where you want it. Of course, you're welcome to try.

If you accidentally drop a selection in the wrong location (say, in the middle of another word), you can just drag it again and drop it in the correct place. I call that mistake "drag and droop."

The quick copy

It's also very easy to copy something with the same technique. The difference between copying and moving is just that the original selection stays where it is and a copy of it appears where you "drop" it.

To copy a selection, just hold down Ctrl and click on it. The mouse pointer will change to the drag-and-drop pointer just as with moving. Then, still holding down Ctrl, drag the pointer and drop the copy in the new location. That's all there is to it.

Be very careful to remember to hold down Ctrl when you want to copy. If you forget to, you'll be moving text instead of copying and you may not notice until later, after you've changed the stuff you moved. I've done that a couple of times and it's incredibly annoying to try to piece something together.

Cut, Copy, and Paste—The Kindergarten Metaphor

If you are planning to move or copy a selection to a location somewhere off the screen, you're better off using the Cut (or Copy) and Paste commands. It's just one more step and it's a little easier to control.

The commands named Cut and Paste are supposed to summon up the image of kindergarten construction-paper projects. You cut a scrap here, and paste it over there. (We lefties always got the lousiest scissors.) Copy is a more computery idea that doesn't fit as well into the arts-and-crafts metaphor.

Move a selection anywhere

Once you've selected the text you want to move, pull down the Edit menu and select Cut. The selection will disappear. (A shortcut for the Cut command is Ctrl-X.)

Next, move the insertion point to the intended destination and then select Edit ➤ Paste. The selection will reappear at the insertion point. (A shortcut for the Paste command is Ctrl-V.)

What's Going On Here? or Who Really Cares As Long As It Works?

When you cut (or copy) a selection, Word copies it to something called the Clipboard. (Cute Windows metaphor alert: The Clipboard is a tool that all Windows programs use to store cut or copied material for pasting. It's called the Clipboard to remind you of the way people clip stray notes to clipboards and then carry them around. You don't need to know any of this.) When you choose the Paste command, the content of the Clipboard is copied to the location of the insertion point. The selection remains on the Clipboard until something new is cut or copied.

Copy a selection anywhere

If you select text and then choose Edit ➤ Copy, nothing will appear to happen, but the selection will now be available for pasting elsewhere without disappearing from its original location. (A shortcut for the Copy command is Ctrl-C.)

Just as with Cut, to complete the act of copying something, you have to position the insertion point and then choose Edit ➤ Paste. The copy will appear.

Editing

Cut, copy, or paste from the Toolbar

There are buttons on the Toolbar for Cut, Copy, and Paste, but they're not particularly *short* shortcuts, since there's hardly any difference between clicking a menu name and dragging to an option, and clicking a button on the Toolbar. But for the record, here they are:

The Cut button shows a pair of scissors. That's easy to remember. The Copy button shows two little documents, which is less useful as a memory aid. And the Paste button shows a clipboard and a tiny document, which is downright useless as a mnemonic.

I never use these "shortcuts," but you might.

Copy a selection over and over

Even after you've pasted a selection, it remains available for pasting (until you cut or copy something new). So if you want to paste something in several locations, you can just use the Paste command over and over, being sure to reposition the insertion point each time.

Why would you ever want to do this? Well, some documents use repeating headings or other such text. Other times, you may want to reuse much of a passage that you've already written, making only minor changes in each occurrence. You can copy the passage, paste it into several locations, and then go back and make the changes necessary. I don't want to make too much of this though—it's not an incredibly useful feature.

Make Across-the-Board Changes

In the previous chapter I showed you how to use the Find command. Now I'll show you Replace, which is really just an extension of Find.

If you realize you've been misspelling a word, or someone's name, for the last 50 pages, or if you suddenly decide you prefer "differently haired" to "bald," you don't have to put yourself to the trouble of combing through your document and making changes one-by-one or worrying that some instance of your error has escaped you and will end up in the final version of the document. Replace lets you make all your changes at once.

Before making across-the-board changes to your document, save it first. That way, if things get really screwed up, you can close the document without saving it again and then open the saved version. If you've forgotten to save first, you can use Undo immediately after replacing.

To begin with, select Replace on the Edit menu. A dialog box appears (you should expect this by now) as shown in Figure 3.2.

FIGURE 3.2:
The Replace dialog box. Put your feet up and let the computer do your editing for you.

Replace	
Fi**n**d What: `The last thing I looked for`	**Find Next**
	Replace
Re**p**lace With:	**Replace All**
	Cancel
☐ Match **W**hole Word Only ☐ Match **C**ase	
─ Find Formatting ─	
Cl**ea**r **Character...** **Paragraph...** **Styles...**	

The last thing searched for with Find *or* Replace (if anything) will appear in the Find What box. Since it's highlighted, you can just type over it if you want to look for something else. After you've typed *bald*, or whatever, press Tab to jump to the Replace With box, and type *differently haired*, or whatever.

If you hit Enter instead of Tab after typing in the first box, Word will take it as if you've clicked the Find Next button (since that's the one that's highlighted). Remember to use Tab to get around a dialog box before you're ready to go to the next step.

Close your eyes and jump

The easiest, fastest, and most reckless way to make all the changes at once is to click the Replace All button. Word will make all the changes and then ask you if it should start looking again from the beginning (unless it was already there). Eventually it will finish or tell you that it didn't find any cases of the text you told it to look for.

Or it might tell you Search text not found. *If so, you'll probably have to figure out what's wrong with the Find What text and retype it, or give up. Maybe you're looking in the wrong document, or maybe you just made a typo.*

The only real danger with this approach is that it will change something you forgot about or don't want it to change. When you choose Replace All, Word doesn't show you all the changes as it makes them, although it does tell you how many changes it made at the end. If you want to have more control over the editing, you can.

Or take it one step at a time

To make your replacements as carefully as possible, start the procedure by clicking Find Next instead of Replace All. Word will find the first example of your Find What word and highlight it so you can make sure it's what you want. If it is what you want and you do want to change it, click the Replace button (not Replace All). Word will change the selection and then highlight the next one it finds. (That's if it finds anything at all. If it finds nothing, you'll have to rethink the Find What text.)

Sometimes this happens so fast that you will think nothing happened.

If Word ever highlights something you didn't intend to change, you can skip changing it by clicking Find Next again, instead of Replace.

If Word is repeatedly finding the wrong stuff, you may have to be more specific about what you want it to look for.

Be more specific

There are two check boxes on the Replace dialog box—Match Whole Word Only and Match Case. They are there so you can rule out some things that might match your Find What text even if you don't want it to. For example, searching for "bald" will result in finding words like "balding," "baldness," and even "Archibald"! Only those four letters of the three words would be highlighted, but it's still a nuisance because you don't want to change "*bald*ing" to "*differently haired*ing," although that is what would happen.

If you check off Match Whole Word Only, Word will refrain from finding examples of your word plus other characters. If you check off Match Case, Word will find only text that matches your Find What text letter for letter, with no switching of capitals and lowercase, so no "Bald," and no "BALD." It's useful for proper nouns and to distinguish the beginnings of sentences and things like that.

Don't forget to turn these options off (uncheck them) when you're done with them. Like a lot of other Word features, these options stay checked even when you return to the Replace command later, and they can therefore screw you up if you don't pay attention.

Or be less specific

Word also allows you to search for several similar things at once, by using the "?" as a wildcard. That means it stands for any character, like a blank scrabble piece. For instance, searching for "shi?" will find "ship" as well as "shin."

The question mark doesn't work in the Replace With box. If you put it there, you'll just get a question mark in your word, and not whatever character was found. I don't know about you, but I find that really annoying.

Tricks for finding tabs and line breaks

If you ever try searching for a tab or a paragraph break, you'll realize that it's not possible, because if you try to type a tab into the Find What box, you'll jump to the Replace With box, and if you try to type Enter, you'll be finding the next match before you even have a chance to type in what you're looking for.

There is a solution, though. It's just a matter of using *other* characters to represent the forbidden characters you're looking for. To find or

Editing

replace with a tab, type ^t. To find or replace a paragraph break, type ^p. Now those aren't too hard to remember, are they?

There's actually a whole bunch of these thingies, but most of them are worthless. Here are the only ones you'll need to know about.

THIS	STANDS FOR THIS
^t	a tab
^p	a paragraph break
^?	a question mark (remember, if you type an actual question mark, it'll be a wildcard)
^^	the ^ character itself (because if you just type ^, Word will think you're trying to represent some other forbidden character)

Hardcore Find and Replace Options for Dedicated Nerds

The row of buttons at the bottom of the Replace dialog box (under Find Formatting) opens up whole worlds of exciting computer-geek options. Actually, the first one just clears any formatting choices from the past. The Character button allows you to choose character formatting (see Chapter 5, *Cosmetics*) for either the Find What or Replace With text, depending on which box the insertion point is in. The Paragraph button works the same way, except for paragraph formatting (things like alignment instead of things like boldfacing, also mostly discussed in Chapter 5). And the Styles button allows you to find or replace Styles (which are confusing but are made crystal clear in Chapter 10, *Styles, Templates—What's the Difference?*).

Don't Forget to Save As

If you're editing your document, don't forget to save your changes when you're done. For that matter, you should be saving now and then anyway just for safety's sake.

Real-Life Editing—Just Like the Good Old Days

Remember the old days when you typed something up double-spaced and then showed it to your boss or your peers? After you read it over and made your own marks, it would be covered with corrections and comments. Then you'd sit down and type it all over again, incorporating changes as you went.

Well, you don't have to do any of that stupid retyping anymore, but you can still edit on paper. Most people prefer it actually to editing on the screen. Sure, it's easier to make the changes with all these slick commands I've been explaining, but they don't make the thinking any easier. They don't make reflection or mulling things over any easier. So here's how to do some good old-fashioned, paper-and-pencil editing.

Make your document double-spaced

First select the entire document. Then pull down the Format menu and select Paragraph. The Paragraph dialog box will appear, as shown in Figure 3.3.

Click the arrow next to the Line Spacing box (next to Auto in Figure 3.3) and then choose Double from the list box that drops down. Then click the OK button. Your document becomes double-spaced. Print it out and make all the marks you want.

What's the Difference between Auto Spacing and Single Spacing? Inquiring Geeks Want to Know

Auto spacing has the same effect as single spacing in most circumstances. The difference is that if you have different-sized text on one line, Auto spacing will adjust the line spacing of that line to accommodate the largest text. Single spacing always keeps the spacing consistent. Aren't you glad you asked?

FIGURE 3.3:
The Paragraph dialog box is where you change line spacing.

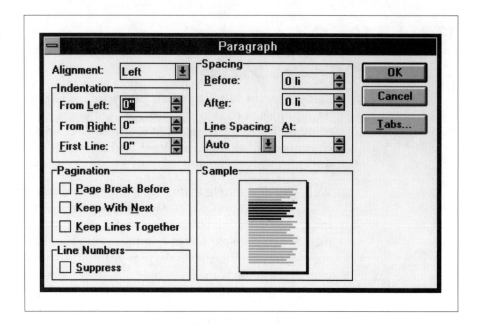

Then change your document back. It's annoying trying to read double-spaced text on the screen because you can only see half as much stuff. Just select Format ➤ Paragraph again (make sure the whole doc is selected) and then choose Auto or Single spacing. Then click OK. The document returns to normal.

Set up one-step double-spacing

If you find yourself double-spacing your documents a lot, you might want to set up a shortcut for yourself by putting double- and single-spacing buttons on your Toolbar. Chapter 16 explains how to do this.

Chapter 4

BUILT-IN PROOFREADING

Hart-Davis' Law of Proofreading:
Proofreaders turn up mistakes you never dreamed
were mistakes; Word does its best to æmulate them

The computer can help you check your work, as long as you don't trust
it too well. Spell-checking can be extremely useful once you get the
hang of it. Just be prepared to do some proofing of your own, because
there are things the computer is going to miss. It's just a dumb
machine after all.

Make Word Check Your Spelling

I was a good speller as a kid, but I recall it was "yacht" that screwed me up in the sixth-grade spelling bee. Of course, on the next round everyone missed a word I knew, so I really should've won it.

Whether you're a good speller or not, you'll probably make typing errors as you go. That's what the spell checker is for. I try to run a spell check right before I turn something in. I recommend waiting until you're just about finished with a document before checking the spelling, or you'll just end up doing it again after you make further changes.

Spell-Check the Whole Document While You're At It

If nothing is selected when you start a spell check, Word will go through the whole document. This is usually what you want to do, so no problems so far. Right?

Go to the top to begin

Word will start a spell check from wherever the insertion point is. If you're going to check the whole document, the most straightforward thing to do to begin with is jump to the beginning of the document (Ctrl-Home).

What If I Start the Spell Check Somewhere in the Middle of the Doc?

It's no big deal, really. In fact, if you want to check just the most recent pages, say, of a document, then start the spell check from the point where those pages begin. When Word gets to the end of the document, it's going to ask you if you want to start again from the beginning anyway, so all your options will still be open. I just like to start at the beginning because then it's clear when I've checked the whole thing.

Start the spell check, already!

To start a spell check, pull down the Tools menu and select Spelling. This button on the Toolbar has the same effect:

But it's one of those shortcuts that isn't really any shorter than the usual approach—you still have to click once. (I guess you don't have to drag, but how hard or time-consuming is that?)

Word will start looking for mistakes and stop when it finds one. The word in question will be highlighted and a dialog box will appear. If the word were "excercise," for example, the dialog box would look like the one shown in Figure 4.1.

FIGURE 4.1:

The Spelling dialog box. Sometimes the suggestions are lame. Sometimes they're amusing. Sometimes (gasp!) they're right.

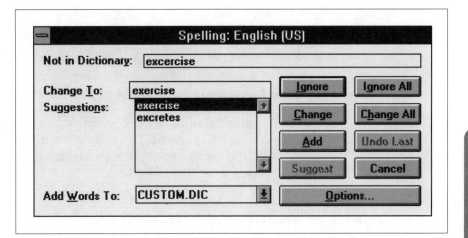

What you do now depends on what kind of mistake Word has found, if any. The most common type of mistake is a misspelling.

Proofreading

If the word is misspelled

If the word in question is truly misspelled, you can either have Word fix it by replacing it with a suggested correct spelling, or you can change it yourself if Word doesn't have a clue what you intended.

A misspelled word will appear in the first text box—the Not in Dictionary box—in the dialog box. Word's best guess about the correct spelling of the word you meant will appear in the Change To box. The best guess and any other suggestions, some reasonable, some ludicrous, will appear in the Suggestions box just below.

Not in What Dictionary?

The spell checker compares the words in your doc to its own dictionary (really, just a list of correctly-spelled words). Word doesn't presume to accuse you of making a mistake. It just lets you know that the word you type is not in its dictionary.

And the best guess is correct

If you recognize the word in the Change To box as the correct spelling of the word you had in mind, you can fix the misspelling in your document by clicking the Change button on the dialog box. The spell checker will then look for another mistake.

And the best guess is correct and you think you've made this mistake a lot

If you realize that the highlighted word is one that you've been misspelling all over the place, you can click the Change All button instead. At first, this will only fix the highlighted word, but after that, any other cases of that same mistake will be fixed as they come up. Word won't show you when it makes the rest of the changes or ask your permission.

And one of the other suggestions is correct

If the first suggestion is not the word you meant, but one of the other suggestions is, click the better suggestion. It will replace the first suggestion in the Change To box. Then click the Change (or Change All) button.

And no suggestion is correct
but the word is definitely wrong

If all the suggestions are lame, you're going to have to fix the word yourself. Try looking in a dictionary if you don't know the correct spelling, or ask a human being. There are two ways to fix a word yourself.

☞ Type the correct spelling in the Change To box and then click Change (or Change All).

☞ Click outside the dialog box, type over the selected (misspelled) word, and then click the Start button on the Spelling dialog box.

If you make the change yourself, Word will ask you if it should start the spell check over from the beginning when it reaches the end, even if you started from the beginning. That's because it forgets that you started at the top. It thinks you started when you clicked start. It's kind of dumb, but it's mostly harmless.

If the Word Is Actually Correct

If the highlighted word is correct but it's someone's name or some jargon or other type of word that's "not in the dictionary," you have two options. You can add the word to the dictionary, ignore the word, or ignore all instances of the word. Three options.

And you're going
to use it a lot (like your name, for example)

If you expect to run into this word in the future, click the Add button. Word will add it to its spelling dictionary and go looking for a new mistake.

And this is the only time it ever appears

If this is a one-shot word, a piece of nonsense, or something else unusual, click the Ignore button and the spell check will continue with the next mistake.

And it appears again in this document

If you don't want to add the word to your dictionary, but you know it comes up again in this document, click the Ignore All button. This just saves you the trouble of hitting Ignore over and over again.

If the Word Is a Repeat

Sometimes, you'll type the same word twice by mistake. This happens when you're distracted or when you continue a sentence you left off previously. Of course, there are also times when the same word appears twice for good reason. The word "to" appears twice in a row in the following sentence, for legitimate grammatical reasons: "You may not like working for a living, but you have to to get ahead in the world." OK, it's not a great sentence, but it works, right? Right.

If you meant to repeat a word that the spell check offers to delete, just click Ignore. If it's a real mistake, click Delete. The repeated word will disappear and the spell check will continue

The Change button turns into the Delete button when the spell check finds a repeated word. Also, **Not in Dictionary** *changes to* **Repeated Word.** *Don't let this disorient you.*

Capitalization Problems

The spell check will also catch mistakes of capitalization, usually two or more letters capitalized at the beginning of a word, or a capital appearing other than at the beginning of a word. A common such typo is *THe.* Unless you intended the unusual capitalization, click Change to accept the correction.

Quit the Spell Check at Any Time

You don't have to complete an entire spell check if you don't want to. At any time you can click the Cancel or Close button and the Spelling dialog box will disappear and leave you back in the document wherever the spell check left off.

You're Done

When the spell check is completed, Word will tell you so in a dialog box with only one button, an OK button. Click OK. I don't really know why they include that button, since you have no choice about whether to click it or not. I guess it's so you can take as long as you want to read *The spelling check is complete.*

Check Just a Single Word or Portion of Your Document

If you are unsure of the correct spelling of a particular word and you don't feel like checking the whole document, you can select the word and then start a spell check by selecting Tools ➥ Spelling or clicking the Spelling button on the toolbar.

If the word checks out okay, you'll then be asked if you want to continue the spell check for the rest of the document. Click No. If the spell check finds something wrong with the word, you will be shown the Spelling dialog box with all the same options outlined in the previous section. After you change or fix the word, you will be asked if you want to continue the spell check. Click No.

There is another shortcut for checking a single word, the F7 key. Press F7 to check the word the insertion point is on or the word immediately to the left of the insertion point. The word will be selected and checked exactly as just outlined.

Undo Part of a Spell Check or the Whole Shebang

At any point during a spell check (except at the very beginning before you've done anything), you can click the Undo Last button and undo the last change made during the spell check. This will work up to five times to undo your last five changes. If you want to undo more changes (or all of them), click Close and then pull down the Edit menu and select Undo Spelling. This will undo all of the changes made during the spell check. Start the spell check over at this point if you want to redo some of the changes.

Undo Spelling will not undo any changes that you hand-typed during the spell check. It's generally a good idea to save your document before running a spell check so that if you really screw it up, you have the earlier version to fall back on.

A Warning about Mistakes the Spelling Checker Won't Find

Remember that there are all kinds of errors that are not technically misspellings and will match entries in the dictionary and therefore not get caught in a spell check. I often type *their* when I mean *there*, and I just have to look out for that mistake myself since *their* is a legitimate word. Likewise, I also type *you're* a lot when I mean *your*. The spelling checker is unable to consider context. Other common mistakes include mixing up *affect* and *effect,* or typing *Yes, sir, I'll get on it right away,* when you really mean *Why don't you do your own work for a change, you lazy bastard!*

Make Word Check Your Grammar, If You Insist

I can't recommend the grammar checker. I don't trust things like that, but I admit that I'm biased because I've been an editor for years, and like everyone else, I don't like to entertain the thought that a computer could do my job as well, or better, than I do it myself. The truth is that grammar checking is still in a crude stage of development, and I find the grammar checker more of a nuisance than a help, because you have to ignore so many off-base suggestions for the occasional good piece of advice. But don't take my word for it, try it for yourself.

A Few Redeeming Features

There are a few things the grammar check can help you with. Overuse of the passive voice, a hallmark of bureaucratic writing and blame-shifting language, should be avoided at all costs. That is, *one* should avoid it at all costs. When a politician says "Mistakes were made," he or she is deliberately avoiding giving a subject to the verb. Of course there are legitimate uses of the passive voice, but the grammar check keeps you on your toes. Unfortunately, it considers almost any instance of the verb "to be" to be an example of the passive voice, so be careful.

The grammar check does catch the *your/you're, there/their* errors that the spell checker overlooks, because it considers the words in the context of the entire sentence.

There are also unlimited grammatical errors that the grammar check will fail to find, so don't assume that just because you've run a grammar check on your document and made all the changes suggested that the grammar and syntax are now perfect. If you're unsure of your own command of these rules, have someone, preferably a trained editor, look your writing over. That's a plug for my editor friends.

Grammar-Check the Whole Document

As with the spell checker, if nothing is selected when you start a grammar check, Word will go through the whole document. So hit Ctrl-Home before starting.

Proofreading

Is Starting a Grammar Check in the Middle of My Document Just like Starting a Spelling Check There? Like, Will It Ask Me If I Want to Start Over at the End?

Yes.

Start the Grammar Check

To start a spell check, pull down the Tools menu and select Grammar. Word will start looking for problems and stop when it finds one. The sentence containing the problem will be highlighted and a dialog box will appear. For example, if your document contained this sentence,

        I ain't got no body.

it would appear in the dialog box shown in Figure 4.2.

As in this example, there will also be a suggestion about what the problem is. Read it and decide if it really applies to your sentence, and if it does, whether you want to change it.

FIGURE 4.2:

The Grammar dialog box. Are you going to let a dumb machine give you advice in a condescending tone?

```
┌─────────────────────────────────────────────────────────┐
│ ▬            Grammar: English (US)                        │
│ Sentence:                                                 │
│ ┌──────────────────────────────────────┐ ▲  ┌──────────┐ │
│ │ I ain't got no body.                 │    │  Ignore  │ │
│ │                                      │    └──────────┘ │
│ │                                      │    ┌──────────┐ │
│ │                                      │    │  Change  │ │
│ │                                      │ ▼  └──────────┘ │
│ └──────────────────────────────────────┘    ┌──────────────┐ │
│                                              │Next Sentence │ │
│ Suggestions:                                 └──────────────┘ │
│ ┌──────────────────────────────────────┐ ▲  ┌──────────┐ │
│ │ Avoid using double negatives.        │    │Ignore Rule│ │
│ │                                      │    └──────────┘ │
│ │                                      │    ┌──────────┐ │
│ │                                      │    │  Cancel  │ │
│ │                                      │    └──────────┘ │
│ │                                      │    ┌──────────┐ │
│ │                                      │    │ Explain… │ │
│ │                                      │ ▼  └──────────┘ │
│ └──────────────────────────────────────┘    ┌──────────┐ │
│                                              │ Options… │ │
│                                              └──────────┘ │
└─────────────────────────────────────────────────────────┘
```

If the suggestion is worthless

If the advice is lame and you don't need to fix anything, click Ignore. The grammar check will then either bring up a new problem in the same sentence or continue to look for problem sentences.

If the suggestion is so worthless you never want to hear about it again

If you think the rule the grammar checker is applying to your sentence is stupid and you don't want to hear about that kind of problem, click Ignore Rule instead of Ignore.

If you don't want to hear any more grief about this same sentence

If you don't want any advice about the highlighted sentence, click Next Sentence, and the grammar checker will stop looking in the current sentence for problems.

If the suggestion is a good one

If you think the grammar checker is correct and the Change button is available (not grayed out), then click Change and Word will fix your sentence. Unfortunately, Word usually can't fix sentences, it can only carp about problems, so you'll probably have to fix it yourself.

To fix a sentence yourself, click outside the Grammar dialog box and retype the sentence. When you are done, click the Start button to continue the grammar check.

If you make a change yourself and then continue, Word will ask you if it should continue from the beginning when it gets to the end of the document.

Proofreading

If you're not sure
if the suggestion is helpful or lame

You can get Word to elaborate a little on the grammar rule it's applying by clicking the Explain button. Word will then show you a discus-
sion of the rule in its own dialog box in front of the Grammar dialog
box. You'll have to scroll through it (or enlarge it) to read more than a
few words. When you're done, double-click in the control box in the
upper-left corner of the dialog box to make it disappear.

If you've had enough
of this stupid grammar checker

Before long, you'll realize that a grammar check takes forever and isn't
very helpful. Remember that you can end it at any time by clicking
Cancel or Close.

You're Doing a Spell Check
Now Whether You Like It or Not

You may not notice this if you've just completed a spell check, but
when you start a grammar check, it starts up the spell checker too. As
it encounters questionable words, it brings up the Spelling dialog box
shown in the previous part of this chapter. If you want to do both, fine. If
you want to skip the spelling part of the grammar check, do the following:
Click the Options button in the Grammar dialog box. In the dialog box
that appears, click the Customize Settings button. Try to ignore all the be-
wildering junk in the dialog box that now appears. In the Grammar box,
scroll down until you see Spelling Errors. Uncheck the box next to this
option (click on it). Then click OK. Click OK again. There you go.

Check Just a Single
Sentence or Part of Your Document

You can check the grammar of any smaller portion of your document
by selecting that portion first and then choosing Tools ➔ Grammar.

When the selected text has been checked, Word will ask you if you want to continue checking the rest of the document. Click No.

So-Called Readability Statistics

When a grammar check is complete, Word displays a dialog box showing what it calls "readability statistics." It will include some useful tidbits about your document, such as how many words, characters, paragraphs, and sentences it contains. It also tells you how many words long your sentences are, on average, sentences per paragraph, and other comparisons like that. Finally, it lists readability information based on some standard methods of judging readability. I would only trust mathematical standards of readability so far, but it's there if you need it. When you're done looking over the stats, click OK.

Figure 4.3 shows the readability statistics for an unedited copy of the previous chapter.

FIGURE 4.3:
Readability Statistics for Chapter 3. Sentences per Paragraph shows an impressively low score!

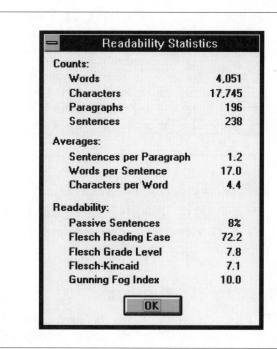

I hope you finished seventh grade, or Chapter 3 must have been pretty tough.

Undo a Grammar Check

If you think you've mangled your document beyond belief, you can undo a grammar check as soon as you've clicked Close. Just select Edit ➠ Undo Grammar. But remember that any changes you made by hand will not be undone by this command.

Look for the Word on the Tip of Your Tongue

One more tool Word provides to help you with your writing is a thesaurus. It helps you search for synonyms so you can keep from repeating yourself. Beware the obvious use of synonyms such as "He imbibed the cool drink," or using "she opined" instead of "she said." That stuff just won't fly.

It's natural to fall into the rut of using a word over and over, however. Some words get stuck somewhere up in the forebrain and offer themselves over and over. Others are ubiquitous because they are vague—words like "thing."

Sometimes you know there's a word you want, but you can't quite remember it. The thesaurus can help you with that as well. Just start with a similar word, ideally a synonym, and the thesaurus will suggest others.

Select the starting word

Start off by selecting the word you want to see synonyms for. If you don't, Word will just use whatever word the insertion point is on or immediately to the right of.

Start the thesaurus

To start the thesaurus (try saying that three times!), pull down the Tools menu and select Thesaurus. A dialog box will then appear. If the word you wanted to replace were *select,* you'd see the Thesaurus dialog box shown in Figure 4.4.

FIGURE 4.4:
The Thesaurus dialog box. Use this for cheating at word-association games.

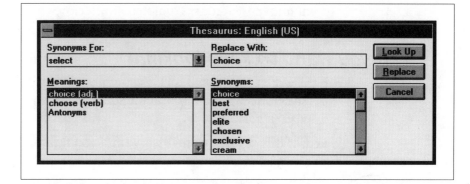

Choose a meaning or part of speech

The dialog box will show you several meanings of the selected word (if there are more than one) in the Meanings box, and it will distinguish between parts of speech. It has to do this. If you wanted synonyms for the noun *select,* synonyms for the verb *select* would be useless. So click the meaning or part of speech that matches what you had in mind.

Why Would I Want to Look Up Antonyms?

Beats me. All computer thesauruses (and real thesauri, such as the venerable Roget's) seem to have that option. If the thesaurus has cross-references for antonyms for your word, it lists Antonyms as an option. I guess some people look up words by thinking of words that are opposite in meaning, but I can't really imagine a situation in which I'd do that. If it's useless for you, ignore it.

Choose a synonym

Scroll through the list of words in the Synonyms box to see if any are what you had in mind, or if any are at least closer to what you had in mind. Click the best one.

Proofreading

If you find the word you were looking for

If the word you selected from the Synonyms box is acceptable, click Replace. The new word will replace the word you selected in your document and the Thesaurus dialog box will close.

If you want to keep looking

If the word you selected is closer, but not quite right, click Look Up and the thesaurus will go through the same routine using your new word as a starting point.

Repeat this as often as necessary until you find the best word available.

All the words you've looked up will remain available in the Synonyms For list box. If you want to backtrack and pursue another synonym of a previous word, pull down the list box and select the earlier word. Then continue as usual.

If you don't find anything you like

If the search is getting you nowhere, click Cancel. The dialog box will close and nothing will change. Sorry.

Human Proofreading Still Rules

One final bit of advice about all of these proofreading tools is that you can only trust them as far as you can throw your computer, which may be fine for those of you using laptops in tall buildings. They can all help in some situations, and I truly believe that the spell checker is a great invention, but it's not time to get rid of your dictionary or your *Roget's* just yet. Proofread your own work and always try to get at least one other person to look something over before you consider it finished. End of sermon.

Chapter 5

COSMETICS

Stephenson's Law of Attractiveness: Beauty is only skin deep, but ugly goes to the bone

FOR REASONS I don't really understand, Word starts you off with a relatively unattractive font at a size a little too small for comfortable viewing. The ribbon shows the name of the font and its size. If you've changed nothing, the second box on the ribbon (the font box) will read "Times New Roman" and the third box (the point-size box) will contain the number 10, as shown at the top of the next page.

Font box   Point-size box

Times New Roman is the font. A font is a typeface or type style. The number 10 indicates 10 points. A point is a unit of measurement for typefaces. An inch is roughly 72 points. Newspapers are often printed with 10-point type, and typewriter fonts are usually around 12 point.

Fix the Scrawny Font Word Sticks You With

In Chapter 6, *Change Your Point of View,* I will explain how to magnify the view of the screen, which would be one way of avoiding eyestrain if you must work with a 10-point font, but then the width of the page probably won't all fit on the screen at once, so you'll have a new problem to deal with. Myself, I usually work in 12-point fonts, which are easier on the eye both on the screen and when printed.

Choose an everyday font you can live with

Times New Roman might be your cup of tea. I'm not insisting that you change it, but if you want to change to a font you like better, here's how.

First type something, so you can see what different fonts look like. Then select everything. (Hold down Ctrl and click in the left margin.) Then click the arrow to the right of the font box on the ribbon. The font box will change into a drop-down list box with a list of fonts. It will also have a scroll bar if the list doesn't all fit.

If the fonts listed are unfamiliar to you, you can click on them one by one to see the effect on your sample text. When you see something you like, stick with it.

You don't have to print with the font you use for everyday typing, as long as you remember to change the font before printing. I've got a lousy dot-matrix printer that can only do a good job with its own fonts, so I use them with it, but I type with whatever I want first.

Choose a size that won't give you eyestrain

Even if you decide to stick with Times New Roman (your other choices may be no better), you should at least work with a larger size than 10 point. Again, make sure you've selected the entire document, then click the arrow to the right of the point-size box. As with the font box, a list box will drop down to give you choices of point sizes. I recommend 12 point, but you can try the different options to see what you're comfortable with.

Again, choose a arrangement that your eyes like, and then just change it to something more suitable when it's time to print. I know people who type in 16 point but still print in 12.

Make your preferences permanent

Once you've decided on a font and size that you're comfortable with, you can choose them whenever you start a new document. Even if the document is blank, select everything (namely, the nonprinting paragraph mark) or else you'll find yourself back in Times New Roman 10 point if you move past the paragraph mark at the end of what you've typed.

If you get tired of always resetting your standard font and size, you can make your preferences permanent. To do so, pull down the Format menu and select Character (or just double-click the ribbon). The Character dialog box will appear, as shown in Figure 5.1.

The "Font" and "Points" boxes work just like the ones on the ribbon. Select the font and point size that you want and then click the Use as Default button. Word asks you if you want to change the font for the Normal Style to whatever you chose. It sounds intimidating, but click Yes. From then on you'll get the font you want in the size you want automatically.

Cosmetics

FIGURE 5.1:
The Character dialog
box lets you change
font, point size, and
more attributes than
we should get into
right now.

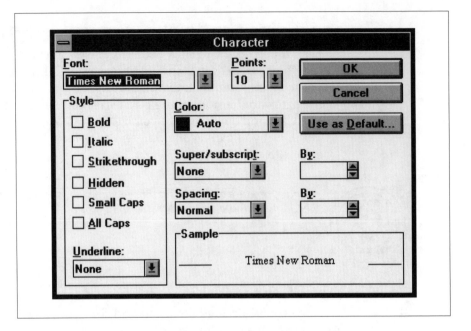

FIGURE 5.1:
The Character dialog
box lets you change
font, point size, and
more attributes than
we should get into
right now.

Ask Dr. Geeky: What Does "Default" Mean?

The word *default* is computer jargon. A default is a setting that exists "by default"; that is, even if you don't do or change anything. To make matters worse, there are defaults, and then there are default defaults. In the relevant example, Times New Roman is the default default. It's the font you get by default. If you select Courier New and make it the default, Times New Roman will no longer be the default. But it was the default by default; that is, before you changed it. I hope that clears everything up.

I'll discuss the Character dialog box again later in this chapter, and there's more on setting defaults in Chapter 16, *Customize Word to Suit Your Needs.*

More Different Types of Character Formatting Than You'll Ever Use

I've just explained to you how to ditch the ugly stick letters Word gives everyone to work with, but there's more to formatting text than choosing a comfortable font. I recommended changing font and size to make your work more pleasant, but the usual reason to make changes to text is to make it communicate better, more clearly.

You're best off writing and editing your work in some simple, unadorned font, and then, when you are ready to print it out and present it to whomever will read it, embellishing the document to make it more engaging and easier to read. There are all kinds of ways to add emphasis or distinguish one part of a document from another. The most basic is using ALL CAPITALS.

Change Capitalization

To some, capitalization is the crudest form of emphasis. After all, even typewriters can do it. And it's true that reading too much text in all caps is bound to give you a headache. All caps are the visual equivalent of shouting, so use them sparingly.

Of course, you can type in all caps just by hitting CapsLock before typing, but if you decide to change capitalization after you've typed something, Word can do it for you. This is another of the small favors that make computers OK. Just select the text you want to affect and hit Shift-F3. That changes all lowercase to all uppercase, all uppercase to initial uppercase only, and initial uppercase only to all lowercase. Here, I'll demonstrate:

SHIFT-F3 TURNS THIS	INTO THIS
anything	ANYTHING
ANYTHING	Anything
Anything	anything

If the text you select is of mixed cases, such as the first two words in a sentence, all text will get the case the first word gets.

You can also select any text and then press Ctrl-A to make it all caps. Pressing Ctrl-A again will change it back to whatever it was.

Change Appearance

There are other, more subtle and sophisticated ways of making some words stand out from others. You can make text bold. **Bold text stands out significantly from regular text, but it's hard to read after a while. It's best for headlines, captions, and short things like that.** You can make text italic. *Italic text is most often used for foreign words, for spoken emphasis, or to represent characters' thoughts in fiction.* And so on.

The favorites—bold, italic, underline

Boldface, italics, and underlining are by far the most common kinds of emphasis, so Word has provided easy access to each on the ribbon. Underlining, though, is actually sort of bush league. It works well in typewritten-looking text, because typewriters don't have italic, but in most cases italic is preferable to underlining.

To turn on one of these type of formatting, just click the appropriate button from the ribbon:

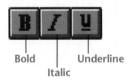

You can do this before you begin typing, or you can select text you've already typed and then click the button.

Watch the Buttons

If you are ever unsure of the formatting applied to text, you can place the insertion point before a character in question—or select characters—and then look at the buttons. The appropriate buttons will be pushed in. If you highlight text that is bold and italic, for example, both of those buttons will be pushed in. If you select text that is mixed—for example, some bold, some not bold—the B on the Bold button will appear outlined instead of solid.

There are easy-to-remember shortcuts for boldface, italic, and underline. The shortcut for Bold is Ctrl-B, Italic is Ctrl-I, and Underline Ctrl-U.

And the rest—small caps, double underline, superscript, and subscript

The slightly less popular character-formatting options are available only through the Character dialog box (shown in Figure 5.1) and shortcuts. Bring up that box with Format ➻ Character or by double-clicking the ribbon.

To apply, for example, small caps to text, select the text, double-click the ribbon, check off Small Caps, and click OK. Formatting that already applies to selected text will already be checked off in the dialog box. Formatting that applies to part of a selection but not all of it will have a grayed check box. If you click such a box, it will become checked and the format is turned on for the whole selection. Click the box to clear it and the formatting will be turned off for the whole selection. Click it a third time and the box will turn gray again and the selection will revert to its original status. When you have made your formatting choices, click OK.

The only tricky choices are the underlining options and the sub- and superscript choices (you can ignore Spacing and Color for now). They are both operated by list boxes instead of check boxes. With underlining, you can select Single or Double underlining, or Word Only, which means that spaces between words will not be underlined. There is no double-underlining word-only choice. With subscripts and superscripts, you are given way more control than you need over the precise details of how far up or down the 'script will go relative to the regular text. Don't mess with the fine-tuning. Just choose superscript or subscript and leave it at that.

One thing you might want to change with subscripts or superscripts is the point size. Word just moves them up or down. If you want them smaller, you have to make them smaller yourself. Do this in the dialog box before you click OK.

Figure 5.2 shows examples of all the non-weird choices available from the Character dialog box. You can safely ignore the other choices.

FIGURE 5.2:
These are the non-weird formatting choices you can get from the Character dialog box.

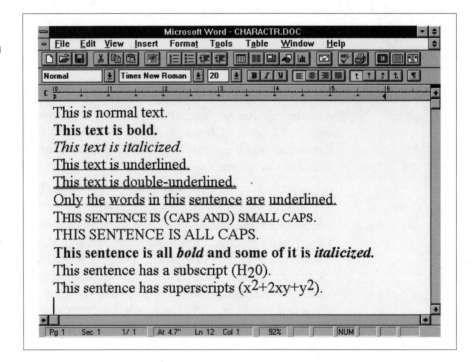

Here are all the shortcuts for character formatting:

TO APPLY	PRESS
Bold	Ctrl-B
Italics	Ctrl-I
Underline	Ctrl-U
Double Underline	Ctrl-D
Word-Only Underline	Ctrl-W
Small Caps (Kaps)	Ctrl-K
All Caps	Ctrl-A
Subscript	Ctrl-=
Superscript	Ctrl-+

Take it off, take it off, take it all off

To remove formatting from a character or selection, either click the button or buttons on the ribbon, until they are all unpushed, check the checkboxes in the Character dialog box until they are all unchecked, choose None on the drop-down list boxes in the dialog box, or, best of all, simply type Ctrl-spacebar.

Fonts of Wisdom

I showed you how to choose an everyday font, but now it's time to look at the big picture for fonts in general. Most documents that are not professional publications will use only one font for all running text. Special fonts are reserved for headings, footnotes, captions, banners, etc. This is all to the good, because most fonts beyond the homely basic set that everyone's issued are display fonts. A display font is one that's not necessarily good for reading but is great for catching your eye and getting you to read a few words, say in a headline.

If you make a selection that contains more than one font, the font box will be empty.

Choose the Font You Want

As described earlier in this chapter, you can choose any of the available fonts from the ribbon, or you can choose from the same list in the Character dialog box. You can choose a font and then start typing or select text and then choose a font to apply to the selection.

There are keyboard shortcuts for the font and point-size boxes. Press Ctrl-F to highlight the font list and ↑ or ↓ to drop it down. Press Ctrl-P to highlight the point-size list and ↑ or ↓ to drop it down. Press either of those Ctrl combination twice to bring up the Character dialog box.

Available fonts are determined by a few factors. Everyone gets five fonts supplied with Word. (They are all TrueType fonts. If you really want to know what that means, hold on, I'll explain in a minute.) Beyond that it depends on your printer and other factors.

The Ctrl-Spacebar shortcut for clearing formatting also returns your text to the "default" font.

If you have a long list of fonts, it can get tiresome always scrolling through the font list. You can start typing the name of the font you want and quickly bring it to the top of the list. Select the font, then just press Enter.

Telling Different Types of Fonts Apart

As you choose fonts to use in your documents, it may help you to understand what type of font you are choosing. You can skip all this if you don't care. The short course is that fonts with TT next to them in the list box will print on any printer (except for daisywheel or line-printer dinosaurs) but slowly on dot-matrix printers, fonts with an icon of a printer next to them will print fast on your printer but possibly not at all on other printers, and fonts with neither symbol are screen fonts that will print slowly and look lousy.

Here's some free advice: Too many fonts spoil the doc. It's tiring on the eyes to see all kinds of fonts slammed together on a page. Choose one or two fonts and stick with them. (If you don't believe me, try it. I think you'll soon be converted.)

Built-in and other TrueType fonts

The built-in TrueType fonts are Arial, Courier New, Times New Roman, Symbol, and Wingdings. Arial seems to be based on Helvetica, a standard sans-serif font. Courier New is a typewriter-looking font based on the traditional Courier typeface. Times New is a rip-off of the standard Times typeface based on the typeface used by the New York Times. Symbol contains a set of useful typographical and general-purpose symbols. And Wingdings is a collection of "dingbats," which are little symbols such as arrows, pointing fingers, smiley faces, and so on that can be used as "bullets" to start lists or fill a graphic role on the page.

You may have other TrueType fonts, depending on what you or anyone else has installed on your machine. Certain other programs, like CorelDRAW, include hundreds of TrueType fonts, and simply installing a program like Corel makes these fonts available to all your Windows programs.

OK, But What the Hell's a TrueType Font?

Glad you asked. TrueType is a system that Microsoft, the makers of Windows and Word for Windows, invented so that typefaces could be shared by all Windows programs. They can be produced on any printer, usually as graphics, but they take a long time on dot-matrix printers and may look heavy and ugly to boot. They usually look fine and take a reasonable amount of time to print on laser printers.

Printer fonts

Printer fonts will always work best with your printer, because they are built into the printer itself. The printer doesn't have to fake or construct these fonts; it was *made* to print them. They are not portable in the sense that TrueType is, though, so they're not too useful if you have to print from a different printer. But you can always work with printer fonts on your own setup and then change fonts when printing else-where. The drawback is that your document will change appearance, lines may break in new places, formatting may look different, and so on.

What is CPI?

CPI stands for characters per inch. Some printer fonts have a different version for each character width. In the typewriter days, 10 CPI was referred to as "pica," and 12 CPI was referred to as "elite."

Use Styles for Better Control of Fonts

In Chapter 10, *Styles, Templates—What's the Difference?*, I explain how to use styles to standardize and gain more control over your use of fonts. By defining styles for certain situations or types of writing, you can apply formatting consistently and then, when necessary, make changes all at once. Read Chapter 10 for the how-to.

A Bang or a Whimper

Of course, you can change size for emphasis as well. You can choose a point size in the point-size box on the ribbon or in the equivalent box in the Character dialog box. The keyboard shortcut to get to the point-size box is Ctrl-P. Press it twice to bring up the Character dialog box.

You can also increase the point size of a selection by pressing Ctrl-F2, or decrease the point size by pressing Ctrl-Shift-F2.

Control the Appearance of the Page

The final aspect of beautifying a document to make it more present-able is controlling the page itself. The issues that affect the appearance of the page are the size of the margins, the alignment of the text, the indentation of the paragraphs, and whatever header or footers will appear outside of the running text.

Choose Proper Margins

Until or unless you change the default, your documents will start off with one-inch margins at the top and bottom of the page and one-and-a-quarter-inch margins at the left and right. This may suit you just fine, but if you want to change them, there are a few ways to do it.

Drag margins into place

There are two ways to set or change margins visually using the mouse. On the Print Preview screen, you can drag margins around until they look right, and on the ruler, you can switch to a margin view and drag the left or right margins into place.

Change margins from Print Preview

To set margins by eye, pull down the File menu and select Print Preview. On the Print Preview screen, click Margins. Lines representing the current margins will appear on the picture of the page. To change a margin, click the "handle" (the little square black box) at the end of the margin and drag the margin in or out. The pointer changes to a cross-hair when you start dragging.

Watch the readout at the upper right to see the exact measurement of the margin you are setting. When you are satisfied with the measurement and or the appearance of the margin, let up the mouse button. To have the text fill out the new margins, click anywhere outside the page. Figure 5.3 shows a top margin being decreased to 1".

When all margins are set to your satisfaction, click Close.

Setting margins on one page in Print Preview affects all pages unless you have split your document into sections. What's a section? Hold on, I'll explain all about them in Chapter 7, **Plan Ahead.**

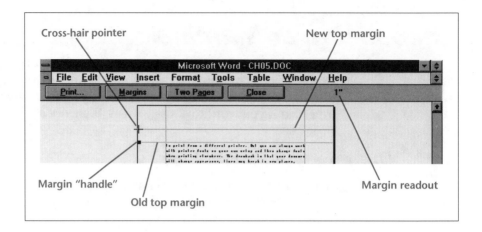

Cross-hair pointer

New top margin

Margin "handle"

Old top margin

Margin readout

Change margins on the ruler

You can set only left and right margins on the ruler, but it's fast and easy to do so. First, click the open-bracket character in the left-margin part of the ruler. The appearance of the ruler will change. The left and right margins will be represented by brackets and the numbers on the ruler will count from the left edge of the page instead of from the left margin. This is so you can tell how big the margins are. To change a margin, click and drag a bracket to the left or right.

To move the left margin further left, you must hold down Shift as you click and drag. (If that doesn't work for you, click the bracket, drag it a little bit to the right, and then *drag it left.) You may have to scroll around a bit to square away the screen after resetting the left margin.*

When you are happy with the new margins, click the split triangle symbol where the bracket used to be in the left margin of the ruler. This returns the ruler to its usual state.

Margins by the numbers

As with all other controls in Word, you can specify margins exactly in a dialog box. To do so, pull down the Format menu and select Page Setup. The Page Setup dialog box will appear, as shown in Figure 5.4.

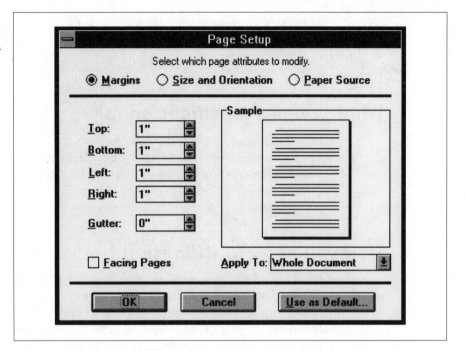

Click Margins if the dot next to it is not selected. You can now set the Top and Bottom, Left and Right Margins in the boxes provided. You can type exact inch measurements or use the little arrow buttons to increase or decrease the current settings.

When you are satisfied with your margin choices, click OK.

Truth, Justification, and the American Way

Justification is a typesetting term that you hear more and more in the word-processing business nowadays. It refers to whether or not the lines of text are aligned along both margins or only one. With *left justification*, the default, text is aligned at the left and "ragged" at the right, so it's also called "ragged right." *Right justification*, the least common, is the exact opposite, ragged left and aligned right. *Full justification* (or simply justification to some), means aligned at both the left and right margins, as most published books are. Finally, *center justification* means that each line is centered.

Cosmetics

Word refers to justification as **alignment***, which means the same thing. The choices are left alignment, center alignment, right alignment, and of course justified alignment.*

What you use justification for

Left justification is the look that typewriters produce, and it's used to suggest an informal, casual style. Full justification is used for most formal publications. It's the classiest style. Right justification appears mainly in magazines with daring layouts. Centering is mostly used for single lines—headlines or titles, for example.

How you apply justification

Unlike font and size, which apply to characters, and margins, which apply to the entire document, justification applies to paragraphs. When you set justification, it applies to whatever paragraph contains the insertion point. To apply it to more than one paragraph, you must first make a selection that starts in the first and ends in the last paragraph you want to affect. To apply justification to the entire document, select it all first.

Easy justification

There are four buttons for justification on the ribbon. So once you've selected the text or at least positioned the insertion point, you just have to click the proper button and you're set. I'll let you guess the alignment each button stands for.

For obvious reasons, only one kind of justification can be set at a time.

The usual dialog-box option

Of course, you can set alignment from the dialog box, but there's no point doing that unless you're not displaying the ribbon, because there aren't any extra options as there sometimes are on some dialog boxes for some types of commands.

To set justification, or "alignment" as Word calls it, first make your selection. Then pull down the Format menu and select Paragraph (or double-click the top half of the ruler). The Paragraph dialog box appears (see Figure 5.5).

FIGURE 5.5:
The Paragraph dialog box—another way to justify (or "align") your paragraphs

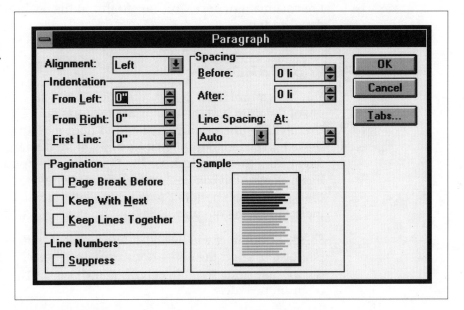

Click the Alignment box and choose Left, Right, Center, or Justified (which means full justification) from the list box that drops down. Then click OK.

There are also keyboard shortcuts for alignment: Ctrl-L for Left, Ctrl-R for Right, Ctrl-E for Center, and Ctrl-J for Justified. Ctrl-E? Yes, indeedy. Remember, Ctrl-C is Copy, as I mentioned in Chapter 3. There's probably a useful mnemonic for remembering that Ctrl-E is Center, but I can't think of it at the moment.

Cosmetics

What Indentation Is For

There are two uses for indentation. The first is to show the beginnings of paragraphs. The second is to temporarily change margins, as when quotations are indented from the left and right in academic papers.

It's true that you can indent paragraphs with tabs, but you have more control if you don't type tabs but simply set the indentation for the entire document at once. You can do this at the beginning or when you're done writing.

Easy indentation

You can control indents from the ruler. The split triangle at the left margin of the ruler and the solid triangle at the right show indentation. Usually they line up with the left and right margins. The triangle on the left is split so that the first-line indent for a paragraph can be different from the main indent. The top half of the triangle shows the first-line indent and it can be moved independently of the bottom. Moving the bottom half changes the main indent and moves the first-line indent the same amount.

So, for example, if you like a half-inch indent at the beginning of each paragraph, select the entire document and then click the top half of the triangle and drag it over half an inch on the ruler. The change will occur immediately.

What's a Hanging Indent and How Do I Make One?

A hanging indent (sometimes called an "outdent") is a first line indent that is to the left of the main indent, so that all subsequent lines of a paragraph are more indented than the first line. Lists often use this sort of format. To produce a hanging indent, first bring the left indent in (to the right) as a whole, and then drag the first-line indent back to the left.

The usual dialog-box option

From the same dialog box just shown (Format ➛ Paragraph, or double-click the top half of the ruler), you can type in or increment your way up or down to exact inch measurement for Left, Right, and First-Line indents. Then click OK.

Line Spacing in All Its Wonderful Variations

I explained in Chapter 3, *Simple Editing and Corrections,* how to double-space your document for easy editing. Now I'll tell you the rest of the options in case you want two-and-a-third line spacing for some reason. (You can also set spacing between paragraphs.)

Line spacing within paragraphs

Line spacing is also set from the Paragraph dialog box (Format ➛ Paragraph, or double-click the top half of the ruler). Besides the Auto, Single, and Double choices discussed in Chapter 3, you can also select 1.5-line spacing from the Line Spacing list box.

Or you can choose At Least or Exactly, and then type in (or jump up or down by .5 increments with the little arrow buttons) some precise weird line spacing. The difference between At Least and Exactly is that if you choose At Least, Word may increase the spacing a bit to get the last line on the page all the way down to the bottom margin. If you choose Exactly, the line spacing will not be adjusted to even out the pages.

There are keyboard shortcuts for the three most common line-spacing shortcuts: Ctrl-1 for single-spacing, Ctrl-2 for double, and Ctrl-5 for 1.5 spacing.

Line spacing between paragraphs

The Paragraph dialog box (Format ➛ Paragraph, or double-click the top half of the ruler) also allows you to set a fixed amount of spacing before and or after paragraphs, in case you like your paragraphs to breathe.

Cosmetics

Remember to select paragraphs first. These controls work like all the others. You can type exact numbers of lines (including decimals) or use the arrow buttons to jump by .5 increments. When you are done, click OK.

Page Numbering, Headers, and Footers

To Word, these three things all go together. They're lumped together because they're all things that repeat automatically from one page to the next and they're all things that you shouldn't have to type more than once. Therefore, they're handled in their own special way and kept out of your sight most of time.

But you don't have to think about all of that, and you needn't worry about the fact that when you turn on page numbering, you're *really* making a footer or header. You can just do it.

Page numbering (without thinking about headers or footers)

The fast, easy way to put page numbers on your documents is to pull down the Insert menu and select Page Numbers. The Page Numbers dialog box will appear:

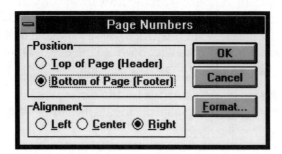

You can just click OK, and you'll get page numbers at the bottom right of each page, starting from the second page. On this dialog box, you can also specify Top, and or Left or Center. If you really want to get fancy, you can click the Format button and choose a different style of numbering (such as Roman numerals), or a starting page number other than 1.

Headers and footers

If you want anything more than just a page number at the top or bottom of each page, or if you want to start page numbers at the first page, you have to deal with headers and or footers.

To make a header or footer, pull down the View menu and select Header/Footer. (Yes, I know this is a bizarre place for this.) The Header/Footer dialog box will appear:

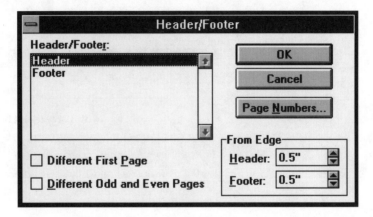

If you want a different header or footer (or none) on the first page, click Different First Page. Two more choices will appear in the box, First Header and First Footer. These choices will already be present if you've previously inserted page numbers.

If you want different headers or footers on odd and even pages, click Different Odd and Even Pages. Four choices will replace Header and Footer—namely, Even Header, Even Footer, Odd Header, and Odd Footer.

A royal pane

You can type and format as usual in a header or footer pane, and additionally, you can insert a few special elements from buttons on the edge of the pane, as shown in Figure 5.6.

FIGURE 5.6:

You can insert special elements from buttons on the border of the header or footer pane.

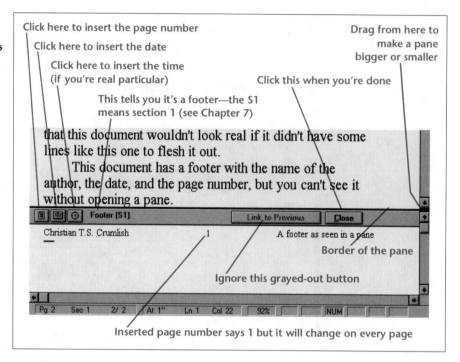

Click here to insert the page number

Click here to insert the date

Click here to insert the time (if you're real particular)

This tells you it's a footer—the S1 means section 1 (see Chapter 7)

Drag from here to make a pane bigger or smaller

Click this when you're done

that this document wouldn't look real if it didn't have some lines like this one to flesh it out.

This document has a footer with the name of the author, the date, and the page number, but you can't see it without opening a pane.

Footer (S1)　　　　　　　　Link to Previous　　Close

Christian T.S. Crumlish　　　　　　　　1

A footer as seen in a pane

Border of the pane

Ignore this grayed-out button

Pg 2　　Sec 1　　2/ 2　　At 1"　　Ln 1　　Col 22　　92%　　　　NUM

Inserted page number says 1 but it will change on every page

If you've changed the margins on your document, you may have to adjust the header or footer tabs to get your page number or other information to align properly with the document. Headers and footers have a center-aligned tab halfway between the left and right margins and a right-aligned tab at the right margin. (See Chapter 8, Organize Your Info, for more on tabs.) For example, I often use 1" left and right margins instead of the 1.25" default margins. I then have to move the right tab in my footer a half inch to the 6.5" mark on the ruler, and the center tab a quarter inch to the 3.25" mark.

Type your name or the title of the document or whatever you want in your header or footer. Insert the page number or date with the buttons on the edge. Click Close when you're done.

Start numbering over

If you want to start numbering over again from 1 somewhere in the middle of the document, then you'll need to break your document out into sections. I'll explain how to do that in the next chapter.

Chapter 6

CHANGE YOUR POINT OF VIEW

Nisbet's Law of Appearances: What you see is never what you get

IF YOU'RE GOING to spend any amount of time working with Word and staring at the screen, you should make sure that your view is as useful and as comfortable as possible. Word allows you a wide range of viewing options. You can simplify the visible formatting so you can concentrate on the text, or you can make nonprinting characters visible. You can remove screen elements to increase the working space, magnify or shrink the text, or view the page as a whole.

If you're happy with the way things are, that's great. But if you want to change your point of view, here's how.

Make the Screen Easier on Your Eyes

As word processors have gotten more sophisticated and complex, the screens they display have gotten busier. With Word, you see the effects of all your formatting. This can be useful, but it can also be distracting.

Also, there's all kinds of buttons, drop-down list boxes, scroll bars, and other doohickeys all over the screen (mostly around the edges, it's true). These things, called graphical elements, are there for your convenience, but they just take up space if you never use them. There are several things you can do if you want to reduce clutter and complication on your screen.

Work in Draft View

Word has an optional view called Draft. If you're in Draft view, you won't see the exact fonts you're using or any text enhancements. Draft view allows you to focus on the words and worry about the appearance later. You can switch back at any time to see how things are working out.

To switch to Draft view, pull down the View menu and select Draft. Figure 6.1 shows a sample document with several appearance and size changes.

Figure 6.2 shows the same document in draft view.

Notice that both bold and italicized text are shown as underlined, and that everything is in the same boring font and the same size that Windows uses for everything else. Now you can see the whole document on the screen.

Draft view still shows alignment and spacing, so if you like to print double-spaced documents, you'll still have to work with them single-spaced to see as much on the screen as possible. Too bad.

FIGURE 6.1:

A sample document in Normal view.

To switch back from Draft view, the procedure is the same. Look at the View menu when you pull it down this time. Draft is checked to show you that it is turned on. When you select it again, the check mark will disappear.

What Is WYSIWYG and Why Should I Care?

First of all, you shouldn't care. WYSIWYG (pronounced *whizzy-wig*—yes, honestly!) is a marketing term, an acronym for "What You See Is What You Get," intended to imply that the document on the screen will look exactly like the document when printed. This is patently false. It's true that things look a lot closer to how they'll look printed than in the old days, but so what? Some fonts are displayed very accurately and some aren't. It hardly matters unless you're desktop publishing with Word and you need to see how your pages look before printing them. If so, good luck.

The sample document in draft view. Both bold and italic text are shown underlined, all the text is in the same boring font and size, and you can see lots more of the document at once.

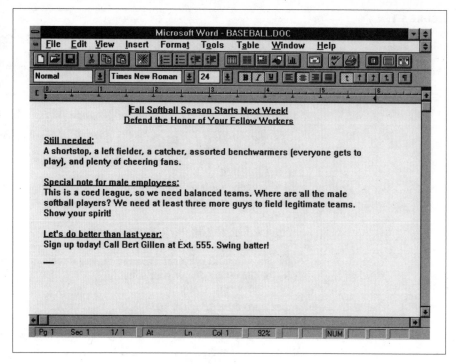

One drawback of Draft view is that the generic font it uses is sort of clunky and no easier on the eye than whatever font you're using. (Although Times New Roman in 10 point, the standard font for Word, can be pretty tough on the eye itself.) But the option is there for you.

Clean the Screen

In a recent computer-magazine article, there was a joke about a new word processor with buttons and sliders and all kinds of graphical elements on the screen, along with an optional view porthole to see a tiny portion of the document being worked on. (Hey, I don't read those magazines. Someone told me about it.)

Fortunately, all the stuff on the Word screen can be hidden, so you can have the entire screen to type on. Former WordPerfect users might appreciate this, since WordPerfect was praised for its almost blank work area.

Hiding the stuff at the top of the screen

You can easily hide the Toolbar, ribbon, and ruler. Do this if you hardly ever use them or even if you know you won't be using them for a while. You can always bring them back.

To hide the Toolbar, pull down the View menu and select Toolbar. To hide the ribbon, pull down the View menu and select Ribbon. To hide the ruler, pull down the View menu and select Ruler. (They're all checked on the menu when visible and unchecked when hidden.)

The procedure is the same to bring any of them back.

Hiding the scroll bars and the status bar

It's a little more complicated to hide the status bar and scroll bars, but just as easy. Pull down the Tools menu and select Options. On the dialog box that appears, scroll to the top of the Category box and click View (unless it's already selected). The dialog box will then look like Figure 6.3.

FIGURE 6.3:

The Options dialog box. Uncheck the boxes for scroll and status bars to hide them then check the Full Screen option. Ignore the other stuff for the time being.

Options — Modify view settings

Category: View, General, Print, Save

Window
- ☒ Horizontal Scroll Bar
- ☒ Vertical Scroll Bar
- ☒ Status Bar
- Style Area Width: 0"

OK
Cancel

Show Text with
- ☒ Table Gridlines
- ☐ Text Boundaries
- ☐ Picture Placeholders
- ☐ Field Codes
- ☐ Line Breaks and Fonts as Printed

Nonprinting Characters
- ☐ Tabs
- ☐ Spaces
- ☐ Paragraph Marks
- ☐ Optional Hyphens
- ☐ Hidden Text
- ☐ All

☐ Full Screen (No Menus - Press Esc to Cancel)

To see more options, click on the category list at left.

Uncheck the three options at the top of the "Window" area (Horizontal Scroll Bar, Vertical Scroll Bar, and Status Bar) by clicking them each, and then check the Full Screen option. Then click OK. Figure 6.4 shows a clean screen. Press Esc to get your menus back.

You'll only have the Full Screen option if you have Word 2.0 or a later version. If you have an earlier version, you won't be able to get rid of the title bar or menu bar.

FIGURE 6.4:
A clean screen: Word stripped to its essentials. Handy for viewing lots of text, but light on buttons and information.

This is what text looks like on a "clean screen." (Select Tools ⇨ Options and then choose Full Screen. You can only do this in Word 2.0b or a later version.)

You can see a lot more text this way, or just write in a huge point size, but it helps to have memorized the menus. You can't perform any commands with the mouse, but the keyboard works fine.

If you get stuck with a blank screen like this, press Esc to get out of it. (What else?)

Notice how the text just runs off the bottom of the screen when you keep typing on

It may be only after you clean your screen this way that you realize that you're used to the shortcuts on the Toolbar or ribbon, or that you like being able to scroll. Just restore whichever screen elements you find useful. Or do all your typing first on a clean screen and your editing and changes later with the tools available.

To restore the scroll bars and the status bar, select Tools ➻ Options again, check the boxes, and click OK.

Make the Hidden Visible

If you're having trouble distinguishing paragraph breaks from regular line breaks, or you want to make sure there's only one space between two words, or you're not sure whether there's a tab in a certain place, all of these things can be made visible.

Show all special characters sometimes

To make all nonprinting characters visible temporarily, click the button on the ribbon with the paragraph symbol on it, the last one on the right:

Paragraph breaks will appear as that same paragraph symbol, spaces will appear as dots (higher up on the line than periods), and tabs will appear as arrows. Figure 6.5 shows an example.

FIGURE 6.5:
Displaying nonprinting characters—spaces, paragraph breaks, and tabs.

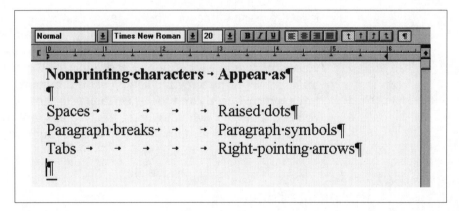

Just click the button again when you want to hide the nonprinting characters again.

Show some special characters all the time

If you decide that you want to see any of these characters as a matter of course, you can set things up that way. For example, some people like to see spaces represented visibly at all times. To make some (or all) nonprinting characters visible automatically, select Tools ➺ Options. On the dialog box that appears, scroll to the top of the Category box and click View (unless it's already selected). In the Nonprinting Characters area, check off Tabs, Spaces, Paragraph Marks, or All. Then click OK.

If you set any combination of tabs, spaces, or paragraph marks to be visible, then clicking the paragraph-symbol button on the ribbon will make any other type of nonprinting character visible (and then invisible if you click it again), without affecting the types of characters you selected to always be visible. If you chose All from the Options dialog box, then the paragraph-symbol button will be "on" (it will appear pushed in) when you start Word and clicking it will turn it off and make all the nonprinting characters invisible.

Who's Zooming Who?

If you're using a line length that lets text run off the right side of the screen, you're going to get tired of all the horizontal scrolling that's going to go on every time you get to the end of a line. You can make your work a whole lot easier by shrinking the view a bit so that an entire line fits on the screen. Likewise, if you're typing something in some tiny point size, you can blow it up bigger to make it easier to read (or you could always switch to Draft view, I guess, but we already covered that). The Zoom command lets you choose any magnification that suits you.

Shrink to fit

The most common uses of the Zoom command are lumped together on the Toolbar. They're the three buttons on the furthest right. From left to right they're Zoom Whole Page, Zoom 100%, and Zoom Page Width:

If your text isn't fitting on the screen, click Zoom Page Width (the rightmost one). Then the widest lines of text will just fit. I often use a 6½ -inch line length and have to use that Zoom button to keep everything on the screen. The percentage that works for the font I use is 92%, but Word will zoom to whatever percentage works best for you. Here's a picture of the bottom of my screen, right now:

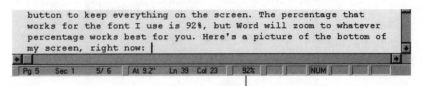

See, the status bar shows my zoom is 92%

Whenever you want to return to regular, full magnification, click the Zoom 100 Percent button (the middle one).

Blow it all out of proportion.

The Zoom Whole Page button, just as it sounds, allows you to zoom out far enough to see the whole page at once. This is only really useful for getting a sense of the layout of the page, its overall appearance, but you actually can type even when everything's so tiny that you can't see what you're doing. Isn't technology amazing?

Zoom Whole Page puts you into Page Layout view, which I'll get to in a minute.

Fine-tune your zoom

If, for whatever reason, you want to make the text huge or tiny, or vary it in some other way, you can specify the zoom percentage exactly. I haven't found much use for that much control yet, but I guess it's nice to have.

Pull down the View menu and select Zoom. The Zoom dialog box will appear:

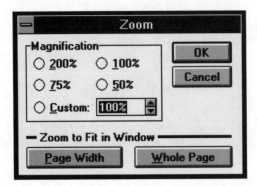

You can click on one of the standard zoom percentages and then click OK, or you can click Custom and type in an exact percentage (or use the little arrow buttons to get to the right number) and then click OK. The two buttons at the bottom of the dialog box are equivalent to two of the Zoom buttons on the Toolbar. Click Cancel if you change your mind.

See the Page as It Really Is

As you know if you've read Chapter 5, *Cosmetics,* there are things that appear on the page but not on the screen, such as page numbers.

As discussed in Chapter 5, you can look at these things in their own little windows (called *panes*). You can also switch to Page Layout view and see the page as a whole, with everything on it. And you can even look at the page (or two pages at once) in Print Preview.

Get a look at the page layout

If you don't do anything about it, you're going to be in Normal view without even realizing it. If you want to see everything on the page, you can switch to Page Layout view. To do so, pull down the View menu (notice the dot next to Normal) and select Page Layout. The zoom percentage will probably get smaller because the view will include empty space to represent the margins and lines to represent the edge of the page. Figure 6.6 shows part of a document in Normal view; Figure 6.7 shows the same document in Page Layout view.

FIGURE 6.6:
Here's a Normal view of a document with real big text.

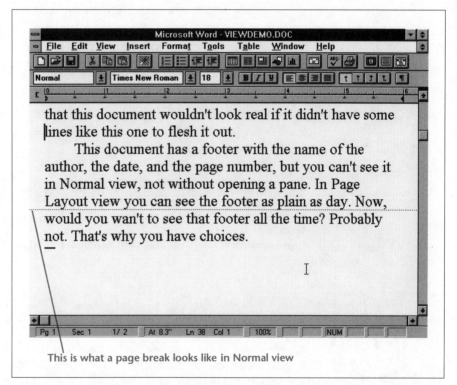

This is what a page break looks like in Normal view

Notice how a page break is a dotted line in Normal view and a solid line in Page Layout view. If you were to click the Zoom Page Width button in Page Layout view, you'd see solid lines at the left and right edges of the pages as well as between pages.

In Page Layout view, you can judge the appearance of headers, footers, etc., and you can type or edit normally, both in the main part of the document and in any of the normally invisible stuff. You can get them out of your face at any time by going back to Normal view.

FIGURE 6.7:
Here's the same
document in Page
Layout view. The footer
has smaller text.

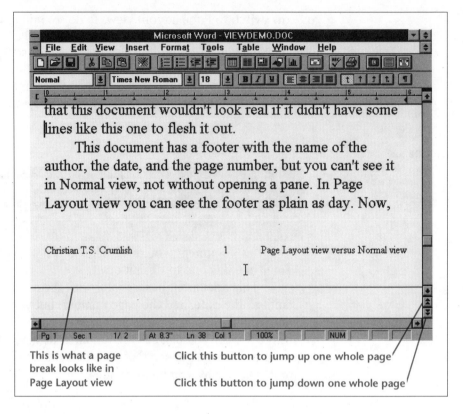

This is what a page
break looks like in
Page Layout view

Click this button to jump up one whole page

Click this button to jump down one whole page

I Just Started Word and It's in Some Funky Mode

Whether you find it useful or not, a lot of Word options are "sticky." This doesn't mean you have to wash your hands after using Word. It's just a geek expression that means they stick the way you set them even when you quit Word. If things look weird right when you start, it's because you or someone else were working that way last time. If Word is in a window and you want it full screen, click the Maximize button in the upper-right corner. If it's in Page Layout view, select View ➥ Normal. If the zoom is off, click the Zoom 100% button. That should straighten things out.

Back to Normalcy

To go back to Normal view, pull down the View menu and select Normal. What did you expect?

The Zoom 100% button automatically puts you into Normal view, if you're not in it already. Zoom Whole Page puts you into Page Layout view, but you can switch back to Normal view and keep everything tiny, if you want. Zoom Page Width does not change what view you're in.

Look Before You Print

You can take one last look at your document before you print it, which is often a good idea. I've often caught errors or problems in Print Preview. As discussed in Chapter 5, *Cosmetics,* you can also use Print Preview for setting margins—in fact, that's one of the easier ways to set them.

To see a preview of your document, pull down the File menu and select Print Preview. You can scroll around the document, set or just look at the margins by clicking the Margins button, and view a two-page spread by clicking the Two Pages button or switch back to a single page by clicking One Page. If everything looks okay, you can print directly by clicking the Print button, or at any time you can quit the print preview by clicking Cancel or Close.

Use Outlines to Get an Overview

One other way to change your view is to go into Outline view. I explain all about outlines in Chapter 7, *Plan Ahead.*

Make Yourself Comfortable

All of these choices are here for you so that you can set Word up to operate the way you're comfortable. Unfortunately, having so many choices can produce the opposite effect, discomfort and worry. Am I in the right view or mode or whatever the hell it is? Don't worry. If you're fine with the way things are, just ignore all this stuff. If you realize after a while that you'd like things to be a little different, you can control the environment (at least on the screen) and have things the way you want.

Mills' Law: Any planning you do ahead of time will become worthless as soon as a project begins

In this part, we'll cover two different ways that you can plan and organize your documents. First, you'll see how to arrange a document so it can have different formatting in different sections. Then I'll show you how Word can help you outline your writing. Finally, you'll find out how to take advantage of tables and lists to make your ideas stand out.

Take a Look at the Big Picture

Chapter 7

PLAN AHEAD

Burns' Law of Planning: The best-laid schemes o' mice an' men gang aft agley

---

EVEN THOUGH WORD almost never makes you stick with your decisions if you change your mind, there are still some aspects of a document that are worth planning out ahead of time. You won't be locked in to any of your decisions, but the techniques we'll explore in this chapter will make it easier to develop some documents.

First we'll see how to tell Word if you're going to use anything other than 8½×11" (letter-sized) paper. Then we'll go through how to apply different formatting to different parts of a document. And finally, you'll learn how to outline a document before or during writing it and how to make structural and organizational changes easily.

Use Whatever Paper You Want

Word assumes you're going to print on letter paper, but you don't have to. If you want to use legal paper or some other weird kind of paper, or if you want to print sideways, along the paper's length, it's easy enough to tell Word what you want.

Pull down the Format menu and select Page Setup. Click Size and Orientation and the Page Setup dialog box will appear (see Figure 7:1).

FIGURE 7.1:
The Page Setup dialog box. Here's where you choose the weird size of paper you want to use.

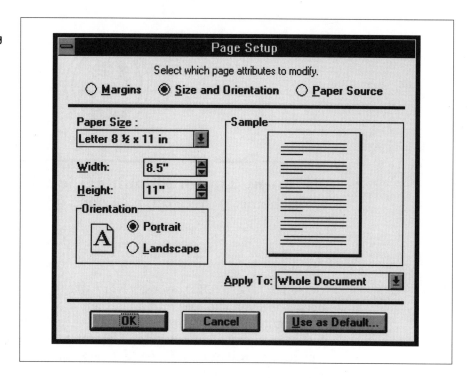

The Paper Size box drops down if you click it and shows you a list of standard paper sizes. If the type of paper you're planning to use is on that list, select it. If not, select Custom Size. Then type inch measurements into the Width and Size boxes. Then click OK.

Turn the paper sideways

To print along the length of paper, instead of along the width, simply click Landscape on the Page Setup box before clicking OK. You'll notice that the length and width measurements will switch boxes.

The page margins will stay the same. So if you have one-inch left and right margins and you switch to Landscape, you'll now have one-inch bottom and top margins, but they're the same margins (the long sides of the paper).

Use nonletter paper all the time

If you use some other kind of paper than letter most or all of the time, you can set up Word so it will assume you are using that other kind of paper unless you tell it different. Follow the same instructions above for choosing paper size, but click the Use as Default button instead of OK. Then click Yes on the box that appears to ask you if you're sure.

Change paper size within your document

If you want part of a document to be landscape, say, or several pages to be legal sized and the rest letter, type the document first. Then put the insertion point on the first line that you want on a different paper size (or orientation). Select Format ➻ Page Setup and choose the type of paper or orientation you want. Then click the Apply To box. On the list that drops down, click This Point Forward, then click OK. A double line will appear across the page above the line the insertion point is on. This is a *section marker,* which I'll explain just up ahead.

Change paper size several times

If you want to change a later part of the document to a third paper style, move the insertion point to the first line that you want to change and repeat the procedure. After you make your paper choices, pull down the Apply To list box. It will now contain a third choice, This Section, but that's not the one you want. You want This Point Forward again. Choose it and click OK. Another section mark will appear.

Change paper size in the middle of your document

If you want to change a portion in the middle of a document to a different paper style, with the sections before and afterward remaining the same, select the portion you want to change before selecting Format ➤ Page Setup. Then, when you have specified the paper you want, choose Selected Text from the Apply To box, and click OK. Word will insert section marks before and after the selection.

How to Get Different Paper Types into Your Printer

If you are arranging to change paper in mid-document (and not just orientation), you'll have to deal with feeding in a different paper type at some point. After designating the paper type in the Page Setup box, choose Format ➤ Page Setup again and click Paper Source. Then, under both First Page and Other Pages, choose Manual Feed. In the Apply To box, choose This Section.

Divide Your Document into Sections

Word lets you break a document into *sections* so that you can apply different formatting to different parts of a document. As explained above, you can even use different types of paper in different sections.

If there are formatting choices that you intend to apply to the entire document, you should make them first, before dividing the document into sections. Then every section will start with the same basic formatting and you can modify the sections separately.

When do I need sections?

If you want your document to contain any of the following, you need to use sections:

☞ Varying margins

☞ Varying paper size

☞ Varying page orientation

☞ A centered page, such as a title page

☞ Varying numbers of columns, or both columns and regular text (see Chapter 9, *The Wonderful World of Desktop Publishing*)

☞ Restarted page numbering

☞ Varying headers or footers beyond odd and even, and different first page

☞ Varying footnotes or line numbers (see Chapter 12, *In the Groves of Academe*)

You don't need separate sections to mix tables with regular text or to vary tab settings (see Chapter 8, *Organize Your Info*). In fact, you don't need sections to vary any character or paragraph formatting (see Chapter 5, *Cosmetics*).

Start a new section

If all you want to change in a new section are the margins, you can force a new section to begin by changing the margins in the Page Setup box, just as you would change paper type, as described above.

Otherwise, you start a new section by pulling down the Insert Menu and selecting Break. The Break dialog box appears (*kazam!*):

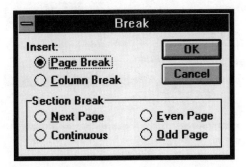

If you want the new section to start on a new page, click Next Page. If you want the new section to start at the location of the insertion point on the current page, click Continuous. If you want the new section to start on the next even or odd page (just as chapters in some books always start on odd pages) click Even Page or Odd Page. Then click OK.

Even if you select Continuous, if you then change the footnote style or paper size or orientation, the effects will start on the next new page. It makes sense when you think about it, but if you don't think, it can screw up your formatting pretty good.

Copy a section

If you've set up a section to your liking and want to copy its format to another location in your document, just select the section break and drag it (holding down Ctrl), or copy it and paste it, to the new location. All the section formatting from the old section will exist in the copy and will apply to all the text preceding the new section mark (up to any previous section mark).

Change how the section starts

To change the way a section starts, double-click the section mark at the end of the section. If you haven't made a section yet, or want to affect the final section, pull down the Format menu and select Section Layout. Either way, the Section Layout dialog box appears:

The section you're in. If you haven't set up any sections yet, it will read 1

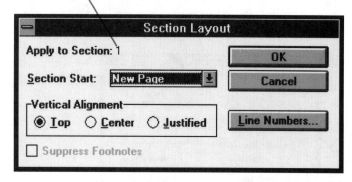

You can also click the left bracket at the left end of the ruler and then double-click anywhere on the lower half of the ruler to bring up the Section Layout box. If you don't click the left bracket first, the first click of a double-click will insert a tab wherever the mouse arrow is, and the second will bring up the Tabs dialog box. (For the terminally curious, double-clicking on the upper half of the ruler produces the Paragraph dialog box.)

The Section Start box contains the options Continuous, New Column, New Page, Even Page, and Odd Page. See Chapter 9, *The Wonderful World of Desktop Publishing,* for an explanation of the New Column option. The rest are identical to the choices in the Insert Break box. (The box won't offer Continuous as an option if it's not possible—if, for instance, the section has a new paper type.)

Important! Use Section Layout First to Set Defaults

The Section Layout box doesn't create sections, but you can use it before you make any section to change how new sections will be created. For instance, if you want new sections to appear continuously after the previous section (by default, they appear on a new page), choose Continuous in the Section Layout box. However, sections created by Page Setup start on new pages regardless of what Section Layout says. So if you want margin changes on a single page, you can change the margins with Page Setup, but you'll then have to go into Section Layout before and after the new margins and change Section Start to Continuous. (This will only change left and right margins. Top and bottom margins are always based on the first section on a page.)

Center a page (or whole section) vertically

To center a page vertically, as a title page, for example, or a business letter, bring up the Section Layout box and choose Center in the Vertical Alignment area. (You could also choose Justified, to have the lines on the page spread out evenly from top to bottom margin.) Then click OK.

Change page numbers in sections

If you do nothing special, page numbers will continue the numbering from previous sections. You can set up page numbering before making sections, or just insert page numbers in the first section and all the rest will follow.

You can also start page numbering in the second section or any section thereafter. Page numbering will then continue in all subsequent sections.

To start page numbering from a specific number at the beginning of a section, select Insert »+ Page Numbers and click the Format button on the box that appears. That will bring up the Page Numbers dialog box:

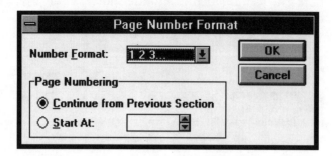

In the Page Numbering area, click Start At and enter the starting page number you want. Then click OK twice.

Page numbers can also be handled in headers or footers.

In fact, if you want a page number on the first page of a section, you **must** *set up the page numbering in a header or footer. To start the numbering at a specific number, click the Page Numbers button in the Header/Footer box. That will bring you to the Page Number Format box.*

Change headers and footers in sections

Like page numbers, headers and footers automatically take after the headers and footers from previous sections unless you tell them different.

If you want a different sort of header or footer to start with a new section (such as a chapter title), place the insertion point in the new section, select View »+ Header/Footer and choose the type of header or footer you want to modify. Then click OK. When you make changes to the header or footer, the Link to Previous button will become available. Click it only if you wish to undo your changes and have the header or footer revert to the format of the previous section.

Figure 7.2 shows a footer created for the second section of a document.

FIGURE 7.2:

A footer created for the second section of a document in which each section is a separate chapter

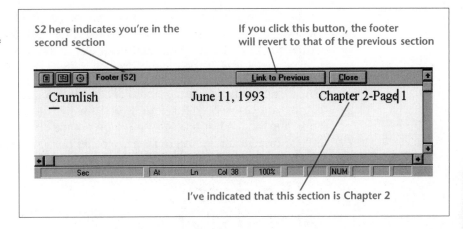

S2 here indicates you're in the second section

If you click this button, the footer will revert to that of the previous section

Crumlish   June 11, 1993   Chapter 2-Page 1

I've indicated that this section is Chapter 2

Getting rid of a section break

You can remove a section break just as you would any character, by deleting it or backspacing over it. The text preceding the section break will then have the formatting of the following section. To reunite two sections and give them both the format of the first section, drag the section break to the end of the second section.

If you delete a section break by mistake, immediately undo the action or you will lose all the formatting of that section. Otherwise, you'll have to put in a new section break and recreate the formatting from scratch. Nothing's more infuriating than having to tell a computer the same thing twice.

A section break is not a page break

The whole matter of section breaks and page breaks can get confusing. A natural page break (or *soft* page break) is shown as a dotted line across the page. An inserted page break (or *hard* page break) is shown as a more tightly dotted line. A section break is shown as a double dotted line. Even if a section starts on a new page, no hard page break will be shown. To make matters worse, a column break (see Chapter 9, *The Wonderful World of Desktop Publishing*) looks just like a soft page break.

Plan Ahead

To see whether a section starts on a new page, check the section layout, view the document in Page Layout view, check out the print preview, or watch the page number readout on the status bar when you move the insertion point past the section break.

One other confusing thing about section breaks and hard page breaks is that you can search for both of them with Find or Replace by using ^d in the Find What box. You have no choice about this. If you're looking for one, you're going to find the other also, so be careful about that.

Outlines—The Best Writing Tool Nobody Loves

Everyone knows you're supposed to make an outline before you write something, but it's like flossing—only the very fastidious do it with any regularity. You think I outline this stuff before I write it? (Actually, I do.) Word's outline feature allows you to start with an outline and expand it into a full-fledged document. Then, at any time, you can revert to the outline view and change or rearrange the outline.

Switch to Outline view

To create or rearrange an outline, pull down the View menu and select Outline. The outline bar will replace the ruler and a little hollow minus sign will appear to the left of the first line of text, as shown.

A style (see Chapter 10) for the first heading level

Preset format choices for the heading 1 style

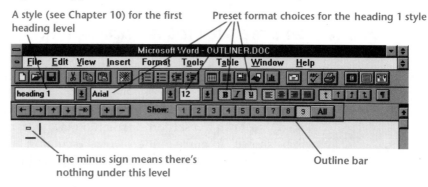

The minus sign means there's nothing under this level

Outline bar

If you've already typed anything, it will appear with a small hollow square to the left of it.

The outline bar allows you to easily expand or deflate the outline and to move parts of it around smoothly.

Enter your outline

To make your outline, just start typing headings. When you begin, you'll be typing a first-level heading. When you hit Enter, the next line will be set up as a first-level heading. Whenever you hit Enter, the new line starts off at the level of the previous line.

To make a new heading subordinate to the previous one, click the right-arrow (Demote Heading Level) button on the outline bar:

A heading that has lower level headings subordinate to it will have a hollow plus sign to its left, instead of a hollow minus sign. Also, you'll notice that the format of each new heading level is different from the previous level. (Actually, levels 7, 8, and 9 are all the same. I guess they figured no one would ever notice.) Each heading level has a style associated with it. I'll explain styles in Chapter 10, *Styles, Template—What's the Difference?*

When you need to create a heading that's at a higher level than the previous one, click the left-arrow (Promote Heading Level) button:

While creating your outline, if you think of something you'll want to write *within* one of the sections you've created, click the double right-arrow (Demote to Body Text) button:

Then when you're done jotting and have hit Enter, click the left-arrow button to start the next heading. Any body text you write will have a little hollow square to the left of it.

Switch back to Normal view

At any time, you can return to Normal view by selecting View ➤ Normal. The outline bar and the pluses and minuses (*pli* and *mini?*) will disappear and the headings will no longer be indented in even steps but will be indented based on the styles, which they retain.

Expand or collapse your outline

Part of the reason for working with an outline is so you can look at only as much of it as you want to see at one time. You can get an overview by looking at only the first-level headings, or only the first two levels, or whatever.

The buttons on the outline bar with numbers on them are for picking the number of heading levels you want to see. If you choose to look at only some of the levels and hide the rest, hidden material will be represented by gray lines. Figure 7.3 shows an outline expanded only to its third heading level.

FIGURE 7.3:

An outline expanded only to its third heading level. The gray lines after Office, Home, Outdoors, and Emergencies indicate hidden material beyond the third level.

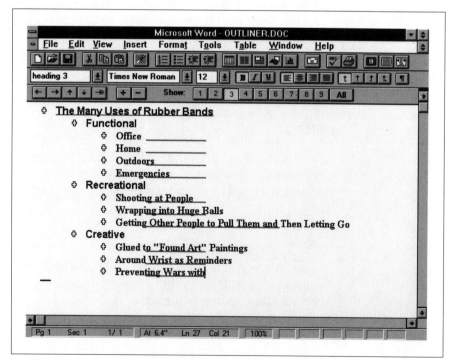

You can also expand or collapse all the material subordinate to a specific heading by double-clicking the hollow plus to its left. Do the same from the outline bar by selecting the heading (or headings) you want to affect and then clicking the plus sign (Show Subtext) button to expand and the minus sign (Hide Subtext) button to collapse. To expand or collapse subordinate headings one level at a time, just place the insertion point inside the highest heading level (rather than selecting the heading) and then use the plus or minus buttons.

You can limit the display of body text to the first line of each paragraph only. To do so, just hit Alt-Shift-F. Hit Alt-Shift-F again to restore full display of body text.

Special rules of selection in outlines

To select any single heading or paragraph of body text, just click to the left of the element you want to select. To select several consecutive headings or paragraphs, click in the first one and drag to the last one.

Be careful not to click the hollow symbols to the left of headings and text if you're trying to select several, or you'll drag stuff to a new location rather than selecting it. If you do drag stuff, remember Undo; if it's too late to undo the damage, drag the stuff back.

To select a heading and all headings and body text subordinate to it, click the hollow symbol to the left of the heading.

Rearrange your outline

To move a heading and everything subordinate to it, either click the hollow symbol to the left of the heading, or collapse the subordinate material and select the heading. When you click a hollow symbol, it turns into a four-headed arrow pointing up, down, left, and right.

To move a single heading independently, make sure everything subordinate to it is fully expanded and then select just the heading. You can also select any number of headings and text and then move them together.

To move a selection to a higher heading level, click the left-arrow button. To move a selection including all subordinate material to a higher level, click the hollow symbol to its left and drag it further left, as shown in Figure 7.4.

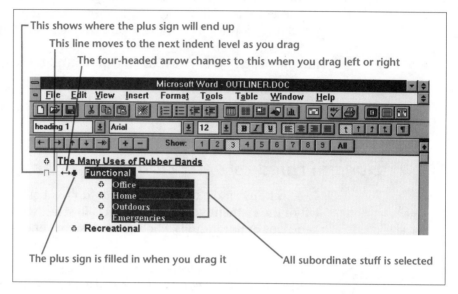

To move a selection to a lower heading level, do the same, click the right-arrow button or drag symbol to the right.

To make a selected heading into body text, click the double–right arrow button.

To move a selection up (earlier in the outline) or down (later in the outline), click the up-arrow or down-arrow button. To move a selection including all subordinate material to a higher or lower level, drag the hollow symbol up or down. When you drag the symbol up or down, it turns to a two-header arrow pointing up and down.

Body text always moves with the heading it's under, no matter what kind of selection you have made.

If nothing is selected and you click one of the arrow buttons, the heading the insertion point is in (and any body text and collapsed subordinate headings) will move left, right, up or down. If you move it up or down, the heading will become selected.

You can type over or drag selected text as in normal editing, as long as you don't click the hollow symbols.

Outline a document you already started

You can convert a regular document into an outline by going into outline view and then promoting text to heading levels. From then you can manipulate the outline as usual.

Change the ugly heading styles Word gave you

If you find the heading styles unattractive (as I do) and would like to change them to styles that suit you better, you can do so pretty easily.

First, select a heading in the style you want to change. Select Format ⇒ Style. On the box that appears, click the Define button. On the box that brings up, click the Character button if you want to change the font, appearance, or size of the text, or the Paragraph button if you want to change alignment, indentation, or spacing. (You can do both, one after the other, as well.)

For more help with styles, check out Chapter 10, Styles, Templates—What's the Difference? I explain how to work with character and paragraph formatting in Chapter 5, Cosmetics.

When you are done with character or paragraph formatting, click OK. When you are satisfied with the formatting choices you've made (they'll be summarized in the Description area of the Style box) click the Change button and click Yes on the box that shows up to ask you if you're sure.

When you next exit Word, you'll be asked something about changes to the template. Click Yes to save the heading style changes and exit.

Make a table of contents out of an outline

Once your document is complete, you can use the outline to create a table of contents with references to the proper page numbers. This will only work automatically if you are using the heading styles Word gave you.

To make the TOC (as we call them in the publishing biz), just place the insertion point at the beginning of the document and select Insert ➤ Table of Contents. If you want all heading levels in the TOC, just click OK. If you want only some heading levels, say the first two, click From and enter the first heading level you want to include, usually 1. Then press Tab and type the last heading level you want to include. Then click OK. (See Chapter 9, *The Wonderful World of Desktop Publishing*, for more on tables of contents.)

Chapter 8

ORGANIZE
YOUR INFO

Krassner's Proof of Entropy: Chaos consumes
any desktop left unattended for over a day

YOU CAN'T ALWAYS rely on normal paragraphs to communicate your
meaning clearly. Readers aren't always willing to wade through pages
of gray-looking text to find specific information they need. In this chapter, we'll consider how you can arrange words on the page in ways that
break up the gray and communicate better.

First, I'll show you how to put information into rows and columns with tables. Tables allow readers to scan easily and pick out the facts they need. They can also be used for simple alignment, for creating forms and invoices, or for mathematics. We'll see what tabs are good for—quick-and-dirty alignment—but tabs can only do so much.

Finally, I'll show you how to create lists, which are often the best way to show step-by-step procedures or to tick off a series of options. Here, I'll use a list now, to prove it.

Visual elements that grab attention better than paragraphs:

1. Tables
2. Tab columns
3. Lists
4. Pull quotes
5. The word **SEX**.

When Do Tables Make Sense?

Use tables when you want to telegraph information, for easy reference and retrieval, for forms, to line up text and figures with no hassle, to put lines on the page easily, or to perform mathematical calculations.

Quick Tables

The easiest and fastest way to make a table is to use the Table button on the Toolbar. It sets things like column width for you automatically, but you can change anything about the table as you go, so there are no real drawbacks to using the button.

You should first figure out how many rows and columns you're going to need. (Yes, you can change that too, at any point, but there's no harm in a little bit of forethought, is there?) To be safe, throw in a few more rows, just in case.

When you know what you want, put the insertion point where you want the table to appear. Then click the Table button and drag the table grid that appears down and to the right until the table has the number of rows and columns you want:

As you can see, the table grid expands as needed and also shows a readout of the number of rows and columns.

You can cancel the table before it's created by dragging back up to the button. Once you've let go of the table and it's too late to drag back up to the button, you can select Undo immediately to remove it.

As soon as you let go of the mouse button, the table will appear at the location of the insertion point in your document, and your insertion point will now appear in the first row and column of the table.

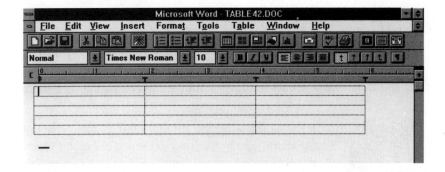

If your table is the first thing in your document, and now you want to type some regular text before the table, you'll find it's easier said than done. The table will seem glued to the top of the document. Never fear—just put the insertion point in the first cell and then press Ctrl-Shift-Enter.

Look at Your Table

A table is represented by gray gridlines that surround each row and column. The rectangles where rows and columns cross are called *cells*. Don't ask me why. Those gray lines don't print out, so they're just there to help you see, but if you don't like them, you can make them disappear. Just pull down the Table menu and select Gridline (it's checked when on and unchecked when off).

You can also turn on and off something called *end-of-cell markers*. They are little notched circles that show the end of the contents of any cell. (There's also a marker at the end of each row.) To show them, click the Show Nonprinting Characters button at the far right of the ribbon (the one with ¶ on it). End-of-cell markers can be turned on even when gridlines are turned off. They're not incredibly useful, although you can use them to select a cell.

One other thing to notice when looking at your table is that the ruler changes appearance when the insertion point is in the table. Upside-down T-shaped markers in the ruler show where the column dividers are in the table.

Getting Around in a Table

After you type whatever you want in the first cell, hit Tab to jump to the next cell over (to the right). If you hit Tab in the last cell of a row, the insertion point will jump to the first cell of the next row.

If you hit Tab in the last cell of the last row, the table will grow a new row and the insertion point will jump to the first cell of the new row. This is great if you wanted to add a row—it means you don't have to specify at first how many rows you need, since you can just keep adding them. But if you didn't want it, remember Edit ➡ Undo (or the Undo button).

If Tab Jumps Me Around, How Do I Type a Real Tab?

Good question. Just hit Ctrl-Tab.

Hit Shift-Tab to jump to the previous cell (or from the first cell of the current row to the last cell of the previous row). If you hit Shift-Tab in the first cell, Word beeps at you and nothing happens.

If you tab or Shift-tab into a cell that already contains text, the text becomes selected.

You can also jump around a table with the arrow keys. If you run into text, the arrow keys will move you one character at a time. Otherwise, they jump you a cell at a time and wrap to the next row when you get to the end of the current one. Arrow keys can jump you right out the end (or beginning) of the table into the regular text.

Finally, you can simply click in any cell to move the insertion point there.

Put Stuff into Your Table

Type into a table just as you would type normally. Remember to hit Tab or → to get to the next cell. Hitting Enter does not move you to another cell, it just adds a new line to the cell you're in and puts the insertion point on it.

You can type text longer than the cell width and Word will just wrap it into a mini-paragraph within the cell, making the cell as many lines "deep" as necessary to accommodate what you type. All the other cells in the same row will expand to the same depth as the cell you're in.

Change Your Table

As you go along entering stuff into your table, you may decide to make changes to it. You may want to add or remove rows or columns, delete text or even whole sections of the table, move or copy stuff, or restructure the table completely. These things can get confusing, but I'll make it as simple as possible.

Know what will be affected

Word distinguishes between the content and structure of a table. There's a difference between deleting text in a cell and deleting a row entirely. Ideally, it's all intuitive, and Word correctly interprets what you're trying to do from context, but things don't always work out that

Tables & Lists

way. Remember you can undo changes that don't work out, and try to notice what you have selected before you do anything to it.

Select a cell

To select a cell, click in the left part of it, when the mouse pointer is a little arrow, or Ctrl-click the contents. You could also just tab your way to it. If there's text in the cell, this will select it. If there's no text, just having the insertion point in the cell is equivalent to selecting it.

Select several cells

To select several cells, click in one cell and drag through the rest; they will all become highlighted. (Or hold down Shift and use arrow keys.)

When you select by dragging, you can continue the selection outside the table to include the text before or after it. This will also change the selection in the table to include entire rows.

Select a row, a column, or the whole schmear

To select an entire row, put the mouse pointer to the left of the row (as a little arrow) and click. To select an entire column, put the mouse pointer at the top of the column. Click when it turns into a black arrow pointing down. To select the whole table, select the first row and drag to the last row, or select the first column and drag to the last column.

You can also select a column by putting the mouse pointer anywhere in the column and clicking the right mouse button.

There are also menu commands for selecting rows, columns, and tables. They are Table ➺ Select Row, Table ➺ Select Column, and Table ➺ Select Table, as you might have guessed.

Delete the contents of a cell or several cells

When you have a single cell or many cells selected, you can delete their contents without removing the empty cells by pressing Delete.

Delete cells entirely

To delete one or more cells so that not just the contents but the entire cells disappear, select them first. Then pull down the Table menu and select Delete Cells. (What else?) The Delete Cells dialog box will appear:

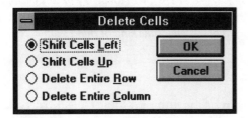

The first two options deal with what to do about the space created by the disappearance of the selected cells. Do you want the cells below them to shift up to take their places, or the cells to the right to shift left? The last two options allow you to delete the entire row or column containing the selected cells. Choose an option and then click OK.

Delete rows or columns

If you know that you want to delete an entire row or rows, select the row or rows. Then select Table ➺ Delete Rows. (The Delete command on the Table menu is "smart." It changes depending on what you've selected.) The rows disappear lickety-split. To delete an entire column or columns, select it or them, then choose Table ➺ Delete Columns.

Delete mixed selections

If you select text outside the table along with rows within the table (by dragging), and then press Delete, the text will disappear and the rows you selected will disappear as well. You can use this as a shortcut for deleting rows at the end of a table.

Tables & Lists

Insert rows

As I described before, to insert a row at the end of a table, just press Tab in the last cell of the last row. To insert a row or rows in the middle of the table, select as many rows as you want to insert, all below the place you want the new rows to appear. Then click the Table button on the ribbon or select Table ➥ Insert Rows. The new rows appear and the selected rows move down to make room for them.

You can only insert as many rows as there are below the point of insertion. To insert more, you have to insert rows repeatedly. If this gets boring, remember the Edit ➥ Repeat command (which repeats whatever you last did, provided it was something legal) or F4. The same kind of thing applies to columns (coming up).

Insert columns

To add a column at the end of a table, select the column of end-of-row marks (they don't have to be visible). Do this by putting the mouse pointer at the top of the table just to the right of the last column until the pointer turns into a black arrow pointing down, then click:

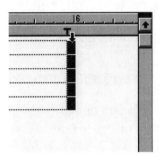

Next, click the table button on the ribbon or select Table ➥ Insert Columns.

*The new column will probably extend past the right margin of the page. To adjust the column widths, see **Change column width,** coming up.*

To insert a column or columns in the middle of the table, select as many columns as you want to insert, all to the right of where you want the new columns to appear. Then click the Table button on the ribbon or select Table ➤ Insert Columns. The new columns appear and the selected columns move to the right to make room.

Insert cells

To insert one or more cells, select the cells that currently occupy the space where you want the new cells to appear. Then click the Table button on the ribbon or select Table ➤ Insert Cells. A box appears just like the one that appears when you delete cells (yes, I know, it says Insert Cells rather than Delete Cells—don't be smart). Check off whether you want cells to shift right or down to make room for the new cells, and then click OK.

If you choose to shift cells right, cells will hang out from the right side of the table. If you shift cells down, entire new rows will appear to include the shifted cells.

Copy or move text

If you select just text and not entire cells, copying and moving work pretty much the same as with regular text. Just be sure not to select the end-of-cell mark when you select the text you want to copy or move. Then drag the selection to the cell you want (or even outside the table entirely). Hold down Ctrl when you drag to copy instead of moving.

If you want to replace some text with the selected text, choose Edit ➤ Cut or Copy. Select the text you want to replace, then choose Edit ➤ Paste.

Copy or move cells

If you copy or move entire cells, they will replace the cells at the destination. To copy or move a single cell, make sure you select the end-of-cell mark along with the contents. If you select more than one cell you don't need to worry about this. Then, holding down Ctrl to copy or not to move, drag the cells to the destination. New cells will be added to the table, if necessary. You can also use Cut, Copy, and Paste Cells on the Edit menu for the same results.

Tables & Lists

Copy or move rows

After selecting an entire row (or rows), you can copy or move it by dragging it, with Ctrl held down or not, to the first cell of the destination row. The row you copy or move it to will move down to make room. If you drag it to any cell that's not the first in a row, it will replace the cells from that cell to the right, and new cells will be added to the end of the row if necessary.

You can use Cut, Copy, and Paste Rows on the Edit menu for the same results. (Columns work similarly.) If you paste other than in the first column, the command on the Edit menu will be Paste Cells.

Copy or move columns

After selecting an entire column (or columns), you can copy or move it by dragging it, with Ctrl held down or not, to the first cell of the destination column. The column you copy or move it to will move to the right to make room. You cannot drag a column to any cell that's not the first in a column, but you can cut or copy the column and then paste it to any cell. It will replace the cells from that cell down, and new rows will be added to the end of the table if necessary.

Evolve Your Table as You Go

You've already seen how to add or delete rows, columns, and cells. There are other alterations you can make to your table as you need them. You can join cells together or split a single cell in two. You can even split the entire table in two. If you want to change the widths of the columns, refer to *Make Your Table Pretty,* coming up.

Combine several cells into one

To merge two or more cells in a row into one, select the cells. Then select Table ➤ Merge Cells. If the cells are empty, hit Delete. If not, the contents of the cells will appear, each in its own paragraph, in the new single cell. The most common reason to merge cells is to create a heading over several columns, as in Figure 8.1.

FIGURE 8.1:
Merging cells to create a heading over several columns

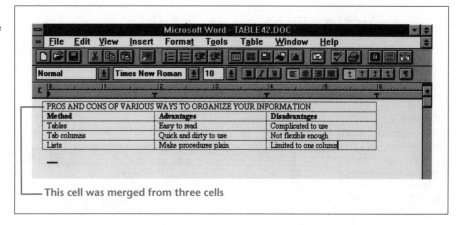

This cell was merged from three cells

You can split up a merged cell into the original cells it was made from by selecting the cell and then selecting Table ↠ Split Cells.

Split your table into pieces

If you decide at some point that your table would work better as two separate tables, you can split the table between any two rows. Just place the insertion point anywhere in the row you want the split to appear above, and then select Table ↠ Split Table (or press Ctrl-Shift-Enter).

You can undo the split if you change your mind right away. Or, at any time, you can delete any paragraph marks between the two pieces of the table to join them into one again.

If you want to split the table and insert a page break at the same time, so that half the table appears on one page and the other half on the next, position the insertion point the same way and then press Ctrl-Enter.

Make Your Table Pretty

Once you've created your table and arranged it to your satisfaction, you might want to pretty it up to make it present the information more effectively. You can add lines to any part of the table (remember, the gridlines don't print). You can format the text in the table. And you can adjust the column widths to make the information fit better.

Putting lines on your table

To put lines on your table, first select the whole thing, then select Format ➺ Border. The Border Table dialog box will appear (see Figure 8.2).

FIGURE 8.2:
The Border Table dialog box. You can add boxes or grids to your table using it. If you want to be fancy, you can change color or even add shading.

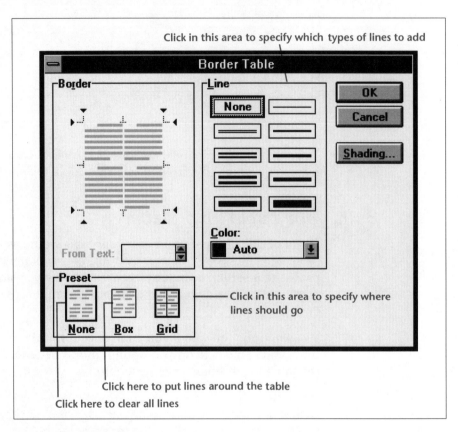

You can click the different areas on this box in any order and you can play with combinations until you get the arrangement you like before clicking OK. If you just want lines around the outside of the table, click Box and then click the type of line you want. If you want lines between every cell, click Grid and then the type of line you want.

If you want different types of lines on different sides of the table or vertically or horizontally between cells, click the specific line you want to affect in the Border area sample and then choose a line type.

You can put lines of one kind on the entire table and then select just part of the table and put different kinds of lines there. If you use this layering method, you'll see ghosts of the lines you've already applied in the sample area.

If you want to put lines around a single cell, make sure you select the whole cell and not just the text in it, or you'll get a paragraph border inside *the cell (see Chapter 9,* **The Wonderful World of Desktop Publishing***).*

For the Very Particular Only: Aligning Table Borders with Margins

Tables are created so that the text in the cells will align with the text in regular paragraphs in the rest of your document. This means that when you add lines to a table, the lines appear outside the normal text margins. To fix this, you have to drag the column gridlines in from both margins, as explained in the upcoming section, *Change column width*.

Formatting text in tables

You format text in a table about the same way you format regular text. You can apply a font, size, or such enhancements as boldface or small caps to any selected text in a table. Likewise, you can change the line spacing, alignment, or indentation of any selected text as you would normal text. The only real difference is the way the ruler works.

Change column width

The off-the-rack tables you get from the Toolbar have columns that are all the same width, wide enough that the table spans the entire page. Once you have entered text into a table, you may realize that you want one column much wider or others narrower. You can make whatever changes you like fairly easily.

Stuff You Can Ignore about Ruler Scales in Tables

When you select part or all of a table and then click whichever symbol in the right part of the ruler, you can switch between three possible ruler "scales." The one that appears automatically when you insert a table is table scale, which shows left and right margins as triangles and column dividers as upside-down T's. If you click the bracket at the left of the ruler, you switch to margin scale, which is no different from margin scale outside of tables. (You can adjust the page margins by dragging the brackets at either end of the table.)

Click the split triangle at the left of the ruler and you arrive at indent scale. This works like indent scale in normal text, but it only shows you the indents for the selected cell or column. You can drag the little triangles in from left or right to increase the indentation from the cell edges, marked by 0 at the left and a vertical line at the right. Clicking the T symbol at the right of the ruler returns it to table scale.

To change the width of an entire column, click on the gridline at its right side and drag it, as shown below:

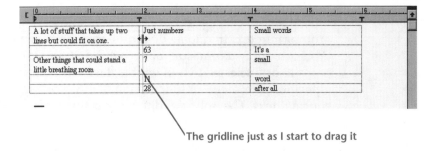

The gridline just as I start to drag it

You can make the same kinds of adjustments to columns widths by dragging the upside-down T's on the ruler when it's in table scale. Ctrl and Shift have the same effect.

This will leave all the columns to the right the same size. They'll just shift right (or left) and the table will change width overall. This may make the table wider than the page, so you might have to adjust the other columns to make it fit. If you want to change a column width without changing the table overall, you have two choices.

You can **hold down Shift as you drag,** and then only the gridline you are dragging will move, so the column to the right of the one you're changing will shrink (or grow) to make up the difference. This limits how much you can widen a column.

Or you can **hold down Ctrl as you drag.** Then the rest of the columns to the right will all adjust evenly to keep the table the same width.

Don't use Ctrl-dragging if you've already fiddled with column widths to the right of the column you're now working on, or else the columns to the right will be moved out and your fine-tuning will be lost.

Drag the gridline at the left of the first column to adjust the table relative to the left margin.

Here's the same table with all the columns adjusted:

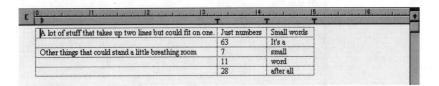

Aligning Tables on the Page When They're Not Full Width and You're Picky about It

If you want to change the alignment of a table, select the entire thing. Then select Table ➔ Row Height. (I know that makes no sense. Hey, I didn't write the program.) The box that appears is shown in *Set a standard row height,* coming up. Then select Left, Center, or Right. Or you can enter a specific indent amount from the left margin. When you are done, click OK. You can even align each row of the table differently if you want. Have a ball.

Tables & Lists

Change cell width

To change the width of a cell or cells but not the entire column, just select the cell or cells and then drag the gridlines of the selected cells. They'll move independently. Ctrl and Shift work the same way as with whole columns, and table scale on the ruler can be used for the same effects.

Set a standard row height

You've already seen how rows of a table expand as needed. You can also set a standard row height. You might want to do this for cosmetic reasons or for reasons of consistency. To set row height, first select the row or rows you want to affect. Then select Table ≫ Row Height. The Row Height dialog box will appear:

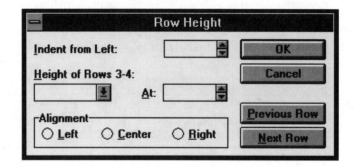

Pull down the Height of Row box and choose At Least. Then select a number of lines in the At box. If you want, use the Previous Row or Next Row buttons to work your way through the table setting row heights like a crazy person.

Make a Table from Regular Text

You can convert text that you've already typed into a table. Say you've been lining things up with tabs and things are getting messy and you realize you'd have been better off working with a table. You don't need to retype, but before you convert it, you might want to prepare the way a little to make things easier.

Word expects you to use Enter to indicate a new row and either commas or tabs to indicate a new column. If there are both commas and tabs in the text, you'll be asked which to use to make the table. The number of columns will be based on the paragraph with the highest number of commas or tabs. If you want to leave a cell blank, put two commas or tabs before the text for the next cell. And if you've been trying to align text with tabs, make sure there's only one tab between entries or you'll get unwanted blank cells.

When the text is ready, select it all and then click the Table button on the ribbon. (Table ➨ Convert Text to Table has the same effect.)

Change a Table to Regular Text

This is even easier than going the other way. Simply select the whole table (or just some rows, even) and then select Table ➨ Convert Table to Text. The Convert Table To Text dialog box will appear:

Select the kind of characters you want to divide the former cells of the table and then click OK.

Use Tabs for Quickie Alignment Only

As you probably know, tab settings appear as little upside-down T's on a normal ruler in indent scale. These are the "default" tab settings and they're each a half-inch apart. You can use these tabs to line things up quickly and avoid getting entangled with tables. You can also set your own tabs fairly easily.

Choose what kind of tab you want

There are four kinds of tabs. Most of the time, you'll want left-aligned tabs, the normal kind, in which case you don't have to do anything special before setting them. You can also have text right-aligned or centered at tab settings, or numbers' decimal points aligned. To choose to set one of these other kinds of tabs, click one of the tab buttons on the ribbon:

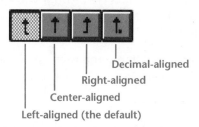

Decimal-aligned

Right-aligned

Center-aligned

Left-aligned (the default)

Click the ruler

Then select the paragraph or paragraphs you want to affect (or the whole document) and then click anywhere on the ruler you want tabs set. As soon as you set a tab, all defaults to the left of it disappear. You can mix different types of tabs. And you can drag tab settings to new positions until you're happy with the results.

TECHNO NOTE

Set New Defaults and Other Boring Things You Can Do with Tabs

If you really want to get into the nitty gritty of it, you can bring up the Tab box. First, select the paragraphs you want to affect. Then select Format ➤ Tabs. (There's a sort of a shortcut for this—double-clicking the bottom half of the ruler, but it makes a tab where you click so it's kinda stupid.) In the box that appears, you can clear any tabs already set. Choose new spacing for default tabs, add leaders to tabs, as well as choose alignment and position for tab settings. What are leaders? Well they are dots or other characters that lead up to the tab position, like the rows of dots that tables of contents sometimes have up to the page numbers. When you've set your fancy tab, click OK.

Make Automatic Lists

Certain types of information are presented best as simple lists, instead of full sentences in paragraph form. Word has a few frills to make lists automatic.

Quick lists

Word gives you a quick way to create numbered or bulleted lists. (Bulleted lists are lists that start with little round dots, called "bullets," or other dingbat characters.) Just type the list straight, hitting Enter at the end of each line, select the text for the list, and then click one of the two list buttons on the Toolbar:

If you rearrange a numbered list, the numbers will not correct themselves. Instead, you'll have to select the list and click the numbered list button again.

Don't get too fancy for your own good

As usual, you can also create numbered or bulleted lists by selecting an option on the menu and then fill out a box and selecting OK. (The command is Tools ➡ Bullets and Numbering.) The box allows you to choose Bullets or Numbered List, and then specify what type of numbering (1, 2, 3 vs. i, ii, iii, for example), or what character to use as a bullet, or any number of other fine-tunings. Play with it if you're interested, but I doubt the time you put in will be rewarding.

Tables & Lists

Tsai's Law: The slicker the publication, the more the typos stand out

If you need to create a newsletter or other publication, or if you just want your documents to look as good as possible, then this is the part for you. You'll see all the layout choices in Word's bag of tricks, and then I'll show you how to save formats that you like so you can reuse them.

Be a Professional, or Just Look Like One

THE WONDERFUL WORLD OF DESKTOP PUBLISHING

Allen's Law: Too many fonts spoil the doc

DO YOU HAVE to put together a newsletter? A notice for the bulletin board? Do you want to make a document that looks really professional? That includes artwork and straight lines? That doesn't look cheesy? This chapter will tell you how to do all those things. And much, much, more! (Sorry, I've always wanted to write that.)

What Does Desktop Publishing Mean?

Desktop publishing is marketing slang that means creating publications with a desktop machine. The idea is that all the professional publishing skills and equipment that used to be needed, such as editing, proofreading, typesetting, layout, and paste-up, are no longer needed if you have a PC on your desktop. If only it were so simple.

What Does It Really Mean?

For all practical purposes, desktop publishing means producing fine-looking documents with your PC and printer. Word has a host of advanced features that allow you to put together great-looking documents, or even "publications," such as newsletters, pamphlets, or handbooks. To make a long story short, I'll explain all those slightly advanced, icing-on-the-cake features in this chapter. You just go through and pick and choose what you want to know.

If you get real interested in this subject or ambitious enough to want to publish a whole book, say, you'll probably want to go out and get yourself another book focused on desktop publishing, or even a program especially designed to create publications, such as PageMaker, Ventura, or QuarkXPress. I'll leave that up to you.

Don't Desktop Publish Your Memos (a Word to the Wise)

Keep your eyes firmly on your own goals when you are making a document. The results covered in this chapter are cosmetic improvements, to help your documents make a good impression, communicate better, or become more presentable. But nobody needs a three-column memo with headlines and captioned illustrations. A lot of time is wasted in offices nowadays desktop publishing interoffice communication. Ask yourself, do I really need to do this?

Useful Things in This Chapter Even if You're Not Making a Publication

There are a few things in this chapter that may prove useful for you even if you have no need to put together a publication. These include:

☞ multiple continuous columns

☞ lines (rules) on the page

☞ paragraph spacing

☞ sarcasm

Tips from the Pros

Here are a few things worth knowing about professional typographical standards. Just following this advice can take you a long way toward giving documents that intangible, boy-you-really-know-what-you're-doing, professional look.

The difference between typing and printing (or publishing)

Typing and printing work differently, and it used to be that they had to look different. With a typewriter, there was no way the lines were going to come out flush at the right margin, unless you looked ahead and typed extra spaces as you went, which would have been a nightmare. In publishing, it's always been central that text could be aligned at both margins, if desired. Typewriters also typically used fonts in which all the characters were the same width (even *w* and *i*). In printing, most of the time you use *proportional* fonts in which characters vary in width as necessary. This looks less clunky. The list goes on, but the point is that printed material has a different look from typewritten stuff, and Word can produce highly polished pages or stuff you'd swear was done on a typewriter.

Desktop Publishing

Do I ever want the typewritten look?

Sure you do. Does it ever bother you to get a letter in the mail that looks too perfect? Some people deliberately cultivate the typewritten look to avoid seeming too slick. To get that look, use one of the Courier fonts, include double-spaces after sentences, and avoid doing most of the things in this chapter.

Professional typographical standards

I'll run down a few things that make the difference between a professional look and a run-of-the-mill look. Don't be thinking about stuff like this while you're writing. Come back to your document later and go over it with this as a checklist.

☞ One space only after sentences and colons. If you can't resist typing two, just use Edit ➠ Replace on a completed document to replace all cases of two spaces with just one space. (See Chapter 3, *Simple Editing and Corrections.*)

☞ Put periods and commas inside quotation marks. This is just an old rule that's still followed today. If you don't do it, you look like a hick. **Important Exception:** Don't mess with the punctuation in lines of computer code unless you are deliberately trying to drive the programmer crazy (which is legitimate).

☞ Don't use underlining. That's a typewriter thing. Use italics most of the time, or bold.

☞ Use real dashes, not multiple hyphens. To insert the short dash between dates or ranges of numbers (as in 10–17), press NumLock to make the NumLock light go on, hold down Alt and type 0150 on the numeric keypad. Remember to let up Alt afterwards. To insert the long dash—like the ones here—to break up a sentence, with NumLock on, hold down Alt and type 0151.

☞ Make "smart quotes." If you look around, you'll notice that printed material uses the curly kind of quotation marks that are like commas. The starting one is different from the ending one. These look better than typewritten quotation marks. With NumLock on and Alt held down, type 0145 to get ‘, 0146 for ’, 0147 for ", or 0148 for ". Let go of Alt afterwards. Use the plain old ' and " for feet and inches.

Don't worry about all these Alt-codes for inserting characters when you're writing a draft. When everything is written and proofed and corrected, then use Replace to substitute typesetting characters for typewriter characters. (If you put Alt-0150, for example, into the Replace With box, you'll only see a black rectangle, but it will come out as a dash. Trust the force.) Replace is explained in Chapter 3, **Simple Editing and Corrections.** *There are also macros that handle some of these typesetting characters. If you're interested, see Chapter 15,* **Automatic for the People.**

Avoid widows and orphans

Widows and orphans are single lines of text left at the bottom and top of the page, respectively, cut off from the rest of the paragraph. It's good form to avoid them, usually, and Word is set up automatically to do that. On the other hand, you may want to allow them sometimes, to make columns of text work out evenly, for example. To allow widows and orphans, select Tools ➥ Options. Choose Print in the Category box, and uncheck Widow/Orphan Control in the Options for Current Document Only area.

Improve character spacing

Real desktop-publishing programs allow you to control *kerning.* That's the spacing between certain characters. For example, if you have capital WA in a headline, there will often be too much space between the *W* and the *A,* because they angle away from each other. So you *kern* those characters closer.

Word doesn't have true kerning, but it does have a character-spacing feature. If you want to tighten or slacken the character spacing of some text, first select the text in question. Then select Format ➥ Character. Then, in the Spacing box, choose Condensed or Expanded, and if you want, change the number of points by which to condense or expand the spacing. You might use this for headlines, when the characters are bigger and spacing matters more, but not for regular text.

You don't actually have to drop down the Spacing list and choose Condensed or Expanded—just click on the up and down arrows in the By box to the right of Spacing instead to expand or condense the selected text in quarter-point steps. This lets you get around the default Expanded and Condensed settings, which tend to be rather dramatic.

Desktop Publishing

The I've-got-twenty-fonts-and-I'm-gonna-use-them mistake

Don't make documents that look like ransom notes. Don't feel like you have to use every font you own in every document. Tasteful documents usually have just a few fonts: An easy-to-read font for most of the text and then one or two others for headlines, captions, and so on. For more on fonts, see *Fonts of Wisdom* in Chapter 5, *Cosmetics*.

You don't have to be nearsighted to use specs

Specs (short for *specifications*) are consistent rules for document format. If you are going to create a publication, you should spec it. This means you should decide and write down how the various elements on a typical page will look. The regular text, is it left-aligned or justified? Single spaced, double, or other? What size is the font? Do this for headlines, captions, photo credits, etc. This will allow you to apply a consistent style to your publication.

The best way to maintain consistency in a publication is to use styles, as explained in the next chapter, *Styles, Templates—What's the Difference?*

Ideas for Newsletters

A newsletter is just a low-key newspaper, published in an office or school or sent to customers to keep everyone informed about what's going on. Figure 9.1 shows the first page of a typical newsletter in Page Layout, zoom whole page view. (You can get a sense of the whole page that way, although some of the details are distorted.)

I'm now going to run down some of the things you'll need to know to make a decent-looking newsletter.

FIGURE 9.1:

I created this page with columns, lines, boxes, headlines, and a figure, and more, all of which I'm about to explain.

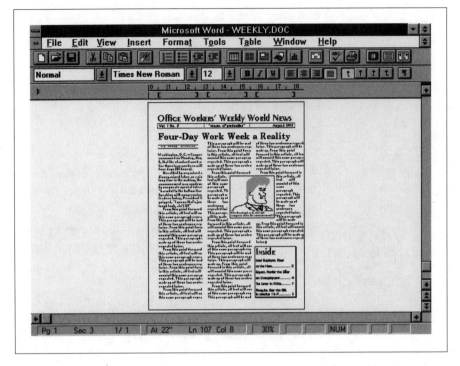

Put Multiple Columns on a Page

Multiple columns, in which the text continues from the bottom of one column to the top of the next, are practically required for any decent newsletter. Setting up and using columns with Word is as simple as pressing a button.

Quick columns

The Columns button—the one to the right of the Table button, showing two columns of lines—on the Toolbar gives you standard, equal-width columns with a standard half-inch between each. As with tables, you can change any of the details later, so there's no reason not to use the button to begin. Click the button (a diagram of columns will appear) and drag to the right until you've highlighted the number of columns you want:

As you can see, the table grid expands as needed and also shows a readout of the number of rows and columns.

You can cancel the columns before they're created by dragging back up to the button. Once you've created them, you can use Undo immediately to get rid of them.

As soon as you let go of the mouse button, the text will narrow on the screen (if you're in Normal view), or you'll actually see the text laid out in the number of columns you specified (if you're in Page Layout View).

If your document is divided into sections, make sure the insertion point is in the section you want your columns in before you click the button.

Look at your columns

As I just mentioned, in Normal view you don't see the columns side-by-side, as they will appear when you print. The text appears as a single long narrow column. But the status bar shows you which column the insertion point is in (Figure 9.2).

If you want to get an idea of how your page is shaping up, or if you want to place figures or control where columns break, you'll need to switch to Page Layout View. Then you'll see the page (roughly) the way it will look when printed. Figure 9.3 shows the same page in Page Layout View.

FIGURE 9.2:

One column (out of three) in Normal view. Note that the status bar tells you which column the insertion point is in.

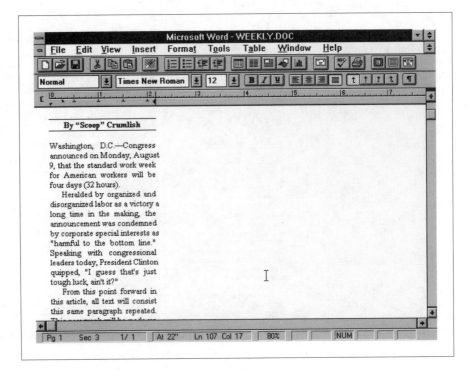

Fine-tune your columns

If you don't like the columns you get off the rack, you can fine-tune them a bit. You can change the space between the columns and you can put a line between them by making selections off a box, or you can change the column widths by eye with the ruler.

Change the space between columns

To fiddle with the space between columns, first put your insertion point in the columns you want to affect. Then select Format ➺ Columns. The Columns dialog box shows up (see Figure 9.4).

Desktop Publishing

FIGURE 9.3:

The same page in Page Layout View. Now you see all the columns (roughly) as they'll appear on the page.

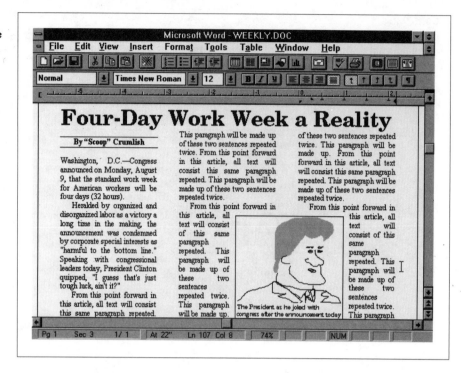

FIGURE 9.4:

The Columns dialog box. Here you can change the number of columns, the space between them, where they will appear, and more.

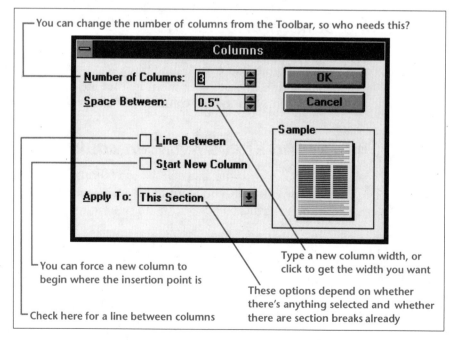

To change the space between columns, hit Tab and type a new measurement (in inches) or click the little arrow buttons till you get to the width you want.

You may have to click in the Apply To box and tell Word where to apply the change. The options will vary depending on the circumstances. For instance, if you've selected text first (and have no section dividers), one of the options will be Selected Text and the other will be Whole Document.

Then click OK. The column width changes to compensate for the change in columns spacing. (All columns are the same width.)

Put a line between columns

In that same box, check off Line Between before clicking OK. (To place other kinds of lines, read *Draw Lines and Boxes*, coming up.)

Change the column width

To change column width, click on the left bracket at the left end of the ruler to bring up column margins, shown as left and right brackets. (If the symbol there is the split triangle, just leave it.) Then drag the right bracket that lines up with the right margin of the first column left or right to get the column width you want (see Figure 9.5).

You can only widen columns so far. When the space between is zero, that's it. The columns change as soon as you let go of the mouse button. (Columns are always all the same width.)

Desktop Publishing

FIGURE 9.5:

Drag the right bracket
to change column width.

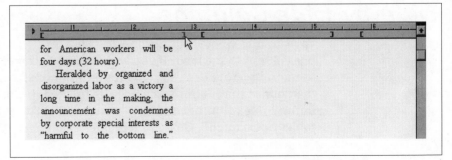

for American workers will be four days (32 hours).

Heralded by organized and disorganized labor as a victory a long time in the making, the announcement was condemned by corporate special interests as "harmful to the bottom line."

Even out uneven columns

When you get to the end of a document with several columns, unless the page just happens to be filled up, the last column will be shorter than the preceding columns. To make them all even—called "bottoming out" in layout parlance—insert a (continuous) section break at the end of the last column.

Force a new column to start

Normally, a column will break at the bottom of the page and the text will continue at the top of the next column. You can, however, force a column to break at any point by inserting a column break yourself. In newsletters, for example, columns sometimes break leaving subheadings separated from text they refer to. If you insert a column break before the subheading in such a case, it will instead appear at the top of the next column, above the text it refers to.

To insert a column break, just position the insertion point and then press Ctrl-Enter. A column break in the last column on a page or in single-column text will work like a page break and the text that follows will start on the next page.

Place graphics amidst your columns

You can put graphics anywhere on the page and make the columns wrap around them if you want to. We'll go through how to place graphics and control text flow around them in *Put Your Picture in a Frame,* later on in this chapter.

Side-by-Side Columns

You can also create columns in which the text does not "snake" from one column to the next. If you want to line up text in parallel columns, as in an itinerary or certain menus or programs, create a table and then adjust the columns as you enter the text. Unlike multiple columns, table columns can be different widths. You can read all about tables in Chapter 8, *Organize Your Info.*

Hyphenate Words to Fix Loose Lines

If you start using narrow columns, you're going to get some very *loose* lines—lines in which there's too much space between words. This happens when the next word is too long to fit on the same line. To fix this, you can hyphenate long words, but you don't want to do it just by typing a hyphen into the word, because if you make changes to the text later, the word may then fit all on one line and you may forget to remove the now-unnecessary hyphen. Words with lame hyphens in them are the hallmark of amateur publications.

Word will break words that have real hyphens in them, if it needs to. So you don't have to do anything special to get Stratford-on-Avon to break between words when necessary.

Put in smart hyphens by hand

Word deals with this problem by having a special character called an *optional hyphen* that appears as a hyphen when needed and is otherwise invisible. You can insert one at any time by just typing Ctrl-- (that's Ctrl and hyphen). If Word breaks the word at that place, then the hyphen will become visible. Otherwise, you won't see anything unless you click the nonprinting characters button on the ribbon (the one at the far right with ¶ on it).

If you always want to see optional hyphens, whether they're in use or not, select Tools ➔ Options. Then click View in the Category box. And then check off Optional Hyphens in the Nonprinting Characters area. Then click OK.

A Note about Preventing Hyphenated Words from Breaking

If you have a hyphenated word that you don't want to break at the end of a line, use a nonbreaking hyphen instead of a regular one. To type a non-breaking hyphen, press Ctrl-Shift-- (Ctrl-Shift-hyphen).

Do all your hyphenation at once

Word can make the hyphenation decisions for you, with as much or as little oversight from you as you want. To hyphenate automatically, go to the beginning of the document and select Tools ➥ Hyphenation. The Hyphenation dialog box will appear:

Uncheck this box if you don't want to hyphenate proper nouns

Hyphenation
Hyphenate At:
☒ **Hyphenate CAPS**   Hot **Z**one: 0.25"
☒ **Confirm**   OK   No   Cancel

Click OK

Ignore this

Leave this one checked or Word will do the hyphenation behind your back

Whether you like it or not, Word will switch you to Page Layout View when you use Hyphenation so you can decide more easily where you need hyphens. This is actually not such a bad idea, especially if you've got columns and want to see how they look side by side.

If you trust Word to make all the decisions (don't), uncheck the Confirm box. Then click OK. If you do uncheck Confirm, Word will go ahead and insert all the hyphens it wants. If you use Confirm, Word will find the first word that can be hyphenated, and the dialog box will look something like this:

The thick line shows where Word thinks you should hyphenate (you can move it with the arrow keys if you have your own ideas on this subject)

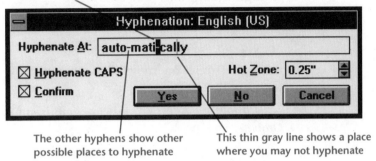

The other hyphens show other possible places to hyphenate

This thin gray line shows a place where you may not hyphenate

Move the insertion point to where the hyphenation will occur if you want, and then click Yes. Or click No, if you don't want to hyphenate this word. Then another word comes up, and so on, until the end of the document. When you're done, go back to Normal view (if you want).

Break Up the Gray

The worst thing a newsletter (or newspaper for that matter) can do is look gray. No one wants to read pages filled with straight text. To make your pages inviting, you have to break up the gray, with lines, boxes, heading, illustrations, and so on.

Draw Lines and Boxes

You can help guide the reader's eye or divide material on the page by strategic placement of lines and boxes. To Word, they're all "borders." Boxes are complete borders around things and lines are partial borders. Generally, you select something to attach the lines to and then choose which sides of the selection will get borders.

Desktop Publishing

What can you put lines on?

You can put lines on any of the following parts of a document:

☞ A single paragraph

☞ Any number of paragraphs

☞ Pictures (illustrations)

☞ A frame. Frames are movable boxes you draw on the page and then put things in

☞ An entire table or any number of cells in a table (see Chapter 8, *Organize Your Info*)

☞ The space between columns (explained earlier in this chapter; these lines are not borders)

Put lines everywhere

To put lines anywhere, you first have to select whatever you want the line or lines to surround or go next to. If the insertion point is in a paragraph, it is considered selected.

Then choose Format ➤ Border. The Border Paragraphs dialog box will appear (see Figure 9.6).

Click the different areas on the box in any order and play with combinations until you get the arrangement you like before clicking OK. If you just want lines around the outside of the paragraph(s), click Box and then click the type of line you want. If you want lines between paragraphs, click in the space between the two paragraphs in the Border area sample. Click Shadow for an extra shadow line at the right and bottom sides of the selection.

If you want different types of lines on different sides of the selection, click the specific line you want to affect in the sample area and then choose a line type.

If you want a line in a footer or header, to separate it from the rest of the page, select the entire "paragraph" in the footer or header and then add a border to the top (for a footer) or the bottom (for a header).

FIGURE 9.6:
The Border Paragraphs
dialog box. It's easier
to use than it looks.
Start clicking the
different areas and
you'll quickly get the
hang of it.

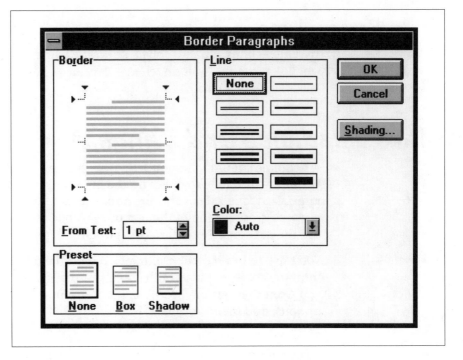

If your selection is text, you can control how close to the text the lines will be. Just type in a number of points in the From Text box or click the arrow buttons till you get to the distance you want.

If your selection contains stuff that you've put borders on earlier, there will be fuzzy gray lines in the sample area. You can click them to make the gray borders disappear or to apply them to your entire new selection.

If Lines Just Aren't Enough, Try Shading

You may notice that there is a button called Shading on the border box. If you click it you get another box that lets you choose from a list of gray shades you can apply to your selection. Choose only a shading—don't mess with the other drop-down lists. Also, don't trust the way the samples look on the list. What really matters is your printer, so you'll probably have to do some test printing to figure out the best shade. Just make sure your text is legible!

Desktop Publishing

Remove lines

To remove lines you've applied, select the same thing you selected when you put the lines on, choose Format ➟ Border, click None in the Preset area, and click OK.

Make Headlines and Banners

A headline should sell an article. It should compel the reader to read it. Headlines also help to break up the monotony of gray with splashy, large-sized text. A *banner* is the name of the publication, usually printed across the top of the first page. A banner might also include art, the date, or other information about the publication.

You have to insert section markers to separate a banner or headline from the column layout of the text. Just place the insertion point where you want to insert the headline, select Insert ➟ Break, click Continuous, and then click OK.

Then type the head before the section break. If necessary, put another section marker before the headline. Experiment with font, size, and things like boldface and italic to get the sort of headline you want. Look at the document in Page Layout view or Print Preview to see how the headline works on the page.

Lay Out Your Page with Frames

Frames are boxes that you draw on the page. You can put stuff in them. You can format the stuff inside them. They can have borders. You can move them around on the page independently. And text can be made to flow around them.

You use frames mainly to put stuff on the page that's not really in the stream of the normal text, or to lay out separate articles on the same page of a publication. Frames can move around with a paragraph or be fixed to one place on the page.

A Few Special Effects Word Can Do to Your Text

You can make curved text, vertical text, text that slants up or down, and more with WordArt. To create your text "art," select Insert ➤ Object. On the box that appears, select MS WordArt and then click OK. A new box will appear. Type in your text and then experiment with the different special effects you can apply to it. When the sample suits you, click OK. The text will be inserted as something called an object. To change it later, double-click on the object and make changes in the WordArt dialog box that appears. Click OK when you're done. To remove the object, just click on it and then press Delete.

To insert a frame, click the Frame button on the toolbar, the one that looks like a little American flag:

(The button is a shortcut for Insert ➤ Frame.) If you're not in Page Layout View, you'll get this dialog box offering to switch you over (so you can really see where the frame is going):

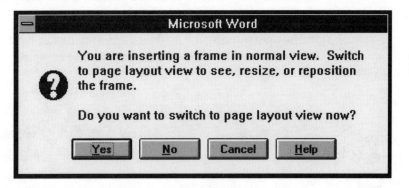

Click Yes. Your pointer will become a cross-hair. Draw a box from one corner to the opposite corner where you want the frame. The frame appears with a border automatically. If you don't want a border on the frame, select Format ➤ Border, click None, and then click OK.

Then type into the frame. You'll have to decide what kind of border you want and how to format the text. Fiddle around with it until you like the way it looks. You'll probably have to adjust the edges of the frame to fit the text well. To do so, just click on the frame and then drag the handles at the sides and corners.

When you switch back to Normal view, you'll notice that the frame appears before the paragraph it interrupts and has a black "handle" to its left in the margin, but if you decide to fool around with a frame after it's placed, you'd best switch back to Page Layout View first.

To control frame placement, size, or text flowaround, select the frame and then select Format ➤ Frame. (I know this terminology gets confusing. There are frames, borders, and pictures, and they're all different, but they can all go together.)

Let Your Paragraphs Breathe

If you still can't get that gray look under control, consider spacing out your paragraphs a bit. We looked at how to control line spacing in Chapters 3 and 5. Spacing before or after paragraphs is handled in a similar way. Select the paragraphs you want to affect. (If there's no selection, the paragraph the insertion point is in is affected.) Then choose Format ➤ Paragraph.

In the Spacing area of the box that appears, enter a number of lines in the Before or After boxes; usually one line is plenty for regular text. Then click OK.

Speaking of Frames, You Can Put One on Anything

You don't have to make a frame and then put something inside it. You can also select something you already have, such as a paragraph or even a graphic that's already placed on the page, and then click the frame button. You'll still be asked if you want to switch to Page Layout View if you're not in it. Click No. The frame will appear around the selection. If you later decide to remove the frame without deleting whatever's in it, select the frame, choose Format ➤ Frame, and then click the Remove Frame button.

Headings should usually have some extra paragraph spacing after them to keep them from running too close to the text. If you're using styles, you can define a heading style with paragraph spacing "after." See Chapter 10, **Styles, Templates—What's the Difference?**, *for more on styles.*

Include Illustrations

Nothing's better for breaking up a gray page than an illustration. A good picture or chart can help clarify what you're writing about. In fact, a picture's supposedly worth 1,000 words, although today I think it's more like 650 words.

With Word you can bring in pre-existing art from other programs, or you can make drawings or charts on the spot. Word supplies two mini-programs, MS Draw and MS Graph, that you can run inside Word to make pictures or charts. If you have other programs you like to draw with, such as Paintbrush, which comes with Windows, or other more sophisticated programs, you can run them inside Word, or import art from them. You can even include scanned photographs this way.

You can also update pictures or graphs at any point by returning to the program they were made in and making changes.

For easy placement, you can put an illustration into a frame and then move the frame around. And you can add a border to a graphic with or without a frame. If you want to go hog-wild, you can make a table, put a frame inside one of the cells, import a picture into the frame, put another frame around the whole table, then put borders on the outer frame, the table, the cell, the inner frame, and the picture. Have a ball.

Insert a Picture

If you want to bring in a graphic that's already been made in some other program, select Insert ➤ Picture. A dialog box just like the Open box will appear. Go to the directory your picture is in and select it from the file list. If you want to make sure you've got the right picture, click the Preview button. The picture will appear in the Preview Picture area, as in Figure 9.7.

FIGURE 9.7:
Using the Picture dialog box to insert a graphic into a document.

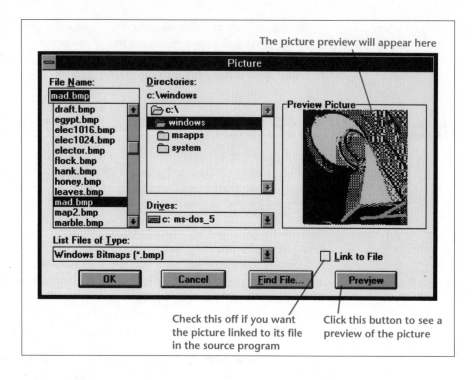

If it's the one you want, click OK. The picture will be inserted into the text at the insertion point. The graphic is then just like a letter in the sentence, and it moves with the paragraph it's attached to. If you want more control over the placement of the graphic, put it in a frame (see *Put your picture in a frame,* coming up).

Make a picture and insert it

If you need to create your own art, you can do it in MS Draw, which comes with Word, or your own drawing program, if you have one. You can fire up MS Draw by clicking the Draw button on the Toolbar, the one with a triangle, a circle, and a square on it:

For other programs, start by selecting Insert ➥ Object. The Object dialog box appears:

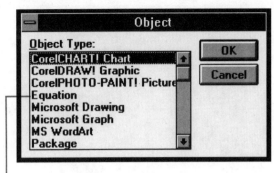

Your list will probably be different, depending on which programs are installed on your computer

Then select the drawing package you want. (You can get to MS Draw from here by clicking Microsoft Drawing.) Then click OK.

The package you selected will appear in a window in front of Word. Resize the new window if you need to. Then make your drawing (Figure 9.8).

When the drawing is done, choose File ➥ Exit and Return. Click Yes when you're asked if you want to update the picture (or No if you've changed your mind). From then on you can treat the picture like any other.

Control Your Picture

Once you've put your picture in your document, you may want to play around with, move it, trim it, enlarge it or shrink it. There are all kinds of things you can do to make the picture look the way you want.

Move your picture

Unless you put the picture in a frame (see *Put your picture in a frame,* coming up), you can only move the picture as you would text. You can cut it and copy it, click it and drag it, but you won't have much control. So if you want to move it, put it in a frame.

FIGURE 9.8:
Here, I've used MS
Draw to create a nearly
photographic likeness
of the president.

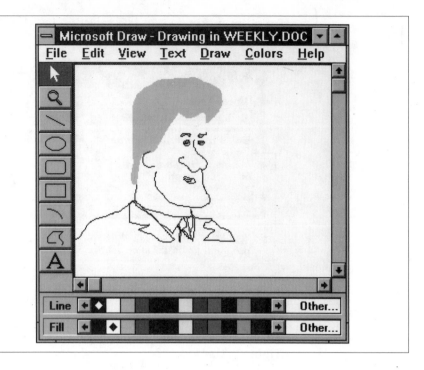

Crop your picture or resize it

To affect the way a picture looks, first click on it anywhere so "handles" appear in the middle of each side and at each corner. If you just want to make the picture bigger or smaller without changing the proportion of height to width, click one of the corner handles and drag. To make the picture fatter or skinnier, click one of the side handles and drag.

If you want to trim out some of the picture (this is called *cropping*), hold down Shift and then click one of the handles. If you drag a corner handle this way the picture will keep the same proportions as it grows or shrinks.

You can also make such changes numerically, by selecting Format ≫ Picture and putting in the measurements you want. If you have precise measurements in mind, that will be a faster and more efficient way to impose them. Otherwise, it's easier to eyeball it.

If you change your mind about cropping or sizing changes, select the graphic, choose Format ➤ Picture, click Reset, and then click OK. Word always remembers how the picture originally looked.

Update your picture

You can modify a picture at any time by double-clicking it to bring up the program it was created in. After you make changes to the picture in the program, select File ➤ Update and then File ➤ Exit and Return. (Or just choose Exit and Return and then click Yes.)

Put a border on your picture

You can put a border directly on a picture or put the picture in a frame and then work with the frame's border (see the next section, *Put your picture in a frame*). You could even do both if you wanted. Borders work the same way with pictures as with everything else. Select the picture, select Format ➤ Border and then choose the type of border you want and click OK. (See *Put lines everywhere,* earlier in this chapter.)

Put your picture in a frame

You can make a frame and then import a picture into it, or select a picture and click the Frame button on the Toolbar to put a frame around it. Then you can move the frame (and the picture) anywhere on the page. Remember that frames come with borders, so you might want to remove the border or change it. Also, remember that the border on a picture is not the same thing as a border on a frame.

If you click a framed picture, the frame is selected first. Click again to select the picture, or double-click to bring up the program the picture was made in, to edit it.

If you want to control the size or position of a frame, or affect whether the text flows around it, select the frame and then select Format ➤ Frame. The Frame dialog box will appear (see Figure 9.9).

FIGURE 9.9:
The Frame dialog box. The main thing you do here is decide whether to have text flow around the frame.

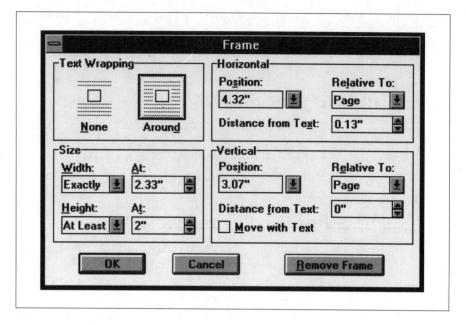

You mostly use this box to put in exact measurements for height, width, and position of the frame. You can affect what the frame is attached to. You can remove a frame with the Remove Frame button. That also closes the box. For other changes, you have to click OK when you're done. You can also make sure that text flows around the frame and doesn't just stop when the frame appears. Figure 9.10 shows a frame set into two columns, with the text flowing around it.

You can also get to this box by clicking the Frame button on the Format Picture box, if you've got a picture inside a frame.

Give your picture a caption

You can put a caption under a picture if it's in a frame. Just position the insertion point so it's a flashing line right next to the right edge of the picture. Then press Enter.

Don't press Enter with the entire picture selected or you'll replace the picture. If you do this, undo it right away.

FIGURE 9.10:
Text Wrapping is set to Around the frame to get this effect

Now you can type your caption and format it how you like. If you want a border that surrounds the picture but not the caption, remove the border (if any) from the frame, select the picture, and add a border to it.

You can also put a title on a picture in the same way. Just put the insertion point at the left side of the picture, type your title, and then press Enter.

Put your picture side-by-side with text

If you want text on one side of the picture, instead of under (or over it), you can do this with a table. Make a one-row, two-column table (see Chapter 8, *Organize Your Info*). Then insert the picture into one of the cells and type the accompanying text into the other cell. You can format the text, add borders to paragraphs, cells, or the entire table. And you can even put the table in a frame if you want to move it around more easily.

Think in Terms of Two-Page Spreads

Whether you're making a newsletter, a pamphlet, or a whole book, remember that publications are usually laid out with different left and right (even and odd) pages. If you want that professional look, think in terms of a two-page spread.

Margins on a two-page spread

You can create margins that are mirrored from left to right page and even include a gutter, some extra space down the middle of a two-page spread to make room for binding, staples, or whatever is holding your publication together.

To set your pages up this way, select Format ➟ Page Setup. Click Margins if it's not already clicked. Check off Facing Pages. The Left and Right margin boxes are relabeled Inside and Outside. As you make changes, you'll see the effects are mirrored on opposing pages in the sample. If you increase the gutter from zero, you'll see a gray pattern appear along the inside margin of each page in the sample. The Apply To area controls how much of the document is affected. When you've got it right, click OK. For more on margins, see Chapter 5, *Cosmetics.*

Page numbers, headers, and footers on a two-page spread

Two-page spreads often have page numbers at the outer edges. (Page numbers are called "folios" in the newspaper business.) And sometimes different headers and footers are used on odd and even pages. For example, in books, often the book title is in the even-page header and the chapter title is in the odd-page header.

To set up the headers, footers, and page numbers for a two-page spread, select View ➟ Header/Footer, click Different Odd and Even Pages, and then choose each of the headers and footers you want to control and set them each up separately. For more on page numbers, headers, and footers, see Chapter 5, *Cosmetics.*

A Very Small Press—Make Your Own Book

Books, pamphlets, or any long publications are difficult to make. The longer something gets, the more can go wrong. And if you're really serious about publishing, you're probably best off with a real desktop-publishing program. I've put out a small book (80 pages) with Page-Maker, for example, and even that wasn't easy.

But I don't want to be too negative about this. Word *is* sophisticated. It's just that getting it to do some of its tricks can be tortuous and might require a lot of study. If you're dedicated to putting out a book and you have limited resources, Word might be your best bet—especially if you've got it already!

As far as designing the look of the book or pamphlet, consider what I explained in the previous section, *Think in Terms of Two-Page Spreads.* Those are some of the easier things about bookmaking. Beyond that, you'll need to deal with book design, separate chapters, a table of contents, and possibly an index. Here's the short course.

Build a Book out of Chapters

There are two different ways you can handle chapters. You can simply create each chapter as a separate document, and even print them all separately. Then you'll have to make sure that each chapter has the same design and you'll have to start page numbering in later chapters from where it left off in previous chapters. The best way to make a design and then use it for all the chapters is to create a template. I explain templates in Chapter 10, *Styles, Templates—What's the Difference?* You can read up on how to start page numbering over in Chapter 5, *Cosmetics.*

The other way to make separate chapters is to make each chapter a different section. You can make all your general design decisions before dividing your document into sections, and then make specific headers, say, for each section. There's a lot about sections in Chapter 7, *Plan Ahead.* Outlines can also be useful for long documents like books. They're also discussed in Chapter 7.

If you're working with a real long document, consider working in Draft mode (select View ➽ Draft). This will speed things up.

Make a Book Design

To make a design and apply it consistently to a whole book, start with setting up pages before you make any section breaks. Select Format ➽ Page Setup and choose the type of paper and the margins you want for your two-page spreads. Then create any headers and footers that will remain the same for the entire document. After you've done that, divide the document into sections. If you have prefacing material before the first chapter (called *frontmatter* in the publishing business), you may want to use the traditional lower-case roman numerals for those page numbers. Then create whatever specialized headers or footers you'll need for each chapter.

Make a Table of Contents

Word gives you a couple of ways to make a table of contents without having to type the whole thing from scratch. There is a certain amount of planning you'll have to do. And you should only create a table of contents (or TOC, for short) when the document is completed.

Make a TOC from outline heads

If you've used outline headings to create your document, you can generate a TOC quite easily. First put the insertion point at the beginning of your document. Select Insert ➤ Table of Contents. The Table of Contents dialog box will appear:

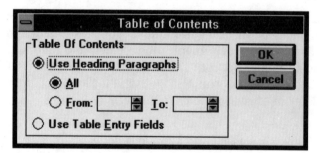

If you want all heading levels included in the TOC, just click OK. If you want only some headings, click From and then enter the first and last heading levels you want in the TOC. Then click OK.

The TOC will appear at the insertion point. Each heading in the document will appear in the TOC. Headings will be indented depending upon their levels. And there will be a dot-leader tab going from the head to the page number of the heading. See Chapter 8, *Organize Your Info,* for more on tabs and dot leaders. You can format the text in the

TOC as you would any text, or change the styles of the TOC entries if you want to make changes that will persist even if you update the TOC.

Make a TOC with fields

If you haven't used the outline headings, you can still make a TOC, but it involves more grunt work. After every heading that you want to appear in the TOC, you have to enter a field code. The less you know about field codes, the better. Just do as I say.

If you want to see what you're doing, click the Nonprinting Characters button on the ribbon (¶). Put the insertion point at the end of the first line you want to appear in the TOC. Then press Ctrl-F9. A bold pair of curly brackets will appear with the insertion point between them.

Type **tc** and a space and then, between quotation marks, the text you want to appear at this point in the TOC. Optionally, if you want some TOC entries indented, you can follow the heading in quotes with a space \l (that's a small L, not a one), another space, and then the number of the heading's level (which will be shown as an amount of indentation in the TOC). Here's an example.

```
tc "The South American Fruit Bat" \l 3
```

Then proceed to the next potential TOC entry and repeat the process, ad infinitum (and ad lib), until you are done. When you are done, hide the nonprinting characters again to get all the field codes out of your face (and to make sure page numbering is not messed up).

After you've entered all the fields, you make the TOC essentially the same way as with outline headings. In the Table of Contents box (shown earlier), select Use Table Entry Fields and then click OK.

Update a TOC

If you ended up having to make changes to your document after making a TOC, you can update the TOC fairly easily. And you should, or the page numbers might be wrong, and there's nothing more annoying than wrong page numbers in a TOC, unless it's wrong page numbers in an index.

Desktop Publishing

If you made your TOC from an outline, you can delete the TOC and insert a new one. Otherwise, just place the insertion point anywhere in the TOC and press F9. Click Yes when Word asks you if you want to replace the existing TOC.

Make an Index

Any technical book or reference book, and even some pamphlets and shorter guides, should have an index. This will enable people to get in and out of the reference most easily. If you want to include an index in your publication, refer to Chapter 12, *In the Groves of Academe.*

You're Not Really Desktop Publishing Unless You're Using Styles

If you're serious about creating professional-looking publications, you'll want to standardize as much as you can, and create reusable, easily modifiable designs. The only way to do this with Word is to use styles (and templates). Styles allow you to make changes to similar elements throughout a document all at once and they make it easier to treat similar elements consistently. Templates allow you to base a new document on the formatting and styles of an old one.

Styles and templates also fit in well with the strategy of layering the work on your publication. You can't design a layout and write an article at the same time. You should write first, then proofread, then edit, and then start formatting. With styles you can apply a consistent format to headlines, bylines, captions, pull quotes, you name it. Is that enough of a plug for Chapter 10?

STYLES, TEMPLATES—WHAT'S THE DIFFERENCE?

Guy's Law of Style: From time to time, style goes out of fashion

---

PEOPLE THROW AROUND terms like *style, style sheet, template, boilerplate,* and *glossary* all the time without knowing what they mean. If that's not confusing enough, different programs use the words to mean different things. It's hard to keep straight, and you're doing just fine without knowing what they mean, right?

Still, if you create a lot of documents, or use formatting a lot, or have a hard time keeping things consistent, you might want to take the time to find out a little bit about styles, at least, and maybe even templates.

Fine, Don't Read This Chapter—See If I Care

Hardly anyone seems to use styles or templates much, except maybe some hardcore desktop-publishing types. Styles are intimidating, and they give off the impression that you'll have to do a lot of work for a small, insignificant advantage. If you have no interest, I don't blame you. Just consider this: Styles make formatting automatic and changing your mind easier. To get the best results, you might have to think ahead, but that's not even required.

What the Hell Is a Style?

First, I'll answer some questions.

What's a style? Styles are formatting shortcuts. They're easy to make and easy to apply. Any type of formatting that you do more than once, you can name as a style and apply in one step.

What's a style sheet? It's just all the styles created for a particular document.

What's a standard style? Standard styles are the predefined styles that are already available when you start a new document. They include Normal, which most people use most of the time, the heading styles for outlines, and a footer style and some other specialized styles that appear when needed. You can always apply the standard styles that come with Word, although they're not very exciting.

What's a base style? Well, that's getting a little ahead of the game. It's a style you base other styles on. More on that later.

What Kind of Formatting Can Be in a Style?

Mainly, any kind of paragraph formats and character formats can be part of a style. Paragraph formats include:

- ☞ indentation
- ☞ alignment
- ☞ line and paragraph spacing
- ☞ tabs
- ☞ borders
- ☞ and even frames

Character formats include:

- ☞ font and size
- ☞ bold, italic, underline (available on the ribbon)
- ☞ and all the other formats available from the Character dialog box (strikethrough, hidden, superscript, subscript, condensed, and so on)

Apply a Style

To apply any style, first select the paragraphs you want to affect.

If you make no selection before applying a style, the paragraph the insertion point is in is affected. As usual, remember that you can use Undo immediately to remove the style; and let me harp on again about saving your irreplaceable work before messing with the copy onscreen, so that if you total it, you can trash the wreck without saving it and reopen your important document unscathed.

Styles & Templates

Then click the arrow button next to the style box in the ribbon (the first box on the left) to drop down a list of available styles (see Figure 10.1).

FIGURE 10.1:
Just standard styles are available at first.

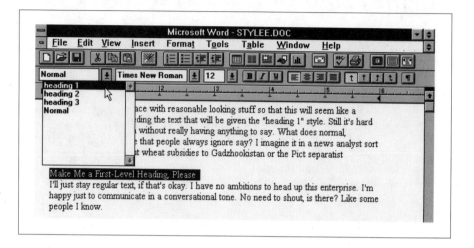

As soon as you release the mouse button, the style is applied. Your selection stays selected until you do something about it:

Remove a Style

To remove a style from text, first select it, then apply the Normal style from the ribbon. All text has to have some style on it, and most text has Normal style even if you didn't realize that. If the text was originally some other style, just apply that old style to the text to remove the new style.

TECHNO NOTE

Stuff You Don't Need to Know about How Style Formatting and Everyday Formatting Work Together

If you've got an italicized word in a paragraph, and then you apply a style that involves italics, the italicized word will be switched back to plain, to retain the contrast between it and the rest of the text. If your whole paragraph is italicized when you apply a style that involves italics, the whole thing is *not* switched back. Word is making a sort of judgment call here. Also, you can add formatting on top of style formatting, just by doing it. If you change the style to something else, the "manual" formatting on top of the style will not change.

If you've added formatting by hand, after applying a style, and you want to get rid of all the extra formatting at once, you can just select the text and press Ctrl-Q. This wipes off any extra formatting. Say you've applied a style to some text that makes it 16-point bold Arial and then you manually make it all underlined. If you select the text and press Ctrl-Q, the underlining disappears but the style formatting remains. If nothing happens, or not everything reverts to the style, that's because Word is guessing you want to keep individual words or phrases highlighted. To clear off all extra *character* formatting, press Ctrl-spacebar.

Make Your Own Style

The standard styles are nothing much to look at, but you can make your own very easily. This is where the term *style sheet* comes in. When you make a style, you're adding it to your document's style sheet, technically.

The easiest way to make a style is to base it on text you've already formatted. That way you know it's what you want.

Make a style from text that's already formatted

Just select the text that's formatted the way you want your style. Then select the style name in the style box on the ribbon (usually Normal). You don't have to click the arrow button, just select the name by dragging. Type a new style name and then press Enter. There, you've done it.

Styles & Templates

Give your styles useful names so that you'll recognize them afterwards, names like Caption, Subheading, Headline Big, Byline, etc. They can be up to 24 characters long. Also, if you've got a series of similar styles to make, give them names that start off the same, such as Headline, Headline Large, Headline Small, rather than names that'll spread them all over the style list (Headline, Large Headline, Small Headline).

Apply your new style just like any other style. Just select the paragraphs you want to format and then choose the style from the style-box list on the ribbon.

Make a style from scratch

You don't have to format a sample paragraph first to make a style, if you already know what you want. To make a style, select Format ➤ Style. This brings up the Style box, which tells you all about the style of the paragraph the insertion point is in. Click Define>> and the box will expand to reveal further options (see Figure 10.2).

FIGURE 10.2:
When you click Define>>, the Style dialog box expands to reveal further options for defining styles.

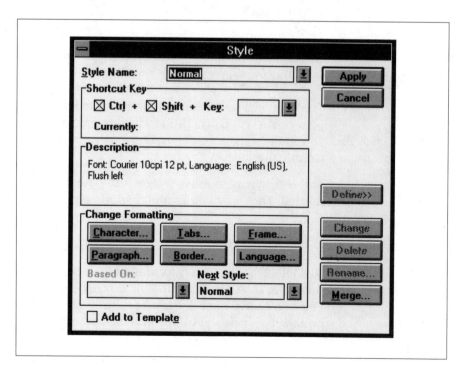

Type a name for your new style. It will replace the style in the Style Name box. Look at the six buttons in the Change Formatting area. Each of them brings up a box you could normally get to from the Format menu. If you want your style to be boldfaced, for example, click the Character button, choose Bold on the Character box, and then click OK. Word will add

    + Bold

to the Description of your style. Repeat this process as often as you need, to specify all your formatting choices.

When the style is right, click the Add button and then Close. (If you want to apply the style to selected text, click Apply instead. This button also has the effect of Add, and it closes the box.)

Styles Don't Have to Be Based on Normal

There's a Based On box in the Style box that allows you to select a style other than Normal to base your new style on. Then the description will start with the base style you pick, not Normal—and you'll be adding formatting to or subtracting it from that style, not Normal.

This can be useful if you plan ahead and decide how you want all your styles to relate. One advantage is that you can change a base style, and all the styles based on it will change accordingly. (I'll explain how to change an existing style soon.)

If you've made a new style and don't want it to change even if the style it's based on changes, you'll have to select the style in the Based On box and delete it. One other thing: All the standard styles are based on Normal. So if you change Normal, you're going to change them all.

Choose a Next Style to follow your new one

Normally, if you apply a style to a paragraph, and then hit Enter to start a new paragraph, the new one gets the same style. Some styles, like the built-in heading styles, for example, are automatically followed by the Normal style, because you don't usually type two headings in a row. (You do type two headings in a row when you're making an outline, of course, but the outline view takes care of that.)

When you make a new style, it will be set up so that the following paragraph gets the same style, unless you change it yourself. On the Style dialog box shown in Figure 10.2 above, the box called Next Style automatically shows the style you're making, but you can pull it down and select a different "next style" if you want.

Postpone the Next Style with Line Breaks

If you're using a style with a different next style, but you want to press Enter to start a new line, and keep using the same style without having to apply it again, press Shift-Enter instead of just Enter. This makes a line break but does not insert a new paragraph mark. So the style stays the same because you're technically in the same paragraph. Watch out, though. If your style has different spacing for between paragraphs from its spacing between lines, you'll get the line spacing, not the paragraph spacing.

Change an Existing Style

One of the advantages of styles is that you can redesign your documents without the grunt work. Just change the styles and all the text that has those styles will change automatically. You can change a style just as easily as making a new one, either by selecting formatted text or by making changes in the Style dialog box.

Change a style from formatted text

First, make formatting changes to text that's already in the style you want to change. Select the text. Then select the style name in the style box on the ribbon (by dragging). Press Enter. Word will check to see if you really want to change the style:

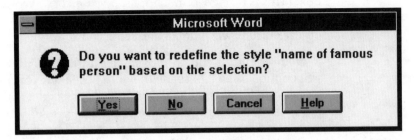

Click Yes and the style is redefined. Everything else in your document with that style will change at the same time. (If you click No, the selected text will revert to the defined style, just as if you had pressed Ctrl-Q, defeating the whole purpose of this exercise.)

If you got no dialog box and nothing happened, Word didn't see anything about your selection as different from the style. You may have to select just the exact text that has the new formatting you want.

Change a style by hand

You can also change a style without formatting a sample. Just select Format ➤ Style. Type the style name and click Define>>. Make all the formatting changes you want by clicking the buttons in the Change Formatting area. When the style is right, click the Change button. (Then click Apply if you want to apply it where the insertion point is. The box will close.) Then click Close (unless you just clicked Apply). The style is redefined, and all instances of it are changed immediately.

Even change a standard style, if you want

You can change standard styles in any of the two ways I just outlined. The change to the style will only occur in the current document. If you want all future documents to have this style changed, you have to check off Add to Template on the Style Box before clicking Change. When you next save the document, you'll get a box asking if you want to save changes to the document template. Click Yes unless you've changed your mind. I'll explain more about templates later in this chapter.

You can also assign any character formatting to the Normal style, including font and size, by checking off Use as Default in the Character box. (This is discussed in Chapter 5, *Cosmetics*.) Word will ask you if you're sure you want to change Normal style for all documents based on the current template. Click Yes if you're sure.

Remember that if you change the Normal style, all the standard styles will change as well because they are based on Normal.

Replacing One Style with Another throughout Your Document

You can search for and replace styles just as you would regular text. (See Chapter 3, *Simple Editing and Corrections,* for more about Replace.) Just click the Styles button in the Find Formatting area of the Replace dialog box while entering the Find What text. A box with a list of the available styles will appear. Choose one and click OK. Then repeat the procedure while entering the Replace With text, except choose the style you want to replace the first style. You don't actually need to enter any text. Then replace as normal. Remember that Replace and Find reuse your entries in the future, so you'll have to clear the formatting when you no longer want to search for styles.

Rename a Style

If you think of a better name for a style, select Format ➡ Style. Type or select the old name of the style you want to rename. Click the Define>> button and then the Rename button. You cannot rename the standard styles.

Type the new name you want in the Rename Style box that appears, click OK to return to the Style dialog box, then click Close.

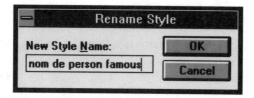

Don't worry—any styles based on the style you renamed will know the new name and won't get "lost."

Remove a Style from the Style Sheet

If you've created styles that you never use anymore, and you're sick of seeing them in the style lists, you can remove them. To remove a style from your document (from its style sheet, to be precise), first select Format ➤ Style. Type or select from the pulldown list the name of the style you want to remove. Click Define>> and then Delete. This dialog box appears to ask you if you're sure:

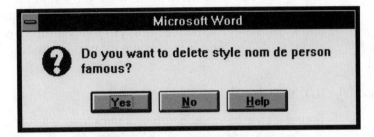

Click Yes to get back to the Style dialog box, then click Close. Any text formatted with the style you removed will revert to Normal style.

You can't remove a standard style, because they're so great, I guess. If you really want to avoid contact with the standard styles, you can create a template with only your own styles in it. I'll get to templates soon.

What Do Styles Have to Do with Desktop Publishing?

I mentioned in the previous chapter that styles are important for desktop publishing. That's because if you're making a publication, you'll want to apply consistent styles to various design elements. You'll want all your page numbers the same, all your bylines, all your captions, and so on. The easiest way to do this is with styles. It's also the easiest way to make across-the-board changes if you want to change your design. Finally, if you use styles and templates, you can easily

Styles & Templates

reuse the styles in later publications. This is especially important for periodical publications that should look the same from one edition to the next.

The Relationship between Styles and Templates

Actually, they're just friends. (Sorry.) Styles are normally part of a document's style sheet. When you create a style, you can attach it to the document's template as well. Then, when you create new documents, you can base them on that template and have all the styles you attached to it available. You can also create templates from scratch and make styles for them or bring in styles from other documents or templates. The standard styles are all part of the Normal template.

Add your style to a template

To add a style to your document's template, select Format ➤ Style. Type or select the style name. Click Define>> and, if necessary, create the style. Next, check off Add to Template. Then click Change or Add, and then Close.

Add your whole style sheet to a template

You can add all the styles from your current document to a template. To do so, select Format ➤ Styles. Click Define>> and then click Merge. The Merge Styles box, which looks a lot like the Open box, will appear. It should show the directory that has your Word templates in it (probably winword). The templates all have .dot extensions. Select the template you want to add your styles to. Then click the To Template button.

A dialog box will appear to warn you that the styles from your document will overwrite any styles in the template with the same names. As long as that won't be a problem, click Yes and then click Close.

If it *is* a problem, click No, and then Cancel; then rename the styles that conflict.

What the Hell Is a Template?

All this talk about templates and I still haven't told you exactly what they are. Templates are very much like documents that you use over and over to create new documents. The advantage of creating a template is that it allows you to set up a standard sort of document once and then reuse that setup in the future without having to recreate it.

Even if you are now willing to use styles, I don't blame you if you don't want to learn about templates. It's a whole nother can of worms. Look, use them only if they'll save you trouble. The idea is that if you're doing something over and over again with the computer, then you can automate it. So if you're creating styles or formatting pages the same way over and over, you should create a template to save yourself work.

Things You Should Know about Templates

Here are a few things you should know about templates:

☞ Every document has one (usually the Normal template).

☞ They have a .dot extension (not .doc as Word documents do).

☞ They're usually "all style, no substance."

Here's what can be assigned to a template:

☞ text (that's what boilerplate is)

☞ formatting, including:

    ☞ page setup

    ☞ section formatting

    ☞ and most importantly, styles

☞ shortcuts, including:

    ☞ glossary entries

    ☞ macros, including automatic macros

    ☞ see Chapter 15, *Automatic for the People (or Make Your Computer Do Your Work for You)*

Styles & Templates

☞ and preferences, including:

   ☞ what's included in the view

   ☞ a customized Toolbar

   ☞ customized menus

   ☞ customized keyboards

   ☞ see Chapter 16, *Customizing Word to Suit Your Needs*

The Normal Template

I think I can explain why you've never realized that your documents were using the Normal template. It's because I oversimplified something in Chapter 1. In that chapter, I told you to create new documents by clicking the New button on the Toolbar. That's actually not exactly the same as selecting File ➠ New. It's a shortcut that skips one step. If you select File ➠ New, before a new document opens up, you'll see the New dialog box:

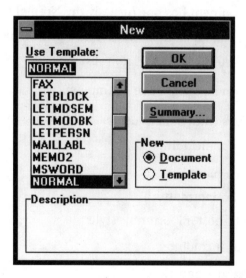

Notice how NORMAL is highlighted in the Use Template box? Normally, you'd just click OK or press Enter at that point (which means that you've accepted Normal as the template). But you could also select another template to base your new document on. When you click the New button, like I recommended, it skips that step and you get the Normal template whether you want it or not.

Change the Normal Template

If you always find yourself changing some of the basic document settings before starting, or before printing—like the 1.25" margins left and right (they're a mite too big for me)—you should consider changing the Normal template. If you want to change margins, select Format ≫ Page Setup, choose the settings you want, and then click Use as Default. This box will appear:

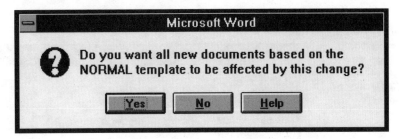

Click Yes.

If you want to change the font, size, or appearance of the Normal style in the Normal template (that's a mouthful), select Format ≫ Character. Then, again, choose the settings you want and click Use as Default. A similar dialog box will appear. Click Yes.

If you don't want to change the Normal template, but you would like to have other standard document layouts available, you should make a new template.

Make Your Own Template

Just as with styles, you can create a template by copying the formatting in a real document that you've already created, or you can start from scratch and create a new template out of thin air. You can also create a template by changing an existing template.

Styles & Templates

Make a template
from a document you've already formatted

Unless you want the same text to appear in every document created from your new template, you should delete all the text in the document. You can leave text in as boilerplate, or replace text with things like "Your name here" if you want. When the document is ready, including all formatting and other selections you want in your template, select File ➥ Save As. In the Save As dialog box that appears, click the Save File as Type box and select Document Template (*.dot). When you do this, the file list shows whatever directory your templates are stored in (probably winword). Figure 10.3 gives an example.

FIGURE 10.3:

Using options in the Save As dialog box to save a document as a template (.dot) rather than as a .doc file.

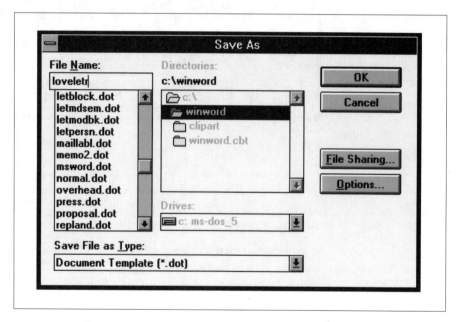

Then replace the name of the document with the name you want for your template under File Name, and click OK.

You're now looking at a template. In the future, when creating a new document based on this template, just start with File ➥ New and then choose this template from the Use Template box.

The only difference if you are creating a template from another template is that you don't have to specify under Save File as Type, because Word assumes you're saving the template as another template.

Make a template from scratch

To make a new template when you don't have a model document, select File ➠ New and then, on the box that appears (shown earlier), click Template. If you want to base your new template on anything besides the Normal template, select the template name or type the document name you want to base it on. Then go ahead and format the template to your heart's content. When you are done, select File ➠ Save As, type a name for your template, and click OK.

Change a Template

If you can think of ways to change or improve your template, you can go ahead and do that. You can only change templates you've created or the Normal template (discussed earlier)—you cannot change the other templates supplied with Word. Changing a template has no effect on documents already created with that template. It only affects documents you create subsequently.

When you change a template, Word asks you to verify the changes when you next save or close the document whose template you changed. When this happens, click Yes.

Change a document's template

If you've got a document open and you want to change its template, you have to change the character formatting, page formatting, and styles all separately.

First select Format ➠ Character and then click Use as Default. This will bring up a dialog box asking if you want to change the template. Click Yes. Then select Format ➠ Page Setup and again click Use as Default. Again click Yes. For any styles you want to add to the document, select Format ➠ Styles. Click Define>>. Check off Add to Template. Click Add. Then click Close.

Styles & Templates

Change a template by opening it

You can also open a template and make changes to it directly. Just select File ➥ Open, choose Document Template (*.dot) under List Files of Type, and then select the template you want to open. Then make any kinds of changes you want, including style changes. When you are done, select File ➥ Save.

What Do Templates Have to Do with Desktop Publishing?

Templates can make it much easier to keep publications consistent. Not only can you apply the same styles over and over, but you can use the same basic page design repeatedly.

The Built-In Templates

Most of the built-in templates are okay, I guess, but you'll probably hardly use any of them. And some of them are so complicated that you'll be more comfortable typing a memo from scratch than answering all the questions the memo template asks you just to get started. Try making new documents from some of the templates, if you're interested. It can be quite a dog-and-pony show watching them do their stuff.

If you pull down the style box on the ribbon, you'll see that all the built-in templates have their own sets of standard styles, some similar to those in the Normal template, and some particular to the type of document.

What kind of built-in templates are there?

Most of the templates are for office workers. These include letter templates, a memo template, a fax cover-sheet template, and an overhead transparency template. There are report templates and a proposal template. (I used the proposal template to propose my first book. It worked!) There's an article template, a press release template, a dissertation template, and mailing-label templates.

Where possible, the templates follow formats established in standard reference guides.

How do they work?

Most of the glitzy stuff the templates can do, asking you the subject of the memo and stuff like that, is done with macros. The template usually has at least one automatic macro that starts as soon as you open a new document. I'll explain all about macros in Chapter 15, *Automatic for the People (or Make the Computer Do Your Work for You)*.

If you don't understand a question a template is asking you, you can usually click an Instructions button on the dialog box. Failing that, you can generally click Cancel or Close and then select Format ➤ Instructions. If you really screw things up, you can just quit without saving and try again. Or give up.

Change built-in templates, if you want

Many of the templates allow you to customize them. There will be a special Set Options command on the Format menu that will allow you to change the default formats of the elements in the template. For example, in the Memo2 template, you can select Format ➤ Set Memo Options to get this Memo Options dialog box:

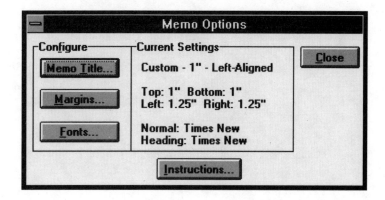

From here you can click any of those buttons and get to more and more dialog boxes that allow you to specify all kinds of formatting choices.

If you want to make more drastic changes than the Set Options dialog box allows, you should probably make a copy of the template first with File ➺ Save As. That way you won't destroy the original template by mistake.

After that, make any changes you want. You can change the styles, change formatting, and change the page setup. You can change the boilerplate text. Whatever you want. When you're done, just choose File ➺ Save to save the changes under the new name.

Styles in built-in templates

You can use the styles that come with built-in templates as you would any styles, but most of them are there for the macros in the templates to use, so you may find you don't need many of them.

You can also add styles to the template if you wish, just as you would add any style to any template (as explained earlier in this chapter).

PART 4

Stone's Law: Any time you gain from productivity, you will spend playing Solitaire

If you use Word on the job, then you may have to use it for mailing or for making forms. If you use it at school, you'll find these tips for the preparation of academic papers handy. I'll also show you how to use Word to work with others on the same documents.

Adapt Word to Your Workplace

Chapter 11

NOT JUST FOR SECRETARIES ANY MORE

Halpern's Law of Direct Mail: You will discover a crucial error only after completing a mass mailing

WHETHER YOU'RE A secretary, an administrative assistant, a manager, an executive, or anything in between, you may at some time have to print an envelope, send out a mass mailing, or create some kind of business or office form with Word. If you're fortunate enough to have someone else who does that sort of thing for you, then let them read this chapter. In the contemporary office, though, most people are now virtually free agents, and odds are you have to do these things yourself.

The Heartache of Envelopes and Labels

Envelopes are always a hassle. Even in the heyday of typewriters, you had to squeeze your envelope onto the cylinder and then type without knocking it askew. Getting an envelope to feed through your printer properly, and then assuring that the address will appear squarely in the right place, can be a nightmare. Even today, some people type or handwrite the addresses on their envelopes for letters they've produced with a computer, which is silly.

Mailing labels have the advantage that they come on $8\frac{1}{2} \times 11"$ sheets of paper and can be fed through the printer in the normal way. The problem with labels is making sure that the text lines up with the stickers and does not print on the space between them. Even though labels are standardized, small variations in paper positioning can screw everything up. On the other hand, with mailing labels you can print up a whole slew of addresses at once.

Automatic Envelopes

Word has managed to automate the process of addressing an envelope. This is something to appreciate. Although you could create an envelope yourself, from scratch, it would require at least some trial and error and quite possibly some tearing of hair and gnashing of teeth. So be thankful at least for that.

Word can even make a pretty good guess about the address to put on the envelope, if you've included the address at the top of your letter. Word takes care of designating the paper type (that's *envelope* type in this case) and, if you include the envelope in your document, it inserts the section break and assigns page number zero to the envelope page, to avoid screwing up your numbering for the rest of your document.

Just press a button

Write your letter before making the envelope. When it is ready, select the addressee's address (this step is optional, but if you're not going to select the address, at least make sure nothing else is selected). Then click the Envelope button on the Toolbar (to the left of the spelling button)—this one:

The Envelope button is a "shortcut" for the Create Envelope command on the Tools menu. Clicking the button and selecting the command from the menu both have exactly the same effect, which is to bring up the Create Envelope dialog box.

This will bring up the Create Envelope dialog box, shown in Figure 11.1.

FIGURE 11.1:
The Create Envelope dialog box grabs the address from your document and will remember your return address after being told only once.

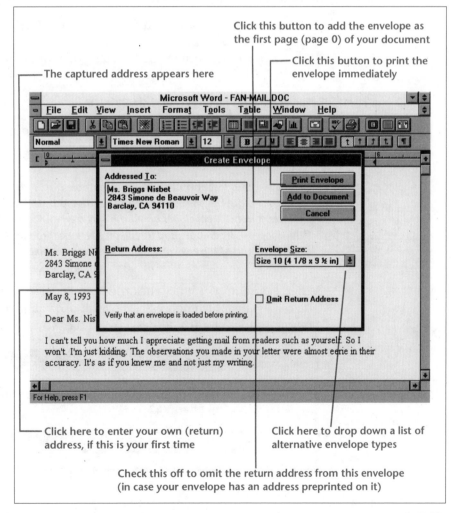

Click this button to add the envelope as the first page (page 0) of your document

Click this button to print the envelope immediately

The captured address appears here

Click here to enter your own (return) address, if this is your first time

Click here to drop down a list of alternative envelope types

Check this off to omit the return address from this envelope (in case your envelope has an address preprinted on it)

Make sure the addresses are correct

Add or correct the address if necessary. You can edit the text in the Addressed To box as you would normally, and it's okay to press Enter at the end of a line. If you've entered a return address in the past, then it will appear in the Return Address area. If there's nothing there, or if the address there is incorrect, click in that area and type your address. If you don't want the return address to appear on this envelope, check off Omit Return Address.

Choose an envelope type

If you are not using standard No. 10 envelopes, click the Envelope Size drop-down list box and choose your envelope type from the list. The box the envelopes came in should tell you what type they are.

Print the envelope immediately

Now, if you're ready to print the envelope, get ready to feed an envelope through your printer.

If you've got a laser printer with an adjustable tray, slide it together all the way and then place the envelope in the tray, left end first. If you've got a dot-matrix printer, it handles envelopes about the way a typewriter does. You'll have to take the paper off the cylinder and thread an envelope through. Put as little as possible of the left end of the envelope up under the paper holder.

When everything's set up, click the Print Envelope button. If you've entered a new return address, Word will ask you if you want to make it your permanent return address (you can always change it again later):

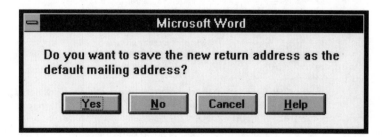

Click Yes or No, and the printing will begin.

Add the envelope to your letter for later printing

If you don't want to print the envelope just now, you can add it to the document by clicking the Add to Document button. The envelope will become the first page of the document (numbered as page 0), and there will be a section divider between it and the former first page.

Don't add the envelope to your letter if you have a dot-matrix printer. You'll always be printing letters and envelopes separately, so there's no point in having them both in the same document.

Figure 11.2 shows what an envelope looks like at the beginning of a letter.

FIGURE 11.2:
The envelope is in its own section, because it's printed in landscape and uses a different paper type.

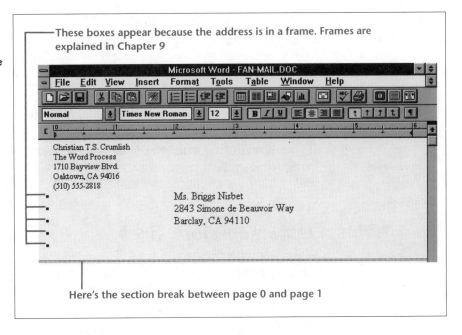

Figure 11.3 shows another view of the envelope and letter, in Print Preview (File ➺ Print Preview).

FIGURE 11.3:
Here you can see the
different paper size
and orientation used
for the envelope.

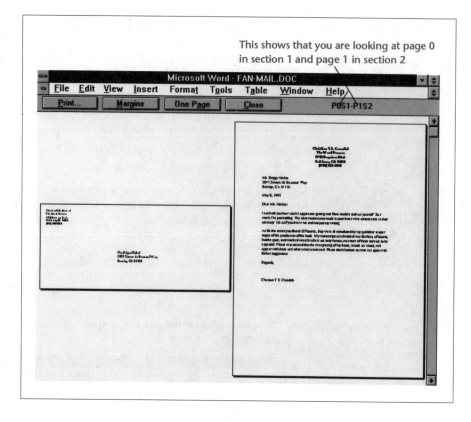

If you play around with the envelope and its section formatting, its
frame, and even its specialized styles, you'll see how complicated it is
and you'll be grateful that Word handles all that for you.

Print a letter, envelope first

When the time comes to print the letter, load an envelope into your
laser printer's sheet feeder. Then the envelope page will print on the envelope and the rest of the letter will print on normal paper from the
paper tray.

To print the whole document, just click the Print button.

Print just the envelope later

Even if you add the envelope to your letter, you can still print just the envelope at any point. All you have to do is set up the printer, select File ➥ Print, and then in the Print dialog box, click Pages, type **0**, hit Tab, and type **0** again. Then click OK. Just the envelope will print.

If you just have a dot-matrix printer and you insist on adding an envelope to your letter, print just the envelope, as described above, and then run the paper back through the printer, select File ➥ Print, click Pages, type 1, and then click OK. All the subsequent pages will then print.

Oh, just go ahead and handwrite the envelope

If I've been unable to convince you that all this envelope rigamarole is worth the trouble, then just go ahead and address your envelopes by hand. I'll admit that, most of the time, I'm one of the silly people who do that. Still, it's not very businesslike, and if impressions count, give the Envelope button a try.

The Pros and Cons of Mailing Labels

Mailing labels are sheets of pull-off, stick-on labels that come in standard sizes and eliminate the necessity of setting up your printer to accept envelopes. However, they bring with them their own alignment problems and usually require some trial and error to get them right.

Labels are probably best used for mass mailings of form letters, which I'll explain later in this chapter.

The mailing label template

Word supplies you with a special template for printing mailing labels. (If you don't know what a template is, read Chapter 10, *Styles, Templates—What's the Difference?*)

Based on the type of labels you're using, it creates a table with cells that line up with the stickers. (I explain all about tables in Chapter 8, *Organize Your Info.*)

To make labels, start by creating a new document with the Maillabl template. Select File ➛ New, click MAILLABL, and then click OK. A dialog box will appear and ask whether you are going to print the labels on a laser printer or a dot-matrix printer:

Word only wants to know this because there are different types of mailing labels for different printers. Click the appropriate button. Word will then prompt you for the exact type of mailing labels you're using (check out Figure 11.4).

FIGURE 11.4:
The Laser Printer Labels Sizes dialog box gives you a list of Avery brand serial numbers to choose from.

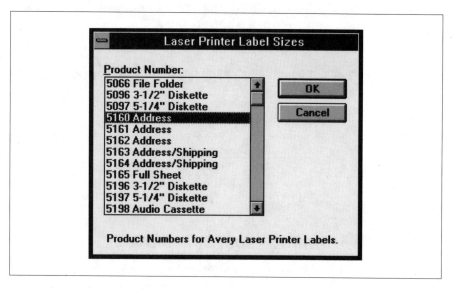

If you're unsure, look at the box the labels came in. Select a label type and click OK.

You can quit the mailing label process at any time, by clicking Cancel on whatever dialog box is showing. You'll get an error message. Click OK. Then close the document that was opened and don't save it.

Watch that template go!

The template's macros then take over and entertain you with a show of creating a table that fits the specifications of the label type you selected. When it's done, Word asks you whether you are printing a single label or many labels at once.

Print a single label

If you're just trying to print one label for a single letter, click the Single Label button. Figure 11.5 shows the Mailing Labels dialog box that appears.

Enter the information for your label and then click Done. The dialog box allows six lines but, depending on the label type you're using, there may be more lines available in the labels themselves. If you need to add more, just type them in directly.

Don't increase the size of the table cells, however, or your label text will print beyond the edge of the label on the sheet. In fact, don't mess with the table at all, if you know what's good for you.

When the label is ready, save it (if you're ever going to use it again), feed the label sheet into your printer, and print the document as you would any other, by clicking the Print button.

FIGURE 11.5:
Enter the information for your one label in this dialog box. Could you have just typed this stuff directly into the document? Yes.

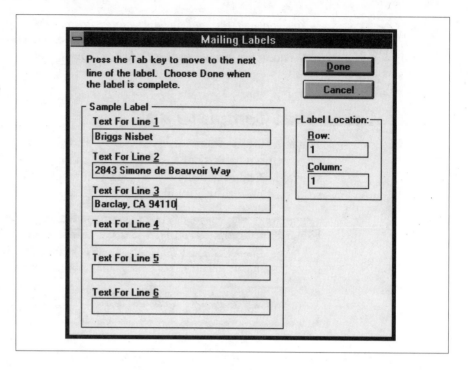

Mailing Labels

Press the Tab key to move to the next line of the label. Choose Done when the label is complete.

Done

Cancel

Sample Label

Text For Line 1

Briggs Nisbet

Text For Line 2

2843 Simone de Beauvoir Way

Text For Line 3

Barclay, CA 94110

Text For Line 4

Text For Line 5

Text For Line 6

Label Location:

Row:

1

Column:

1

Try printing a sample on plain paper first, to see if the text is aligning properly. Word does its best to match the label type you're using, but the printer—especially if it's a dot-matrix printer—may misalign things. After printing on regular paper, hold the paper up in front of a sheet of the label stock to see if the label aligned properly. If the label is off, try adjusting the table slightly to compensate. Tables are explained in Chapter 8, **Organize Your Info.**

Print a whole bunch of labels

If you want to print a bunch of labels at once, you can either type them all in yourself or do a *merge print* to bring the addresses in automatically from a *data file*. I'll explain merge printing (and data files) in the next section.

If you have just a handful of labels to print, type them directly into the table, being careful not to add lines to any of the cells. When you finish, save the document (if you'll ever want to print these labels again), and then click the Print button. (See the Tip about printing a sample page first, above.)

Form Letters without Going Nuts

Form letters are those things we hate to get from Publisher's Clearing House. It's especially annoying to get a letter with the same mistake repeated throughout, like when they try to use your first name to make it sound personal, but they keep repeating your whole name instead. Remember what it's like to get a lousy form letter like that when you're making your own. People really don't seem to mind form letters when there's nothing to remind them that that's what they are.

The whole process of merge printing can get pretty boring and convoluted. I'm just warning you about this now. If you decide to forget all about it when you're halfway through, I don't blame you. But if you've got no choice but to plug away, I'll try to keep things as simple as possible.

Some Words I Can't Avoid Using to Talk About Form Letters

There's no way around explaining some of these specialized terms. But if everything isn't crystal clear for you right away, hold your questions. Once I get into the nitty gritty, these terms will make more sense. First of all, *merge printing* means combining a fill-in-the-blanks type document (the *main document*) with another document that has all the information in it (the *data file*). You write the generic letter or whatever in the main document, and then you merge the data (information) from the data file one-by-one into the main document. The main document is then printed over and over, each time with different data.

I called the main document a fill-in-the-blanks document, but it's really a fill-in-the-*field* kind of thing. *Fields* are variables or placeholders that tell Word which information to put where. The *field names* in the main document have to match the field names in the data file. Each set of information for one printing is called a *record*. Records are made up of fields. I hope you're with me so far, because we haven't done anything yet.

All this dweeby-sounding terminology comes from the database world. So remember, things could be much worse.

Write the main document

The first step in a mass mailing is to write the main document. That's the skeleton of the letter that every recipient of the mailing will get, with the personalizing details left out. If it's easier for you, write everything out as you would normally and then delete the address, salutation, and other pertinent information. When the main document is written and formatted the way you want, you have to create the data file (or attach an existing data file, if appropriate).

Some Things to Think About Before Creating a Data File

The data file will contain all the information (in fields) that gets merged into the main document. When you create the data file, think about what information you'll want to put into each letter. Any information that you might want to treat separately, such as first and last names, parts of an address, etc., you should put into separate fields in your data file. When you have determined all the fields you'll want to put into your data file, you're ready to create it.

When you're ready to attach or create a data file, select File ➤ Print Merge. Figure 11.6 shows the Print Merge Setup dialog box that appears.

Click the Attach Data File button. This will bring up the (surprise!) Attach Data File dialog box (see Figure 11.7).

As you can see, it's another variation on the Open dialog box. If you've already got a data file ready, skip to the next section, *Reuse an Existing Data File*.

Make a data file

Just click the Create Data File button. That brings up, of course, the Create Data File dialog box (shown in Figure 11.8).

FIGURE 11.6:
The Print Merge Setup dialog box. Only some buttons are available at first.

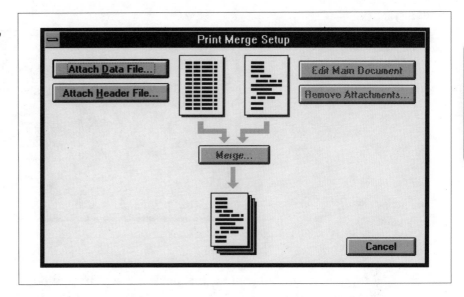

FIGURE 11.7:
The Attach Data File dialog box. Here you can select a pre-existing data file or click the Create Data File button to make a new one.

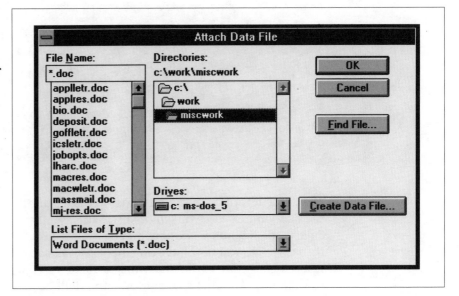

Mailing & Forms

FIGURE 11.8:

The Create Data File dialog box. Add fields one by one here.

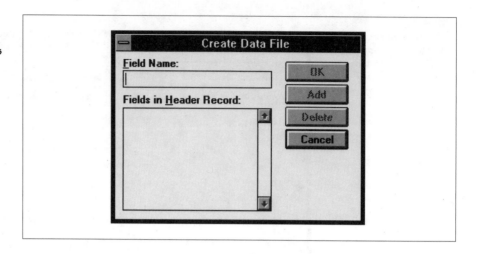

Type the name of the first field you want in your data file. Then click Add.

If You're Looking to Get Silly with Field Names, You Better Go Back to from Where You Came, Because the Geeks Don't Need You, and Man, They Expect the Same

A field name must be one "word," that is, must have no spaces; it can be up to 20 characters long, and it must consist of letters and numbers only. Can you live with that?

Now, repeat that as many times as necessary until you have added all the field names you want to the list. When you are done, click OK. The Save As dialog box will appear. Type a file name for your data file and then click OK. You now have an empty data file on the screen. It's really just a table with as many columns as fields you entered and just one row (so far). The first row contains the field names, all in boldface. Figure 11.9 shows an example.

FIGURE 11.9:
An empty data file waiting for data. The first row contains the field names.

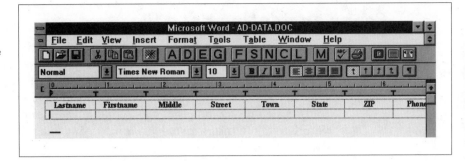

Now enter the data. That is, put in all the information for each record, for each person you want to send your form letter to. When you have completed a field entry, press Tab to jump to the next field. At the end of a record, press Tab to start a new record. Don't worry if the cells need to expand to accommodate the text you enter. It doesn't matter how the words are wrapped in the data file. Press Enter only if you want part of the field to appear on a second line. Also, leave fields blank if there's nothing to put in them.

Figure 11.10 shows several records in a completed version of the same data file as in the previous figure.

FIGURE 11.10:
Here's the same data file with several records entered.

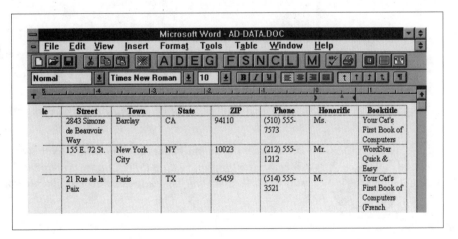

Now skip ahead to *Put field codes in the main document,* coming up.

Mailing & Forms

Reuse an existing data file

If you've already got a data file ready for your form letter (and you're better off reusing data files than recreating them every time you need to mail), you can attach the existing data file instead of creating a new one. In the Attach Data File dialog box, find the file just as you would in the Open dialog box (or type the file name), and then click OK. Now you're ready to insert merge fields into your main document.

Put field codes in the main document

Now switch back to the main document (use the Window menu). Notice that there's now something called the Print Merge bar between the ribbon and the ruler. To begin inserting field codes, place the insertion point where you want the first code to appear, and then click the Insert Merge Field button on the Print Merge bar. That brings up the Insert Merge Field dialog box:

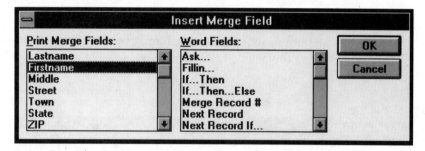

Choose the field you want and then click OK. The field code name will appear between French quotation marks (<< and >>). Now repeat that process until you have filled in all the blanks in your letter.

Don't forget the normal spaces and punctuation you would put between words. Only the exact text in the data file will appear where the field codes are, so make sure that the results will look like normal sentences when you do the merge print.

Figure 11.11 shows a sample letter with all necessary field codes added from my attached data file.

FIGURE 11.11:
The letter to my readers is completed with fields from the data file. Note that I've left spaces between the fields that appear on the same line, so that the resulting text will look normal.

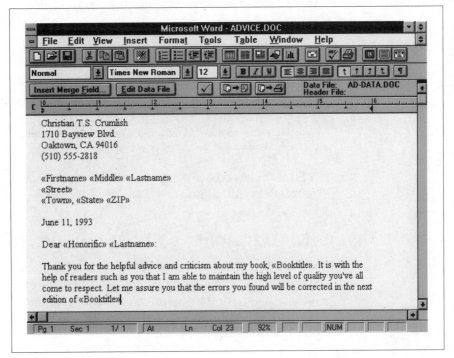

Format the fields

Although the text that will replace the fields is not there yet, you can format the field codes themselves and that same formatting will apply to the text when it is merged from the data file into the main document. So format to your heart's content.

The main event—merge printing

When you are ready to print, click the button on the Print Merge bar that shows several documents going to a printer—the right one here:

Click this button to send all the merged letters to a single file
to be printed at another time

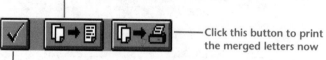

Click this button to print
the merged letters now

Click this button to make sure there are no errors in your main
document or data file (or just cross your fingers)

A Print dialog box will appear with some options grayed out. Click OK. Your letters will all print.

Things I'm not going to tell you about

There's a lot more to merge printing that I'm not going to tell you, and you should thank me. You know how to get through a straightforward mass mailing, and my general advice is keep it simple. I *will* explain how to merge print envelopes and labels, because one or the other is absolutely essential.

Envelopes for your mass mailing

The best way to handle envelopes is to create a separate envelope document. You can just add the envelope as explained earlier in *Automatic Envelopes*, copy the first (envelope) page to a new document, and then delete the first page. This will allow you to attach the same data file to the new envelope main document and then print all the envelopes at once as a merge print of its own.

Mailing labels for your mass mailing

Begin as explained earlier in this chapter by opening a new document and selecting the MAILLABL template for it. Tell Word whether you have a laser or dot-matrix printer, then choose the brand number of the label type you're using and click OK. Word will then create a table to match your label type and then ask if you are printing a single label or many labels at once. Click the Multiple Labels button. A dialog box will appear and ask you if the data and header are in separate files:

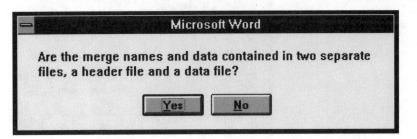

Microsoft Word

Are the merge names and data contained in two separate files, a header file and a data file?

Yes   No

Why Does Word Want to Know If the Data and Header Are in Separate Files?

This is one of the things I didn't tell you about. Don't worry about it. If you've created your data files the way I told you, then you don't have a separate header file. Yes, it's possible to do things that way, but don't bother unless you've got a reason to.

Click No. This brings up the (by now familiar?) Attach Data File dialog box. Select the data file and click OK. The Layout Mailing Labels dialog box appears (see Figure 11.12).

Select the first field you want on the label and choose a space or any punctuation you may want to come immediately after the field. Then click Add to Label. If you make a mistake or change your mind, click Cancel Last Add. When you've completed the label, click Done. Now you get your reward for the terribly slow process of entering fields: You can sit back and relax as Word adds those fields to every label in the document.

When it's done, Word displays a dialog box to tell you what to do next. Click OK. If you're printing to a dot-matrix printer, you'll see a dialog box recommending a macro you can run to fine-tune the alignment of the labels; click OK. (See Chapter 15, *Automatic for the People*, for more on macros.)

FIGURE 11.12:
Have patience. Choose the fields you want on your labels from this dialog box, and insert whatever punctuation you need as you go.

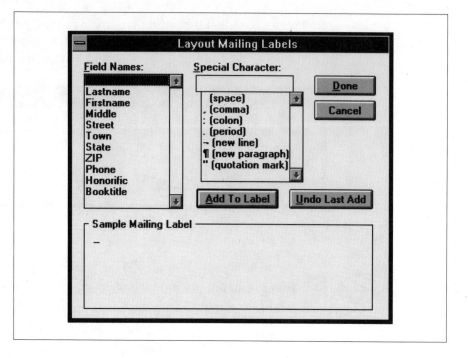

You can now see the fields laid out in the table, repeated in each cell (as shown in Figure 11.13).

To print the labels, first load your labels into the sheet feeder. Then click the button on the Merge Print bar that shows documents going to a printer, and then click OK in the Print dialog box that appears. That's it.

Make Your Own Forms

Here's one other bit of specialized office information that has absolutely nothing to do with mailing! If you need to create a business form for your office, the easiest way is to use a table. With a table you can put text in boxes, line the boxes up, adjust the widths and heights as much as you want, and add lines. You can even shade certain parts of the table and put "For Office Use Only" in that area.

FIGURE 11.13:
These mailing labels use fields from my AD-DATA file.

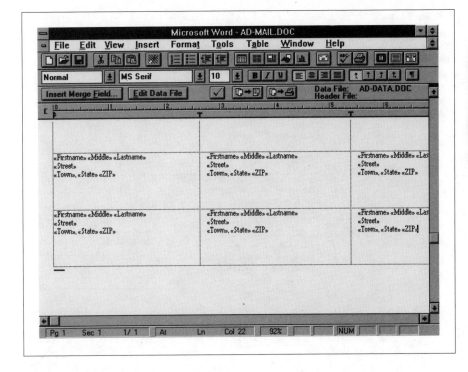

Mailing & Forms

Figure 11.14 shows an example of a form created as a table. If you need to brush up on creating, editing, and formatting tables, refer to Chapter 8, *Organize Your Info*.

Originally the table had 11 columns in each row. By strategically resizing the columns and then merging them here and there, I was able to make the different-sized areas I needed on my form. I formatted different types of text differently and then put borders on cells or groups of cells to create the specific blanks on the form. The logo at the top is WordArt in a frame, and the other two blocks of text above the table are also in frames. The text at the end is regular text.

A form this complicated will probably require you to suffer through some trial and error and a little frustration, but once you get the hang of things, it becomes relatively easy, mindless work.

FIGURE 11.14:

I made this form in about an hour. It consists mainly of a table with variously merged and bordered cells, and some frames and WordArt.

Funkedelic Hi-Fi & Stereo

Funkedelic Hi-Fi & Stereo
6952 Telegram Ave.
Barclay, CA 94407
Phone: (510) 555-3531
Fax: (510) 555-3353
Store Hours: Mon–Fri 10 to 6, Sat 10 to 5

Work Order

Order No.:....................................
Date:....................................
Rep:....................................

CUSTOMER INFORMATION	SERVICE REQUESTED
Name:	__ Diagnostic __ Repair __Warranty __Rush

Address:
City: State: Zip:
Phone:

ESTIMATE

Standard Labor: __ Hrs. @ $45/Hr.
Rush/On-site Labor: __ Hrs. @ $60/Hr.
Part & Materials:
Estimated Total Charge:

SERVICE AUTHORIZATION

I authorize theh ere riefsdf jdsf asdjfg asd d kdfg dsfg dsjkfg djksfg

dfdfsdfsdfsdafsdfsdf sdfsdfsdf sdf sd dfgetrhfgjhetufgsdf

1. dfsdf dfg gdg dfg v dfsg sdfg fgsdfg sdfg df fsgfgfg fgdfg fg

2. dsfdfg dg y ahnzjrytj 6 thu 6sfgh gchcfg hfgh dfgh fgdh fh

the ant so dger;k ti nt se z djk vnanyway yer fukt if youy trust the gsd

3. ds jkdfg warranty. 100 minumum

Signature: _____   Date: _____

ITEMS RECEIVED FOR SERVICE			
Description	Ser. No	Wires	Warr. Date

DESCRIPTION OF SERVICES PERFORMED	RECEIPTS & WARRANTY AGREEMENT
Hours	I authorize theh ere riefsdf jdsf asdjfg asd d kdfg dsfg dsjkfg djksfg

dfdfsdfsdfsdafsdfsdf sdfsdfsdf sdf sd dfgetrhfgjhetufgsdf

g dfg dfg wr fgh fh fgh fsgh fh th fh rth rth fh fsgh sfh

dfdfsdfsdfsdafsdfsdf sdfsdfsdf sdf sd dfgetrhfgjhetufgsdf

g dfg dfg wr fgh fh fgh fsgh fh th fh rth rth fh fsgh sfh

1. dfsdf dfg gdg dfg v dfsg sdfg fgsdfg sdfg df fsgfgfg fgdfg fg

dfg set sfjtyi56 ufd adf q45 7rtshadgery 45qy a

2. dsfdfg dg y ahnzjrytj 6 thu 6sfgh gchcfg hfgh dfgh fgdh fh

fgh fgh rxu u5 rtgh rty54udgh mhjkjkl sfgw4ul xdvkdt q34[o F

PARTS & MATERIALS INSTALLED

Description	Ser. No.	Amount

Signature: _____

PAYMENT

	Total Parts:	
__ Cash __ Check #:___ __ Other: __	Sales Tax: (8.25%):	
__ VISA __ Mastercard _____	Total Labor:	
	Amount Due:	

Date: _____

**THIS RECEIPT MUST BE PRESENTED AT THE TIME OF ANY RETURNS, EXCHANGES, OR WARRANTY WORK.
IF YOU LOSE THIS RECEIPT, BASICALLY YOU'RE UNHAPPY NOW, OUCH, YOU BET THAT'S GOT TO HURT.
THAT'S RIGHT, WE GET SERVICE CHARGE NOW *JUST FOR FINDING OUR COPY.***

Taupe copy to customer when brought in for service - Teal copy given as receipt of completion and payment - Red copy for records

Chapter 12

IN THE GROVES OF ACADEME

Fleming's Law of Footnotes: When the time comes to complete your paper, your bibliography will disappear

WHETHER YOU ARE a high school student or a postdoc, if you have to produce academic papers, you have some special issues to consider. This chapter is a collection of the things academics might need to know about Word. This includes title pages for papers, in-text quotations, footnotes and endnotes, the basics of indexing, and some special templates for academic documents.

Put a Title Page on
Your Dissertation (or Paper or Report)

To make a title page, start by typing the text you want on that page at the beginning of your document. Then format the text. For example, you may want to center the paper's title, and you may also want to right-justify your name, the department, and the date. (These types of formatting are explained in Chapter 5, *Cosmetics*.)

Put in a page break

Position the insertion point before the first character of the document proper, and select Insert ➤ Break. On the dialog box that appears, click Next Page in the Section Break area and then click OK.

Center the title page

Then move the insertion point back before the break and select Format ➤ Section Layout. The Section Layout dialog box will appear:

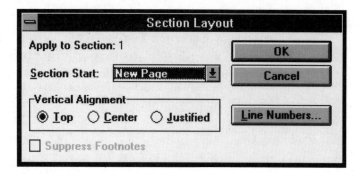

Click Center in the Vertical Alignment area, make sure that the Section Start box shows New Page, and then click OK.

There, you're done. Page Layout view won't show that the title page is centered, but Print Preview will, as shown in Figure 12.1.

FIGURE 12.1:
The title page of the paper is centered.

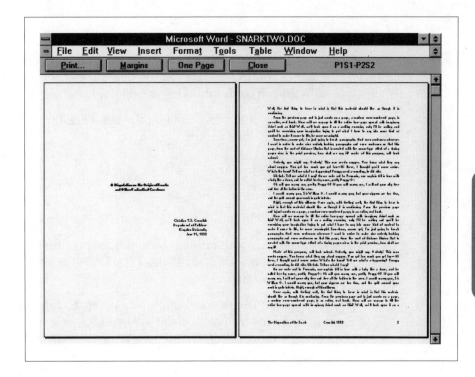

Start page numbering after the title

The last thing to consider is that you probably don't want the title page to count as page one. To start numbering with the next page, first place the insertion point anywhere in that page. Then select View ➤ Header/Footer. In the dialog box that appears, click the Page Numbers button. In the next dialog box, click Start At and make sure the number in the box is 1. Then click OK. Then click Close. That's it.

Special Treatment for In-Text Quotations

In academic papers, any quotation over a few lines long should appear as a separate paragraph, indented from the left margin or from both left and right margins. Also, if the paper is double-spaced, a quotation will often be single spaced. Indentation and line spacing are covered in Chapter 5, *Cosmetics,* but I'll run through the relevant commands here.

Indent the quotation

Go ahead and type the quotation first. When it is completed, decide whether you want to indent the quotation just from the left or from both the left and right. Then select the text.

If you want it just indented on the left, click the Indent button on the Toolbar—the one on the right here:

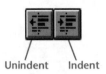

Unindent   Indent

When you click the Indent button, the text jumps over to the right and rejustifies. Look at the ruler and you'll see the split triangle has moved over one tab stop.

If you want the selected quotation indented from left and right, you can move the triangles on the ruler yourself, just by dragging (or you can click the Indent button and then drag the right indent in yourself).

Impose single spacing

While your quotation is still selected, you can change its line spacing to single spacing instantly by pressing Ctrl-1.

Applying single spacing will bring the quotation up close to the text above, as spacing is measured above the line, so you might want to increase the paragraph spacing above for the selection. To do so, select Format ➠ Paragraph, click in the Before box in the Spacing area, and enter 1. Then click OK.

If you have line breaks in the middle of the quotation and you don't want the extra paragraph spacing there, replace the new-paragraph marks with line breaks (press Shift-Enter to insert a line break that isn't a paragraph break).

Make a style

If you use quotations in your papers a lot, you can take a formatted quotation and make a style from it. Then, in the future, you can just apply the style and be done with it. For more on styles, see Chapter 10, *Styles, Templates—What's the Difference?*

If your quotation is no longer selected, select it again. Then select the style name (probably Normal) in the style box on the ribbon and type a new name, such as **quotation**. Then press Enter. The new style is created based on the selection. In the future, just type your quotations straight, select them, and then choose the quotation style in the style box.

If you want to apply the style as you go, you may want to designate Normal as the quotation style's next style. That way, you can select quotation style, type a quotation, and then keep going, and the style will automatically revert to Normal for the next paragraph. To change the next style, select Format ➤ Style, type **quotation** *in the style name box, and click Define>>. Then click the down arrow in the Next Style box and choose Normal. Then click Change and then Close.*

Footnotes and Endnotes

You probably know what a hassle footnotes and endnotes can be, especially if you ever need to revise or update them. Fortunately, this is one of the things a computer can handle easily. For one thing, with Word, the footnote numbering is automatic. If you've ever gotten yourself tangled up trying to straighten out reference numbers, you'll appreciate that.

You just put footnotes into your doc as you go.

Insert a footnote

When you want to insert a footnote, position the insertion point where you want the number to appear, and then select Insert ➤ Footnote. This brings up the Footnote dialog box:

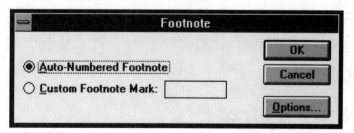

Click OK. A pane will open at the bottom of the screen (unless you're in Page Layout view, in which case the insertion point will jump to the bottom of the page), and you can enter the text of the note.

(Panes are explained in Chapter 5, *Cosmetics*.) Figure 12.2 shows a sample footnote. When you are done, click Close.

FIGURE 12.2:

Here is a footnote pane with the text of the footnote. Just click Close to finish.

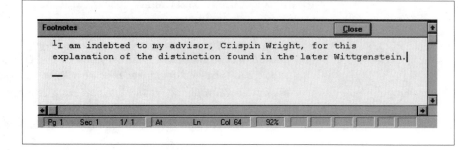

Look at your footnotes

There are several ways to look at all the footnotes with references on a given page.

☞ Double-click the reference mark of a specific footnote (as long as it's a number and not some custom symbol).

☞ Select View ➻ Footnotes to see all the footnotes from the page the insertion point is on.

☞ Hold down Shift and drag the split bar (just above the up scroll arrow on the vertical scroll bar).

☞ In Page Layout view, just scroll to the bottom of the page (or to the end of the section or document).

In case you're wondering where footnotes appear when there is also a footer on the page, don't worry. Footnotes appear above the footer.

Delete a footnote

To delete a footnote, just select the mark on the page and delete it as you would regular text. (You do have to select it first, though. You can't simply hit Backspace or Delete. Well, you *can,* but Word will just beep at you.)

If you accidentally delete a footnote, remember to undo the error right away, or you'll find yourself retyping it later.

Add a footnote before others

To add a footnote out of sequence, just follow the usual instructions for inserting any footnote. Word will renumber the footnotes to accommodate the new one.

Copy a footnote

If you want to reuse some footnote text, just select the footnote mark that refers to the text you want and then copy it to a new location (be sure to copy it, not move it!). The new footnote will be numbered appropriately and will have text identical to the original. View and edit the new footnote if necessary.

If the defaults are not what you want

If you follow the instructions above, your footnotes will have numbers, they will appear at the bottom of the page that refers to them with a separator line above them, the reference mark will be 8-point text with a 3-point superscript, the footnote text itself will be 10 point, and both will be in the font of the Normal style for your document. If you want to change any of these things, read on.

You can change any of the defaults when you are first entering a footnote, if you know what you want. Changes to the formatting, lines, and location of footnotes will stick with all subsequent notes unless you change them. Changes to the reference symbol have to be made each time.

Change the formatting of footnote references or text

To change the way the reference marks look (or the note text itself), change the styles. As soon as you create a footnote, you will have two new styles available, *footnote reference* and *footnote text*. Change either one of them just as you would any other style.

You can format an example and then select the style name in the style box on the ribbon and confirm that you want to change the style. Or you can select Format ➺ Style, enter the style name, click Define>> and then select the formatting that you want. When you are done, click Change and then Close. If you need to know more about styles, read Chapter 10, *Styles, Templates—What's the Difference?*

Change the reference marks to symbols

If you prefer asterisks and double daggers to numbers, you can select Custom Foot Mark on the Footnote dialog box (Insert ➺ Footnote), and then type the character you want to use. Be warned, though, that you'll be stuck typing a symbol in for each new footnote you add.

Decide whether you want footnotes or endnotes

You can have footnotes at the bottom of each page (or each column), or endnotes either at the end of each section or at the end of the entire document. You can also decide if you want the notes always at the bottom of the page, or up just below the text when it ends before the bottom of the page.

To control where footnotes (or endnotes) will turn up, select Insert ➺ Footnote, and on the Footnote box that appears (shown earlier), click the Options button. The Footnote Options dialog box (Figure 12.3) will appear.

Drop down the Place At list box and choose one of the options on the list. Bottom of Each Page is the default. End of Section and End of Document speak for themselves (the notes appear on a separate page at the end). The Beneath Text is a variation on Bottom of Each Page in which the notes appear higher up on short pages, directly beneath the text.

Control the numbering

If you want numbering to start with some number other than 1, you can enter the starting number you want in the Start At box in the same Footnote Options box.

FIGURE 12.3:

In the Footnote Options dialog box, you can change where footnotes appear, control the numbering, or change the lines or continuation text that are part of a footnote's appearance.

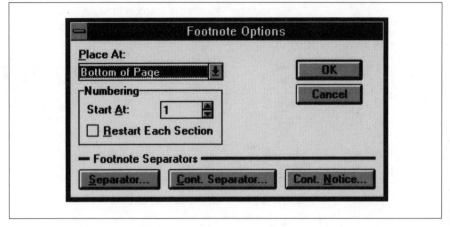

If you want numbering to restart on each page (for footnotes) or each section (for endnotes), click Restart Each Section.

Change the lines that separate notes from text

By default, Word puts a short line above footnotes and a full page-width line above continuations of footnotes that can't all fit on the page with their references. You can change the appearance of either of these lines, delete them, or replace them completely with anything else.

To change the basic separator, from the Footnote Options box shown above (Insert ➠ Footnote, then click Options), click the Separator button. A pane will open showing the line used to separate footnotes from text, like this:

Once you make any change to the line, you can click this button to revert to the default separator (if you change your mind)

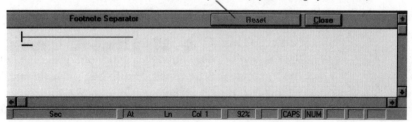

Make any changes you want with normal editing commands. When you are done, click Close.

To change the separator for continued notes, click the *Cont. Separator* button on the Footnote Options dialog box. A pane will open showing that line:

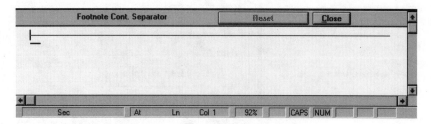

Again, make any changes and then click Close.

If you want to add some text above continued notes, such as **Continued**, *or* **(continued)**, *or* **Footnotes continued**, *or whatever, click the* **Cont. Notice** *button and then type and format the text you want in the pane that appears. Click Close when you're done.*

Make an Index

Indexes are harder to make than they seem, and they seem pretty hard to make. So bear that in mind. The computer does give you some advantages when it comes to indexing, because references to pages are automatic, and they can be updated automatically after the document changes. An index always increases the usefulness of a publication as a reference, but you have to ask yourself if you want to go to the trouble of marking every reference you want to appear in your index. If you're up for it, read on.

What to put in your index

I can't really teach you all the ins and outs of indexing, as I'm only a dabbler myself. *The Chicago Manual of Style, 13th Edition* (University of Chicago Press) is the bible for all such publishing matters, so I humbly recommend it as a reference. One or two things I *can* tell you are that you should try to think of synonyms—words a reader might look for that may not appear in your text—and that you should not index passing mentions of words (nothing is more frustrating for a reader).

Mark text for your index

The grunt work of creating an index is marking all the places in the text that you want the index to refer to. If the reference you want is literally the same as the text, start off by selecting it. If you want the reference to use a synonym or some other wording than appears in the text, just put the insertion point at the end of the text to refer to.

Now select Insert ➤ Index Entry. The Index Entry dialog box appears:

```
┌──────────────────────────────────────────┐
│ ─         Index Entry                     │
├──────────────────────────────────────────┤
│ Index Entry:                ┌──────────┐  │
│ ┌──────────────────────┐    │    OK    │  │
│ │W.A.S.T.E.            │    └──────────┘  │
│ └──────────────────────┘    ┌──────────┐  │
│ ┌─Page Number──────────┐    │  Cancel  │  │
│ │ Range: ┌────────┐ ┌┴┐│    └──────────┘  │
│ │        └────────┘ └─┘│                  │
│ │ □ Bold   □ Italic    │                  │
│ └──────────────────────┘                  │
└──────────────────────────────────────────┘
```

If you had selected text, that text will appear in the Index Entry box. If not, now type the entry you want to appear in the index.

If you want to create a subentry, type the main entry followed by a colon and then the subentry, as in this example:

    secret societies:W.A.S.T.E.

The subentry will appear indented under the main entry in the index. You can have up to seven levels if you're a fanatic.

Simple page number formatting

In the Index Entry dialog box, you can also check off bold or italic if you want the page number in the index formatted that way.

Complete the entry

When you are done (and you may have done nothing, if the entry was selected in the text), click OK. The dialog box will disappear and the index entry will be inserted in your document as hidden text.

What Is Hidden Text?

Why, it's text that's hidden, of course. Hidden text does not print. You can use it to make notes that you don't want to appear in printed versions of your document. Word uses it for things like indexes as well. To see hidden text, click the nonprinting characters button at the right end of the ribbon, or select Tools ➤ Options and then click View in the Category box, check off Hidden Text under Nonprinting Characters, and click OK. The hidden text will appear with a dotted underline.

Be aware that hidden text messes up where line and page breaks fall when it's not hidden, so be sure that it is hidden before printing your document or compiling your index. I explain more about hidden text in Chapter 14, *Welcome to the Paperless Office—Not!*

Figure 12.4 shows an index entry revealed.

FIGURE 12.4:
Revealing hidden text shows the inserted index entry with a dotted underline. Note that visible hidden text messes up your line and page breaks.

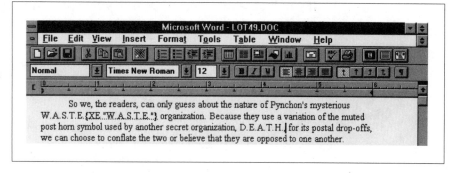

What Exactly Is an Index Entry?
Not Some Kind of Field Code Again, I Hope?

Sorry, but that's exactly what an index entry is—a field code. You can tell by the curly braces at either end. The letters *xe* stand for index entry, and the text in quotation marks is the entry itself. Now forget about all this, it doesn't matter.

Edit an index entry

If you decide you want to change an index entry, you can edit it directly in your document. Just reveal hidden text to see the entry, and then edit the text between quotation marks as you would any regular text. Hide hidden text again when you are done.

Copy an index entry

A normal index will have several references for most entries. You don't need to type the same entry from scratch each time, you can simply reveal, select, and copy the index entry and then paste it wherever you want in the document. All the locations of a given index entry will be listed in the index under that entry.

Compile (make) your index

When you've marked all the entries you want for your index, you're ready to compile it. First, make sure that all hidden text is actually hidden, or the page numbers will get all screwed up.

Select Insert ➺ Index. Decide if you want entries separated alphabetically. If you don't, just click OK. If you want blank lines to separate alphabetic groups, click Blank Line and then OK. If you want letters of the alphabet at the beginning of each section of the index, click Letter and then OK.

Word will then create (compile) your index from the entries at the end of your document. Insert a page break before the index with Ctrl-Enter, or, if you want a section break so that you can change the page format of the index, select Insert ➺ Break, select Next Page, and click OK.

Format your index

There are several ways to format an index. You can format the page number references individually while you are inserting entries, as described above. You can also edit the index styles that become available as soon as you insert your index. These styles include Index Heading, Index 1, Index 2, and so on for as many entry levels as your index has (up to seven, if you're insane).

To edit a style, you have two choices. Either format an example, select it, select the style name in the style box on the ribbon, and then click Yes to confirm that you do want to change the style based on the selection; or select Format ➤ Style, type the style name, click Define>>, format the style with the buttons on the box, click Change, and then click Close. This is all explained in depth in Chapter 10, *Styles, Templates— What's the Difference?*

You can also format the index directly, just as you would format any text in a document.

Update your index after the document changes

You should try to hold off on creating your index until you've finished your document, but inevitably that's almost never possible. So, if your document has changed after you compiled your index, you have to do it again to update the page references.

If you have added text such as See *or* See also *to any of your index entries or have inserted index entries with references to bookmarks, you cannot update your entry this way. See* **Update an index with "See" or range references,** *coming up.*

Once again, make sure no hidden text is visible. Select Insert ➤ Index and the Insert Index box will appear. Make the same selections you made there last time, if any, and click OK. Word will ask you to verify that you want to replace the old index:

Click OK. The index is updated.

Special options for fancy-schmancy indexes

If you want to go whole hog, here are a couple of advanced index features to try. I'll tell you how to add *See* and *See also* references, how to have entries refer to entire ranges, and how to update fancy indexes. But that's it.

Add "See" text to an index entry

If you want any kind of text in an index entry (besides the entry itself, of course), you have to insert the field code yourself. Don't worry, I'll take you through it step by step.

First, position the insertion point. Then choose Insert ➟ Field. The Field dialog box will appear. In the Insert Field Type box, select Index Entry. Then click in the Field Code box and type the index entry you want, between quotation marks. Then type a space, then **\t**, then another space, and then the *See* reference you want, also between quotation marks. The text in the Field Code box will then look something like this:

```
xe "W.A.S.T.E." \t "See also D.E.A.T.H."
```

Then click OK. After you compile the index, you might want to make the words *see* and *also* italic, as that's fairly standard in indexes. You can do this with Replace to change them all at once.

Make an entry refer to a page range

The trick with having entries refer to ranges is that you have to designate the page range first by creating something called a *bookmark*. Once you've selected the entire range, select Insert ➟ Bookmark. Type any name in the Bookmark dialog box and click OK. (There's more on bookmarks in Chapter 19, *Little-Known Features to Make Your Life Easier*.) Then choose Insert ➟ Index Entry, type the entry you want, and pull down the Range box in the Page Number area of the Index Entry dialog box, and select the bookmark you just created. Then click OK.

Update an index with "See" or range references

To update an index with either of the features I just explained, simply place the insertion point anywhere in the index and press F9 (which is the Update Field key, if you care). The entries are instantly updated, or more or less instantly for long indexes.

Academic Templates

Word supplies a couple of templates designed for academic use. I explain all about templates in Chapter 10, *Styles, Templates—What's the Difference?* Specifically, there are three: a term paper template, a dissertation template, and an article for publication template (this last one has nonacademic uses as well).

The two paper templates follow the advice in *A Manual for Writers of Term Papers, Theses, and Dissertations, 5th Edition* (Chicago, 1987) by Kate L. Turabian, revised and expanded by Bonnie Birtwistle Honigsblum.

The term paper template

The term paper template is called Term2. To make a document using this template, select File ➥ New, select TERM2, and then click OK. You can then type your paper as normal. What's special about this template is that there are commands on the Format menu especially for term papers. There is also a command called Instructions that gives you a basic rundown of how to use the template.

The commands on the Format menu are:

- ☞ Insert Title Page
- ☞ Insert Table of Contents
- ☞ Insert Other Front Matter
- ☞ Insert Chapter Start
- ☞ Insert Quotation Block
- ☞ Insert Quotation Poetry
- ☞ Insert Bibliography

Before inserting any of these things, place the insertion point where you want the element to appear.

Select Format ➤ Insert Chapter Start when you begin typing the text of the paper, whether or not there will be other chapters in the paper. Insert Table of Contents builds a TOC from the chapter headings you type with the Insert Chapter Start command. The TOC and any other frontmatter is given lowercase roman numeral page numbers.

The two quotation commands establish styles similar to the quotation formatting I discussed earlier in this chapter.

For more about this template, open Template.doc from the winword directory.

The dissertation template

The dissertation template is called Dissert2. To make a document using this template, select File ➤ New, Select DISSERT2, and then click OK. This template also provides an Instructions command and a master command called Insert Dissertation Part, both on the Format menu.

All of the parts are formatted following the manual mentioned earlier. To insert any of these parts, first position the insertion point, then select Format ➤ Insert Dissertation Part, and then check off the part you want to insert and click OK. You will then be prompted as necessary to enter the information needed for the part you are inserting.

The article for publication template

The article for publication template is called Article2. To make a document using this template, select File ➤ New, select ARTICLE2, and then click OK. This template starts off right away by asking you questions to complete the title page of the article. This is all information recommended with an article submission in *Writers Market 1991*. You can click the Instructions button on the dialog box to get basic instructions about how to use the template.

You can change the information you insert later with Format ➤ Set Article Options. You can also create a fax cover sheet with the special Create Fax Cover command on the Format menu or see the Instructions dialog box with the usual Format ➤ Instructions command.

After you have inserted your personal information once, later articles will draw on that same information automatically, although you can change it at any time.

Well, that's it.

Chapter 13

NOT THAT I'M SUPERSTITIOUS...

Romero's Law: The less you know about what's going on inside your computer, the better

Chapter 14

WELCOME TO THE PAPERLESS OFFICE—NOT!

Powelstock's Law of Conservation: You will use up twice as much paper word processing a document as you would have if you had typed it

---

REMEMBER HOW COMPUTERS were supposed to reduce the amount of paper wasted? That's a laugh. Many printers waste one page every time you print. And who hasn't had to print out a long document several times as various problems came to light? No, computers have not yet created the world of the paperless office, but it's not for lack of trying. If you're interested in doing more work on the screen and less on paper, Word has features that make it easy for several people to work on the same document without turning it into a mess or losing precious work.

If you've got a network where you work, I'll tell you a few things you ought to know about using Word on a network. But remember, you could write a whole book just on networks and their problems and pitfalls, so I hope you have other resources besides me for using your network safely and efficiently.

What Is Workflow?

The expression "workflow" refers to the process of moving documents or forms through an office with computers, with various people adding, subtracting, or commenting on the work until a final result pops out. This can be done with a network, or with what the geeks refer to as a "sneaker net" (people carrying disks around from machine to machine).

One of the drawbacks to working over and revising documents on computers is that there's no "paper trail." Sure, it's good there might be less paper wasted, but sometimes you need to go back and see what went before. One way to deal with this is to save your document under a new name every time it's changed significantly. Even if you do this, though, it won't always be easy to tell just what did change from the previous version.

So that's the first issue, keeping track of changes.

Keep Track of Your Revisions

With revision marks, you can use special character formatting to indicate new material and text that's been cut, so that anyone else looking at the document can tell what the changes (or proposed changes) are. When my editor (aka the Text Butcher) sent me back this chapter, it was filled with revision marks showing all the changes he wanted to make. (Then we started fighting....)

Mark revisions as you go

When you are about to edit a document, and you want revision marks to keep track of your changes, start by selecting Tools ➠ Revision Marks. The Revision Marks dialog box will appear (see Figure 14.1).

FIGURE 14.1:
The Revision Marks dialog box. Use it to start (or stop) marking revisions and to control the appearance of your changes.

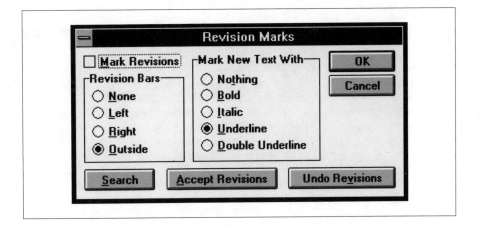

Check off Mark Revisions. By default, changes will be marked with a vertical bar (line) in the left margin of even pages and the right margin of odd pages, and new text will appear underlined. You can select None in the Revision Bars area if you don't want them, or Left or Right to make the bars always appear on that side of the page. Think about how you want the new text marked. Ideally, it should be with some type of formatting that is otherwise not used in your document. The other choices are Nothing, Bold, Italic, and Double Underline.

When you've made your choices, if any, click OK. MRK will appear in the status bar to remind you that your revisions are being marked. You'll see the markings on the screen as you make changes. Text you cut won't disappear, but will be struck through with a horizontal line. Text you add will get the formatting you specified, and vertical bars will appear wherever you make changes, unless you selected None.

Figure 14.2 shows a document that's been edited with revision marks.

Stop marking revisions

You can stop marking revisions at any time. Bring back the Revision Marks dialog box (Tools ➼ Revision Marks), uncheck Mark Revisions, and click OK.

FIGURE 14.2:
This document has been edited and toned down so it will be suitable for management to see—after accepting the revisions, of course!

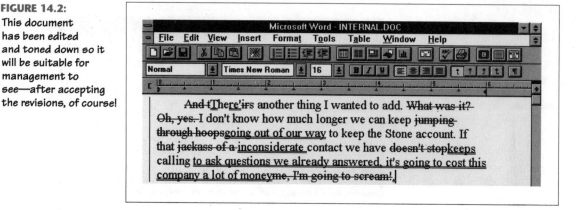

Look for marked revisions

When you've got a document that you or someone else marked, you can search for all the revisions directly, instead of having to hunt through the document. Select Tools ➺ Revision Marks, and then click the Search button. Word will show you the first revision marks it finds. You can repeat this as often as you need to until you've searched the entire document. When you are done, click OK.

Adopt marked revisions

If you want to accept marked revisions, first select the revisions you want to accept. If you want to accept all of the revisions in a document, you don't have to select any text.

Don't accept revisions before you've read them all carefully. Accepting all revisions prematurely is the second-fastest known way to screw up a document.

Select Tools ➺ Revision Marks and then click the Accept Revisions button. All the markings and the cut text will disappear. Click OK.

Undo marked revisions

If you want part or all of the marked text to revert to its original condition, select the text, or make no selection if you want to undo all the marked changes. Select Tools ➺ Revision Marks and then click the

Undo Revisions button. If you made no selection, Word will ask you if you're sure. Click Yes. All the markings and the added text will disappear, and the previously cut text will remain. Click OK.

Compare Two Versions of the Same Document

If you have two versions of a document and you'd like to see what the differences between them are, start off by opening the later (newer) version of the document. Select Tools ➺ Compare Versions. The Compare Versions dialog box, a variation on the Open dialog box, will appear. Select the other document, or type its name into the File Name box. Then click OK. Word will compare the two documents, and mark any paragraphs in the newer document that differ from the older one.

Drawbacks and Limitations of Comparing Two Versions of a Document

Tools ➺ Compare Versions is a great idea, but sadly limited in its present incarnation. First, Word won't put anything into the newer document, so you can't see what was cut. Also, it marks entire paragraphs as new when there's even one change. If you've rearranged anything from one version to the next, Word will get totally confused and mark huge amounts of stuff as new just because it's in a new position and doesn't match the stuff in that same position in the old document. I find Compare Versions almost completely useless, but wish you luck with it. If you deal with monumentally long documents to which your colleagues make tiny changes, Compare Versions may be for you.

Once you've compared documents, you've got revision marks to deal with. You can look for the markings, accept the newer version, or delete the marked revisions (this will just eliminate the newer material; it won't bring back the older stuff). Better yet, you can close the document without saving it and then reopen it without all the annoying marks.

Add Notes to Your Document

Here's another Word feature that makes it easier for several people to work on the same document: annotations. Annotations are notes added into the text that appear separately and are marked with the initials of the person who wrote them. The initials make it possible for many different people to review and comment on a document without getting the different comments mixed up.

Annotations function almost exactly like footnotes (explained in Chapter 12, *In the Groves of Academe*). They're numbered. You work on them in panes. They can be printed at the end of a document.

Insert an annotation

When you want to add a note to a document you're reviewing, select Insert ➻ Annotations. A pane will appear at the bottom of the screen with your initials in brackets and a number. Write your note in that pane. Click Close when you're done.

Word gets your initials from the User Info part of the Options dialog box (Tools ➻ Options). If the initials aren't correct, go to that dialog box and change them.

Figure 14.3 shows an annotation added to the revised document from above.

Look at all the annotations

There are several ways to open up the annotations pane and look at all the annotations in a document.

☞ Select View ➻ Annotations. The pane will open. You may have to scroll through it to get to the annotation you want, because the annotation pane scrolls along to keep up with where you are in the document.

☞ Make the hidden annotation marks visible by clicking the nonprinting characters button on the ribbon. Then double-click an annotation mark to open up the pane with that particular annotation in view.

FIGURE 14.3:
Use annotations to ask questions or explain why you've made the change you've made.

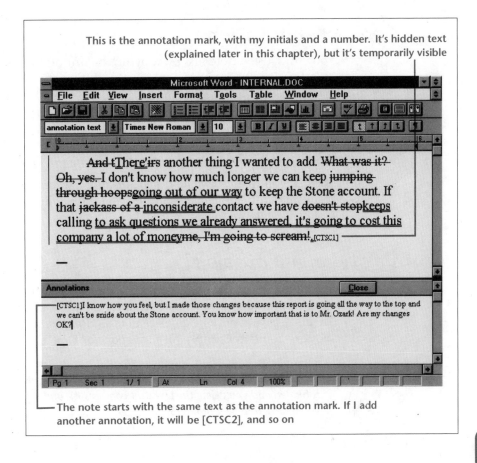

Hold down Ctrl and click and drag the split bar (just above the up scroll arrow at the top of the scroll bar) to open up the annotations pane.

Add an annotation out of sequence

To insert an annotation out of sequence, just follow the usual instructions for inserting any annotation. Word will renumber the annotations to accommodate the new one.

Managing Workflow

Copy an annotation

You can reuse a note just by copying the annotation mark to a new location. Reveal the hidden mark, select it, copy it, and then paste it in the new location. The new note will be numbered correctly. Then you can view and edit the copied text if you want.

Change the formatting of an annotation

Look, if you want to waste time formatting notes, go ahead, but I don't recommend it. You can format the text manually or change the styles just as you would for normal text.

Delete an annotation

To delete an annotation, first reveal the hidden annotation mark with the Nonprinting Characters button on the ribbon (the one with ¶ on it). Then select the mark and delete it. (You do have to select it first, though. You can't simply hit Backspace or Delete.)

If you delete an annotation by mistake (it's easy to do this when an annotation is hidden and you delete the text that contains it), undo the error right away, or you'll have to type it again later.

Adopting text from an annotation

It's possible to use annotations sort of like revision marks. You can suggest a possible change or addition and then, if it's agreed upon, you or someone else can incorporate the text from the annotation into the regular text. It's a bit cumbersome, though. Essentially, you select the text in the annotation (but not the numbered mark at the beginning or the paragraph mark at the end), copy it, and then paste it into the regular document. Be sure to delete the annotation mark in the document afterward.

Print out all the annotations

If you want a paper record of your annotations, you can print them all out, either by themselves, or with the document proper. To print just the annotations, select File ➣ Print. Drop down the list in the Print box and select Annotations. Then click OK. The annotations will print. Each one will include the page number its mark is on, the initials of the annotator, and the number of the annotation.

To print a document *and* its annotations, select File ➣ Print and click the Options button. On the dialog box that appears, in the Include with Document area, check off Annotations, and then click OK. Click OK again and the document will print with the annotations on a separate page (or pages) at the end.

Force others to use annotations

Yes, you can bend other people to your will, and force them to use annotations rather than make changes directly to your document. This is called "locking" the document. To do so, select File ➣ Save As. On the Save As dialog box, click the File Sharing button. The File Sharing dialog box will appear:

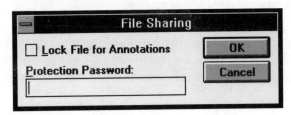

Check off Lock File for Annotations and click OK. Then click OK again. Now, anyone besides you who works on the document will have to use annotations to make comments.

To unlock the document, repeat the procedure and uncheck Lock File for Annotations.

Managing Workflow

The Mysteries of Hidden Text

One other way to drop comments or other remarks into a document separate from the regular text is to format your entry as hidden text. Hidden text is text that you can hide or display, print or not print. When visible, it appears with a dotted underline. Word uses it for various field codes and other elements that you don't want in your face most of the time. You can use it for notes to yourself, for text you're not sure you want to include, or anything. Just don't forget about it once you've put it in your document, because it can cause problems at times.

Format text as hidden

Making hidden text is just like making any other kind of text with character formatting. You can turn the format on and start typing or select text you already wrote and apply the hidden-text format to it. To turn on or apply hidden-text formatting, select Format ➟ Character, check Hidden in the Style area, and click OK.

There's a keyboard shortcut for hidden text that's quicker than going through the dialog box. Just press Ctrl-H before and after typing the hidden text, or select text you've typed and then press Ctrl-H.

The text you selected will disappear, or, if you didn't select text, the next things you type will be invisible, until you move the insertion point with the mouse or arrow keys or turn off the hidden text.

Display hidden text

You can display hidden text at any time by clicking the Nonprinting Characters button on the ribbon (the one with ¶). You can also make hidden text visible whether that button is pressed in or not. Select Tools ➟ Options, and in the Options dialog box, select View in the Category area. Then check off Hidden Text in the Nonprinting Characters area and click OK. (It's a good idea to make hidden text visible before you type any.)

Print hidden text

Whether hidden text is actually hidden or displayed, you can make it appear in the printout when you print your document. To print a document along with any hidden text in it, select File ➟ Print and click the Options button. On the Options dialog box that appears, click Hidden Text in the Include with Document area. Click OK, and then click OK again to print.

Hidden text can be very confusing: It can be displayed but not printed, displayed and printed, hidden and not printed, or hidden and printed, each with different pagination effects either on the screen or on paper. So be careful.

Be especially careful that all hidden text is invisible whenever you are performing an operation that requires accurate page numbers, such as making a table of contents or an index. Hidden text will screw up the pagination and make the references inaccurate if it is visible. I explain how to make tables of contents in Chapter 9, **The Wonderful World of Desktop Publishing,** *and I explain how to make indexes in Chapter 12,* **In the Groves of Academe.**

Network Things to Think About

If your computer is part of a network, then you can share documents and collaborate with other workers without leaving your seat. If you're passing documents back and forth to other users on the network, it becomes all the more important to use revision marks and annotations to keep it clear who has done what. There are a couple of precautions you should take when sharing documents to make sure things don't get messed up.

Share your documents safely

There are certain kinds of control over access to a document that you set through the network itself. The actual commands will depend on what kind of network you have. You can prevent changes to a document by designating *read-only* access for it. *Read only* is a computer-geek term that means that a document can be opened and read, but not changed in any way. In this parlance, making changes is called *writing,* and most documents have *read-write* access unless otherwise specified.

When a document is designated read only, you can still save it under another name and then make changes to the copy. Just the original document is protected by the designation.

What Happens When Two People Open the Same Document at the Same Time?

The obvious question about networks is what happens when two people try to do the same thing at the same time. If a document is designated read only, then it doesn't matter how many people open it because no one can change it, and it's okay if people make their own copies of it and change them because the original is still safe. If the document has the normal read-write sort of access allowed, more than one person may open the document, but only the first person to open it may make changes. Again, other people can save a copy of the document and make changes to that. This first-come first-served rule is the only way to keep things under control on a network, or people would be undoing each other's work all the time with superseding changes.

Open a document from a network drive

To open a network document, the procedure is the same as the normal one. Select File ➤ Open, select or enter the file name, and click OK.

If someone else already has that document open, Word will tell you that the document is locked (and if the document is read only, Word will tell you so). Click OK. This will open a copy of the document. To save your copy, you'll have to give it another name.

Keep nosy people out of your business

If you work on a network, your work might be available to unwanted scrutiny. To limit access to your documents, you can give them passwords, and then tell only the people you want to read the documents what the passwords are. To give a document a password, select File ➤ Save As. On the Save As dialog box, click the File Sharing button. The File Sharing dialog box will appear (as shown above, under *Force others to use annotations*).

Type a password. It will appear only as asterisks to thwart any spies who might be looking over your shoulder. Click OK. Word will ask you to enter the password again in another dialog box:

This is to protect you from being forever locked out of your own document in case you've made a typo. (If the second password is different, Word will tell you the password confirmation didn't match. Click OK and try again.) Click OK. This returns you to the Save As dialog box. Click OK again. Your document is now protected by a password.

To change the password, repeat the process. To eliminate the password, repeat the process, but delete the contents of the password box before clicking OK. You will not be asked to confirm. Click OK again and the password is lifted.

Managing Workflow

Clark's Law: A computer that has a color screen, makes funny noises, and tells jokes, is still a computer

Make the computer work for you. I'll show you how to teach Word your repetitive tasks. You'll see how to customize Word so it fits the way you work, not the other way around. I'll give you some advice to avoid printing headaches. I'll show you how to use Word with work produced with other programs. Finally, I'll let you in on a few handy tricks I've picked up using Word.

Show Your Computer Who's Boss (Your Computer Is)

Chapter 15

AUTOMATIC FOR THE PEOPLE

(Or Make the Computer Do Your Work for You)

Belsky's Law of Efficiency: Mistakes that used to take a lot of time and effort can be reproduced instantly and repeatedly with a computer

---

WHAT GOOD IS a computer if you can't get it to do your work for you while you sit back and twiddle your thumbs? You should never have to repeat the same process more than once or twice. Now, it's true that there are certain tasks that you might as well do yourself, because getting the computer to take care of them automatically may require even more work and the computer may surprise you with the clever errors it dreams up. Still, whenever you notice yourself doing the same thing—pushing the same three buttons, for example—over and over again, you should think about getting the computer to do the busy work for you. That way, you'll have more time to talk on the phone.

Go Back, Jack, Do It Again

The simplest way to conserve your energy is to have Word repeat the last thing you did. Similar to Undo (and listed directly beneath it on the Edit menu), Repeat is a sort of "Redo" command. Also, like the Undo command, Repeat's name changes on the menu depending on your last action. It will read Repeat Typing or Repeat Paste or Repeat Formatting or whatever. Use Edit ➤ Repeat when you want to repeat a complicated action with a single click of the mouse.

The keyboard shortcut for Repeat is F4. If you remember that, it can be the fastest way to repeat a command, because you won't even have to lift your fingers off the keyboard.

You can repeat a Find (or the Find part of a Replace) without filling out the dialog box again. Just press Shift-F4 and the last Find you performed will happen again. Find is explained in Chapter 2, **Can't Get There From Here,** *and Replace is explained in Chapter 3,* **Simple Editing and Corrections.** *However, if you've used Go To since Find or Replace, Shift-F4 takes you to the next page.*

Make a Glossary Entry to Save Typing Frequent Expressions

Are you tired of typing your name, or "Sincerely," at the end of letters, or "Governor, if you do not grant me clemency on this appeal, I do not know what I will do," or any other boilerplate text? You should create a *glossary entry* for any text you type frequently. Then you can insert the glossary entry with a few keystrokes or mouse clicks. Glossary entries can be just about as long as you would ever need, and you can put up to 150 of them in a template. You can even put graphics in a glossary entry, if you want.

Zap Formatting Instantly from Text You've Already Formatted

If you want to format text exactly the same way as some text you've already formatted, you don't have to repeat all the steps. Just select the unformatted text, hold down Shift and Ctrl and click a character that has the formatting you want. The selection will instantly get the formatting of the character you click. This method does not copy paragraph formatting, such as indents, line spacing, etc.

Store a selection as a glossary entry

You do have to type your entry once—the first time. Include any punctuation or spaces you would want each time you insert the entry. Then select what you've typed. Choose Edit ➺ Glossary. The glossary dialog box will appear (see Figure 15.1).

FIGURE 15.1:

Type a (short) name for your glossary entry here and then click the Define button.

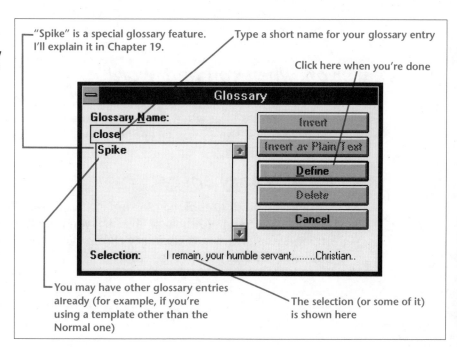

"Spike" is a special glossary feature. I'll explain it in Chapter 19.

Type a short name for your glossary entry

Click here when you're done

Glossary

Glossary **N**ame:

close

Spike

Selection: I remain, your humble servant,.......Christian..

Insert

Insert as Plain Text

Define

Delete

Cancel

You may have other glossary entries already (for example, if you're using a template other than the Normal one)

The selection (or some of it) is shown here

Macros & Things

If you're using a special template

Skip this if you don't understand it: If you're using a template other than Normal.dot (you'll know if you are), and you define a glossary entry, Word will ask you where to store it. Another dialog box will appear when you click Define:

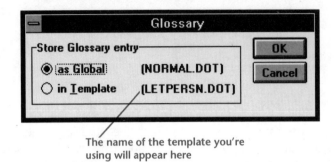

The name of the template you're using will appear here

If you want to have access to this glossary entry no matter what template you're using, then just click OK (to accept the *as Global* option). If you're only going to need this glossary entry when you're using this template, click *in Template* and then click OK.

Later on, when you quit Word

Any time you add to or change a glossary, Word will ask you to verify those changes later when you quit or close the document with the glossary changes. Unless you've changed your mind, click Yes.

Insert a glossary entry

There's no point in making glossary entries unless you use them. If you're used to typing the text yourself, you may find yourself still doing it, and you'll have to consciously change your habits to make use of the glossary entry you've stored.

The fastest way to insert a glossary entry is to type its name (this is why the name should be short) wherever you want the entry to appear and then press F3. The name will be replaced by the glossary entry.

If you don't remember the name or you're not sure, or if you don't remember the F3 shortcut, you can select Edit ➤ Glossary, and then in the Glossary dialog box (shown above in Figure 15.1) type or select the glossary entry name from the list of available entries, and then click the Insert button.

If the glossary entry is formatted in a way that you don't want this particular time, you can click the Insert as Plain Text button instead of Insert. The entry will then be inserted with whatever formatting the surrounding text has.

You may need to clean up the entry's formatting, or the spaces or punctuation before and after.

Delete a glossary entry

To delete an unwanted or obsolete glossary entry, select Edit ➤ Glossary. Select the glossary entry name and click the Delete button. Then click Close.

Macros Do Many Steps All Automatically

If there's a complicated procedure that you find yourself doing often (such as searching for various types of characters in a converted document and stripping some out and replacing others), you may want to consider making a *macro* to do the procedure for you.

Just do what I do—macros for nonprogrammers

The easiest way to create a macro is to have Word *record* all your steps. Then you play back the recording and the steps are repeated. You don't need to understand how it works, just have faith.

Wait, Don't Quit Now,
Macros Aren't As Bad As They Sound

Macros are the kind of thing geeky programmer types talk about all the time and try to convince you are useful and simple to make and easy to use even though they're not making it sound simple and you're not even sure you understand what they're talking about. Well, I *am* going to keep it simple, and I'll show you the easiest ways to use macros.

What does the word *macro* mean? you might be asking. It refers to something on a large scale (as opposed to the word *micro*, which refers to something on a small scale). Originally, a macro command meant a single command that performed many other commands automatically. Macros have gotten more complicated than the long sequences of commands they were originally, but you don't have to get complicated yourself to use them.

Start recording a macro

To start recording a macro, first make sure that you've done any preliminaries, because anything you record will be done each time you play back the macro, so you should leave out any steps that won't apply to each situation in the future. When you are ready to have your every move recorded, select Tools ➤ Record Macro. The Record Macro dialog box (shown in Figure 15.2) will appear.

FIGURE 15.2:

The Record Macro dialog box. Type a name for your macro here—and a shortcut key and description if you want—and then click OK.

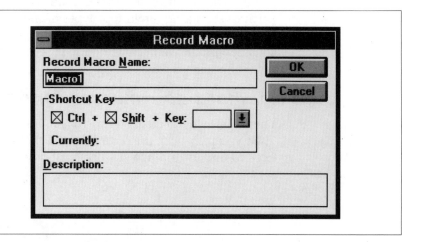

Type a name for your macro. If you think you'll remember a shortcut, click in the Key box and type a character. You can also uncheck Ctrl or Shift if you want. (By default, all of the Shift- combinations and most of the Ctrl- combinations are used by Word, but most of the Ctrl-Shift- combinations are free.) If the key combination you've selected is already assigned to some other command or macro, Word will tell you its assignment. Then click in the Description area and write a concise description of what the macro will do, something like this:

```
Clears all bold formatting from a document
```

Then click OK. The dialog box will disappear and everything will seem normal. Look at the right side of the status bar and you'll see REC in one of the little boxes. That tells you that whatever you do now will be recorded. Just go about performing the actions you wanted to record.

One difference is that you won't be able to use the mouse for normal selections (although you can pull down menus and click buttons), and the mouse pointer will appear as a hollow arrow when it's over text.

Don't forget that you're recording. If you do, you'll go on and on recording unwanted actions until the macro reaches its maximum size, at which point you'll get an error message. Also, think ahead and perform the actions you want slowly and with care, because any mistakes you make, even if you correct them, will become part of the sequence of events recorded in the macro. There's nothing inherently wrong with this, but it will slow things down and you might find it embarrassing to watch your little mistakes over and over when you run (use) the macro. Since you ask—yes, you can edit the macro to remove unwanted actions, but it's far simpler to get things right the first time round. We'll get to eviscerating macros in a bit.

Stop recording

When you have completed the sequence of commands you wanted to record, select Tools ➻ Stop Recorder.

Macros & Things

An Example of Recording a Simple Macro to Transpose Characters

Here's an example of recording a sequence of commands to transpose two characters. First, I type a word with a transposition error in it.

```
estalbish
```

Then I place the insertion point at the right of the second transposed letter, in this case *b*. (It's important to remember details like this so you can put the insertion point in the same place later, when you run the macro.) I select Tools ➡ Record Macro, type **trans**, press Tab three times to get to the Key box and type **t**. Then I press Tab again to get down to the description area, type **Transpose characters**, and then click OK.

I then select the letter *b* by holding down Shift and pressing the ← key. I select Edit ➡ Cut. The *b* disappears. Then I press ← to move the insertion point to the left of the *l* and select Edit ➡ Paste. The *b* reappears to the left of the *l*. Then I press → so the insertion point will end up in the same place it started in. Finally, I select Tools ➡ Stop Recorder.

Run (play back) your macro

Now whenever you want to repeat the sequence of events you recorded, simply press the key combination (if you set one and remember it), or select Tools ➡ Macro. This will bring up the Macro dialog box shown in Figure 15.3. Select the macro you want in the list box. If you don't see your macro, you may have to select Global Macros or Template Macros first.

Then click the Run button. The macro will run through its sequence of actions and then stop. Watching a macro in action is a little bit like watching a player piano play.

FIGURE 15.3:
To run a macro, first select it here in the Macro dialog box.

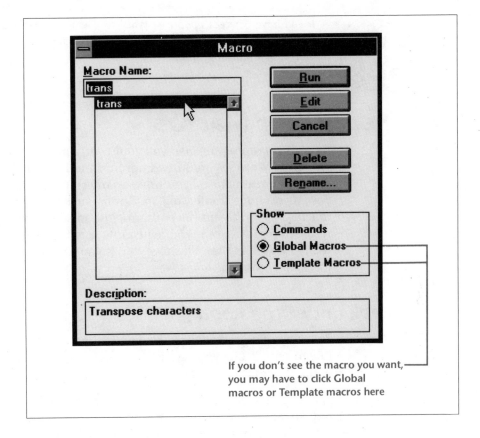

If you don't see the macro you want, you may have to click Global macros or Template macros here

Built-in macros that come with Word

There are a bunch of ready-made macros you can take a look at if you're interested. They're in a document called Newmacro.doc in your winword directory. They include some deletion shortcuts, desktop-publishing macros such as a drop cap macro and a macro for producing "smart" quotation marks, and many others. To see these macros demonstrated, open Newmacro.doc, choose the macro you're interested in from the list that appears, and click the Demo button.

If you want to use any of these macros in your own documents, select the macro you want to install, and then click the Install button. Word will ask you which template you'd like the macro to be added to. Choose the Normal template if you want all your documents to have access to the macro. Then click the Copy button.

Macros & Things

If you have a recent update of Word, you may also have a document called Pss.doc, with yet another set of macros. Use it with caution, because some of the macros in it appear unstable.

Get Inside Your Macros

If you were a programmer, you could write macros yourself from scratch in Word's WordBasic programming language, but I bet you're not a programmer and you have no interest in becoming one. Good for you. If you have small-scale ambitions, such as improving a recorded macro or clearing out the embarrassing mistakes you made when you recorded a macro, or if you're just interested in seeing what a macro really looks like, then I'll show you. If you're not interested, that's fine—just skip on ahead.

Look under the hood

To see what a macro looks like, you first have to record one. If you haven't made one yourself yet, consider following the steps I explained earlier to make a transposer macro.

Select Tools ➤ Macro. The Macro dialog box shown in Figure 15.3 will appear. Select the macro you want to see and then click the Edit button. A listing of the commands stored in the macro will appear on the screen and the title bar will change to the name and location of the macro (see Figure 15.4).

If there are lines with instructions followed by the Undo command, you can delete them, just as you would regular text, only don't mess up the line breaks. Later, when you quit Word or close all the documents, you will be asked to verify the changes to the template (the dialog box may also mention glossaries). When this happens, click Yes.

If you want to get clever

If you feel like modifying a recorded macro, you can type away in the macro window. The Help system has a whole section on the WordBasic programming language, which is the language the macros are recorded in. Be careful, though. Some of the commands are more

FIGURE 15.4:
A listing of the "trans" macro I created earlier

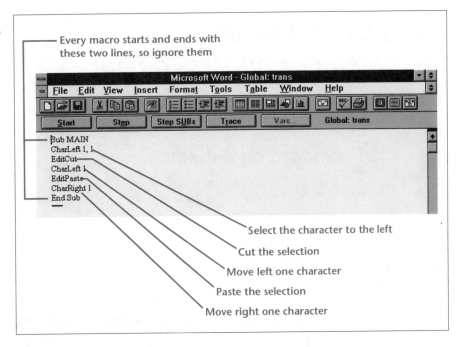

Every macro starts and ends with
these two lines, so ignore them

Microsoft Word - Global: trans

File Edit View Insert Format Tools Table Window Help

Start | Step | Step SUBs | Trace | Vars... | Global: trans

```
Sub MAIN
CharLeft 1, 1
EditCut
CharLeft 1
EditPaste
CharRight 1
End Sub
```

Select the character to the left

Cut the selection

Move left one character

Paste the selection

Move right one character

powerful than you might like and can cause disasters if used indis-
criminately. Most of the commands, though, are variations on the
menu commands you are already familiar with.

TECHNO NOTE

Yes, Commands Are Sort of Macros Too, but Don't Come Running to Me If You Edit Your Commands and Screw Everything Up

In the Macro dialog box shown in Figure 15.3, you might have noticed the
Commands option in the Show area. If you click there, you can edit regular
Word commands just as you would macros (in a sense, the commands are
macros), but **DON'T DO THIS!** I'm only telling you this because you could
do it by mistake and then wonder why the File ➡ Exit command no longer
works, or whatever. Don't mess around with the inner workings of Word unless you're so sure of yourself that you won't mind if there's no one who can
help you if you botch the job.

Macros & Things

Put a Useful Macro on a Menu or on the Toolbar

If you've got a macro that you use all the time, you can add it to any menu or make it a button on the Toolbar. It's easier than it sounds.

Put a macro on a menu

To put a macro on a menu, select Tools ➡ Options. Then, in the Category box, select Menus. Figure 15.5 shows the Options dialog box at this point.

FIGURE 15.5:
The Options dialog box with the Menus category selected

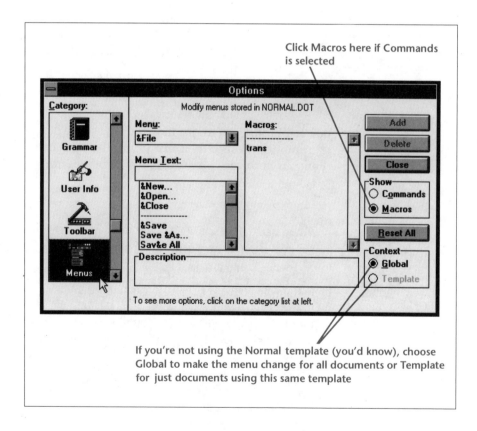

Click Macros here if Commands is selected

If you're not using the Normal template (you'd know), choose Global to make the menu change for all documents or Template for just documents using this same template

First select a menu to add the macro to. (Don't let those ampersands [&] distract you. A character with an ampersand before it gets underlined in the menu as an Alt- shortcut key.) Then go to the Select Macros area and click on the macro you want to add. The macro's name will appear in the Menu Text area. If you want to rename it or change the & character, click in that area and edit the text. When you are satisfied, click the Add button (see Figure 15.6).

Then click Close (or repeat the procedure to add other macros to menus and then click Close). When you want to use the macro, you can now select it off a menu like a "real" Windows command. Here's my new Edit menu:

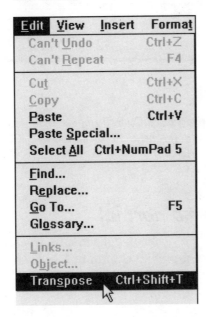

Take a macro back off a menu

If you don't want the macro on your menu any longer, select Tools ➻ Options. Select Menus in the Category Box. Then select the menu name in the Menu area, select the macro's command name in the Menu Text area, and then click Delete. Then click Close.

FIGURE 15.6:
I'm putting the "trans" macro on the Edit menu (the "p" was the first letter in "Transpose" not already used as a shortcut by some other command on the menu.

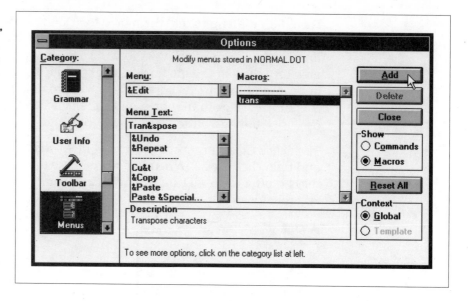

Be careful. You can remove "real" menu commands in exactly the same way as you remove macros from the menus. If you do this by mistake, though, all is not lost. Read the next section.

Return your menus to normal

If you don't want any macros on your menus any longer or you want to restore all the original menu commands, or both, select Tools ➡ Options. Select Menus in the Category box. Click the Reset All button, and then click Close.

Put a macro on the Toolbar

To put a macro on the Toolbar, select Tools ➡ Options. Then, in the Category box, select Toolbar. Figure 15.7 shows the Options dialog box at this point.

FIGURE 15.7:
The Options dialog box
with the Toolbar
category selected

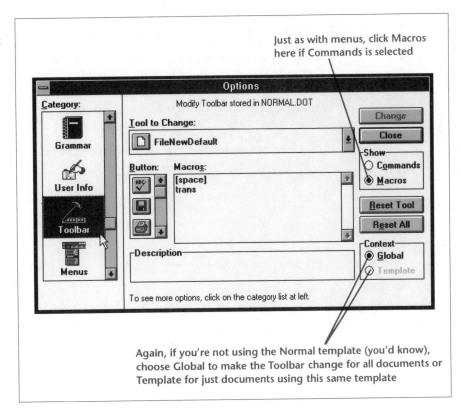

Just as with menus, click Macros
here if Commands is selected

Again, if you're not using the Normal template (you'd know),
choose Global to make the Toolbar change for all documents or
Template for just documents using this same template

In the Tool to Change box, select either one of the current buttons or
one of the places where it says *[space]*. Then scroll through the Button
box to select a button for your macro. Don't use one of the ones already in use unless you want to confuse yourself later. There are some
graphical ones and then a bunch with letters and numbers on them.

When you've selected the button you want, go to the Macros box and
select the macro you want assigned to the selected button. Then click
the Change button. Then click Close (or repeat the procedure to add
other macros to the Toolbar and then click Close). Now, when you want
to use the macro, you can just press a button on the Toolbar. Here's
where I put my "trans" macro:

Macros & Things

Take a macro back off the Toolbar

If you don't want the macro on the Toolbar any longer, select Tools ➺
Options. Select Toolbar in the Category Box. Then select the macro's
button in the Tool to Change box. Click the Reset Tool button, and it
will return to its original assignment or become a space again. Then
click Close.

To make the entire Toolbar revert to its original condition, select Tools
➺ Options, select Toolbar, and then click the Reset All button.

Chapter 16

CUSTOMIZE WORD TO SUIT YOUR NEEDS

Robert's Law of Interfaces: A customized computer program will still mangle your document, but you'll feel more comfortable when it happens

CUSTOMIZABILITY IS FALLOUT from the computer program–features race. You have to remember that the companies that make programs like Word need to sell them to the same people over and over again, every year or so. So they're constantly trying to absorb their competitors' features and grant whole wish-lists for their loyal users.

The benefits for you are mixed. As a result, you can tweak and shave your copy of Word until it's exactly the way you want it or until it's unrecognizable to anyone else. But face it, you're probably not going to spend a lot of time tinkering with your setup. You have better things to do.

You *could* arrange it so that every key on your keyboard types the letter *p*, but if you do, you're in serious need of psychological "help." Also, you can customize your computer setup all you want and it's still not going to turn into a day at the movies.

Treat this chapter (like so many others in this book) as a grab bag. Flip through it. If you see anything you might like, try it out. You can always undo customization if your new "shortcut" doesn't work out. If you really wish something about Word worked differently, maybe I've got a solution for you here.

You May Not Yet Know What Your Preferences Are, and That's Okay

So what are your preferences? If your answer is "Who knows?" then you're like the rest of us. Don't go looking for problems, but try to notice when something about Word bugs you, or when you're always having to reset something. You may be able to nail down something annoying like that so it doesn't keep changing back.

Some things "stick" from one Word session to the next. If you just saved or closed a document in Page Layout view, the next document you create or open will be in Page Layout view as well. The zoom percentage sticks the same way, as does the appearance of nonprinting characters, and the presence or absence of the ruler, ribbon, and Toolbar.

I'll start off with ways to customize how Word starts up. Then I'll talk about the way Word appears or works. And finally, I'll point out a few things about Word that are controlled in Windows.

Start Word the Way You Want

In Chapter 1, I explained how to start Word from the DOS prompt and also from within Windows. If you tend to start Word from within Windows, you can have Word start the way you want and you can even have it start automatically whenever you run Windows.

Assign a working directory

Do you always have to change directories the first time you go to open a document? If so, you should establish a default directory for Word so that it starts you off already looking in the right place. This is something you do in Windows.

Select (single-click) the Microsoft Word icon in the Program Manager and then select File ➟ Properties. The Program Item Properties dialog box will appear (as shown in Figure 16.1).

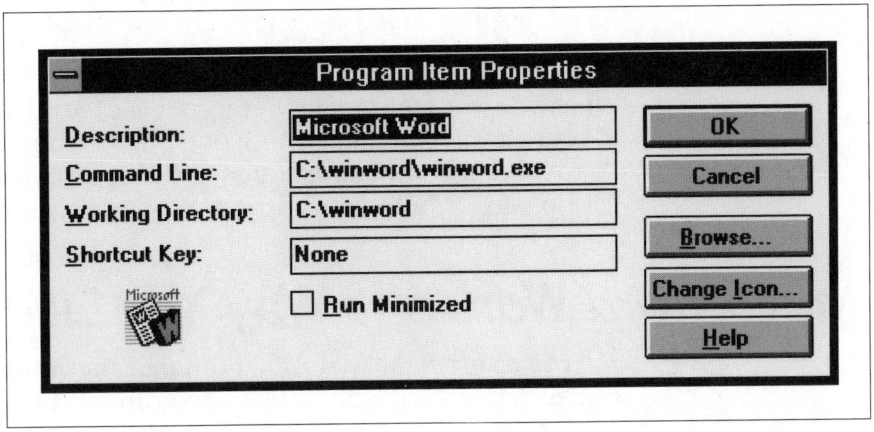

FIGURE 16.1:
In the Program Item Properties dialog box, you can pick a working directory for your Word sessions.

Hit Tab twice to get you to the Working Directory box, then type to replace the text there now or press an arrow key and then edit the contents of the box. (You can also click the Browse button and select a directory, and then click OK.) Then click OK.

Make Word start automatically

The Program Manager will start any programs in its StartUp group whenever you start Windows. So if you want any program to start up automatically, you just have to put a copy of its icon in the StartUp group.

If you haven't got a StartUp group, you can make one easily. In the Program Manager, select File ➤ New. In the New Program Object dialog box that appears, click Program Group. Then, in the Description box of the Program Group Properties dialog box that appears, type StartUp and then click OK. That's it.

Open your StartUp group and open the Applications group, or whichever one your Microsoft Word icon is in. Then hold down Ctrl, click (don't double-click) the Word icon, and hold down the mouse button. The mouse pointer will turn to a copy of the Word icon. Drag it into the StartUp group and let go.

Now whenever you start Windows, Word will also start. You may want it to start minimized, though, so it's not in your face until you need it. That's easy to arrange. Select (don't double-click) the Word icon in the StartUp directory and then select File ➤ Properties. The Program Item Properties dialog box shown in Figure 16.1 will appear. Check off Run Minimized and then click OK.

When you want to work in Word, double-click the icon at the bottom of your screen, or hold down Alt and press Tab until you arrive at Word. Click the maximize button in the upper-right corner of the window to make Word run full-screen.

Make Word Work the Way You Like

You can do a number of things to change the Word *interface*, the way you tell it what you want it to do. You can add buttons to the Toolbar (or remove buttons from it). You can add commands to the menus (or remove commands from them). You can change keyboard shortcut assignments. And so on. Only do these things if it really matters to you.

When you quit or save a document after making these kinds of changes to the Toolbar, the menus, or the keyboard assignments, you'll be asked to confirm any changes to the current glossary and template. Just click Yes (unless you've changed your mind, in which case, click No).

Oh, one other thing. Everything in this section is incredibly easy to do.

Put commands on the Toolbar

If there's a command you use all the time, and you're tired of making your way through menu choices to get to it and you don't remember the keyboard shortcut (or there is none), you can put the command on the Toolbar where you can always get to it easily.

To put a command on the Toolbar, select Tools ➤ Options. Then, in the Category box, select Toolbar. Figure 16.2 shows the Options dialog box at this point.

FIGURE 16.2:
The Options dialog box with the Toolbar category selected. Here's where you stick buttons on the Toolbar—or rip them off it.

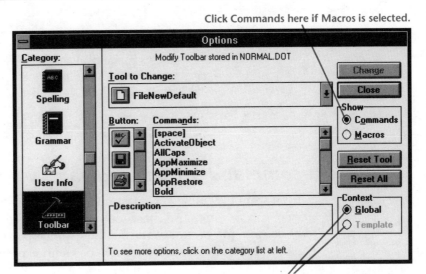

Click Commands here if Macros is selected.

If you're not using the Normal template (you'd know), you'll have to choose Global to make the menu change for all documents or Template to make the change for just documents using this same template.

In the Tool to Change box, select either one of the current buttons, or one of the places where it says *[space]*. Next, scroll through the commands box to find the command you want to put on the Toolbar. Many of the names are abbreviations of the command menu sequences; other commands are shortcuts for Toolbar buttons (for example, the Print button executes a command called FilePrintDefault); others aren't connected to anything till you hook them up.

When you've selected the command you want, scroll through the Button box to select a button for your macro. Pick one you'll recognize, then click the Change button. Then click Close (or repeat the procedure to add other commands to the Toolbar and then click Close). Now, when you want to execute that command, you can just click the button on the Toolbar.

Set Up a Double-Spacing Shortcut on the Toolbar

Here's an example of a useful command to put on the Toolbar, the double-spacing command. (Word used to have a spacing shortcut on the ribbon but "they" took it off when they decided it wasn't as useful as decimal tabs. Hah.) Select Tools ➤ Options, select Toolbar in the Category box, and make sure Commands is selected in the Show box. In the Tools to Change box, select InsertChart. In the Commands box, choose SpacePara2, and in the Button box, select the button with two horizontal lines spaced well apart (about halfway through the list of choices). Then click Change, and then Close.

Take a command off the Toolbar

If you want to remove a command you never use from the Toolbar, select Tools ➤ Options. Select Toolbar in the Category Box. Then select the command's button in the Tool to Change box and select *[space]* in the Commands box. Then click the Change button, and then click Close.

To make the entire Toolbar revert to its original condition, select Tools ➤ Options, select Toolbar, and then click the Reset All button.

Put a command on a menu

To put a command on a menu, select Tools ➤ Options. Then, in the Category box, select Menus. Figure 16.3 shows the Options dialog box at this point.

FIGURE 16.3:
The Options dialog box
with the Menus
category selected

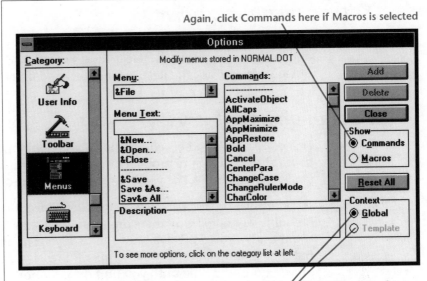

Again, click Commands here if Macros is selected

If you're not in the Normal template (you'd know), you'll have to choose
Global to make the menu change for all documents or Template to
make the change for just documents using this same template.

Customizing Word

First, select a menu to add the command to. (Don't let those ampersands [&] distract you. A character with an ampersand before it gets
underlined in the menu as an Alt- shortcut key.) Then go to the Commands box, scroll through, and click on the command you want to
add. The command's name will appear in the Menu Text area. If you
want to rename it or change the & character, click in that area and
edit the text. When you are satisfied, click the Add button.

Then click Close (or repeat the procedure to add other commands to
menus and then click Close). When you want to use the command,
you can now select it off a menu like a "real" Windows command.

Take a command off a menu

If you don't want the new command on your menu any longer, or if
you want to delete a command you never use, select Tools ➺ Options.
Select Menus in the Category Box. Then select the menu name in the
Menu area, select the command's command name in the Menu Text
area, and then click Delete. Then click Close.

Return menus to normal

If you want to undo all your menu customization and restore all the original menu commands, select Tools ➤ Options. Select Menus in the Category box. Click the Reset All button, and then click Close.

Assign shortcut keys

First of all, don't bother reading this if you don't normally use keyboard shortcuts. You're probably not about to start. Come back when you're hitting Shift-F12 to save your document and we'll talk.

If you *are* the type of person who uses keyboard shortcuts, you've probably wondered why there aren't more. It's the fastest way to select commands—you don't even have to take your hands off the keyboard. But they're much harder to remember. At least with menus you can browse around a little until you find the command you want. If you don't know what Alt-F4 does, for instance, don't hit it.

If you're a refugee from a failed word-processing program of the past, and you're still attached to the "classic" key assignments in that program, then get a life. No, just kidding, you can easily make key assignments to mimic WordStar, for example. There is a special command in the General category Options dialog box to enable WordPerfect key assignments.

Well, you can make as many keyboard shortcuts as you want. If there's a command you'd like to give a shortcut to, select Tools ➤ Options and select the Keyboard category. The Options dialog box will look like Figure 16.4.

Find the command you want in the Commands box. The box will show you if there already is a shortcut for the command. The Current Keys For box below will show you if there's already more than one key combo assigned to that command. (There's no limit.) Finally, describe a shortcut key combination in the Shortcut Key box at the top by choosing a key and adding Ctrl or Shift or both to it. If the key combination you choose is already assigned to a command, it will show up after the word Currently in that area. (You *can* reassign keys.)

FIGURE 16.4:
The Options dialog box with the Keyboard category selected. Here's where you change your key assignments to something suitably bizarre.

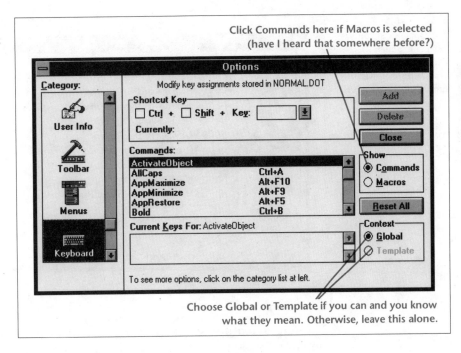

Click Commands here if Macros is selected (have I heard that somewhere before?)

Choose Global or Template if you can and you know what they mean. Otherwise, leave this alone.

When you've made your selections, click Add and then Close (or make more assignments and finally click Close).

Remove shortcut assignments

You can remove a key assignment just as easily. Select the command and then select the key assignment in the Key Assignment For box. Then click the Delete button.

You can also restore all key assignments to the defaults by clicking the Reset All button.

Change how editing works

If you like the way Word lets you edit your docs, then skip ahead, you'll be bored by this. If you've got any gripes, though, there are some things you can change. Select Tools ➺ Options and then select the General Category (see Figure 16.5).

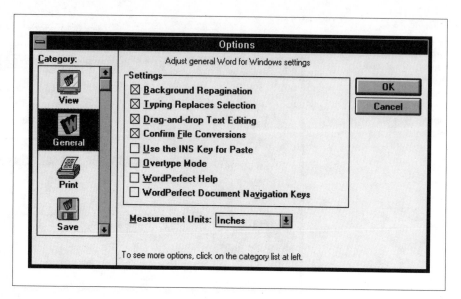

The editing features you can change are called Typing Replaces Selection and Drag-and-drop Text Editing (which are both "turned on" by default), and Use the INS Key for Paste and Overtype Mode (which are both "turned off" by default). If it bugs you that you can so easily type over selected text, turn off Typing Replaces Selection. It won't happen any more.

If you're against drag and drop, turn it off. If you want to use the Insert key as a shortcut for Edit ➧ Paste (as some other programs do), turn on Use the INS Key for Paste. If you actually like overtype and use it most of the time, you can turn it on so it's the default.

When you've made your selections, click OK.

For Wonks Only—Change the Units of Measurement

If you want to work in centimeters instead of inches, or if you prefer to use typesetter's measurements of picas or points, you can choose one of those other measuring systems on this dialog box. Just drop down the Measurement Units box and choose the type you want. Then click OK. Notice how the ruler changes?

Customizing Word

Control the proofreading tools

There are things you can do to fine-tune the spelling and grammar checkers, but they're really only useful if something about those proofreading tools is bothering you. Otherwise you're wasting your time.

Control the spelling checker

To change the spelling checker's defaults, select Tools ➻ Options and then select the Spelling category (see Figure 16.6).

If your spell checks are always getting tripped up on proper nouns or technical jargon or file names, you can check off Words in UPPERCASE or Words with Numbers (or both) in the Ignore area. If you don't want Word to automatically suggest correct spellings for misspelled words, uncheck Always Suggest. And if you want to create different custom dictionaries (word lists) for different types of work, click the Add button and then type a file name for each new custom dictionary you want to create. Then, when a word comes up during a spell check that's particular to a given field, choose the correct dictionary to add the word to.

When you've made all your choices, click OK.

FIGURE 16.6:
The Options dialog box with the Spelling category selected. Are you sure you're not just wasting time now?

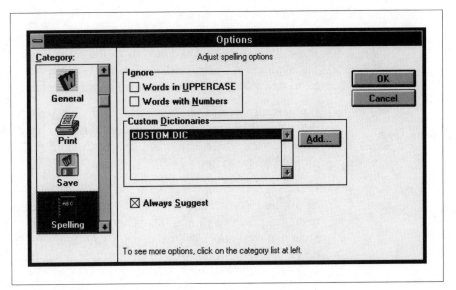

Control the grammar checker

To change the grammar checker's defaults, select Tools ➟ Options and then select the Grammar category (see Figure 16.7).

FIGURE 16.7:
The Options dialog box with the Grammar category selected. Do you really want to get into this stuff?

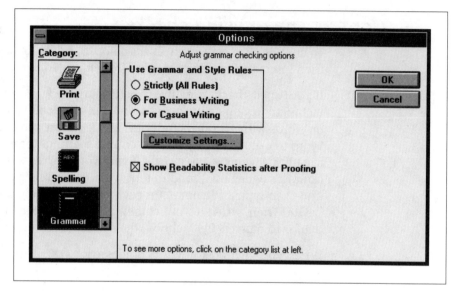

Here you can select the degree of strictness of the grammar check, from three choices under Use Grammar and Style Rules: Strictly (All Rules), For Business Writing, and For Casual Writing. You can uncheck Show Readability Statistics after Proofing if you have no use for those statistics.

If you really want to get involved in the nitty gritty (or nitty gritty nitty ditty great bird) of grammar and style rules, click the Customize Settings button, which will bring up the Customize Grammar Settings dialog box (see Figure 16.8).

Here you can select which grammar and style rules, specifically, should be applied to your documents. Start off by selecting one of the options from the previous dialog box. Then scroll through the Grammar and Style lists and check the rules you want used and uncheck the rules you don't. If you're unsure what a rule means, select it and click the Explain

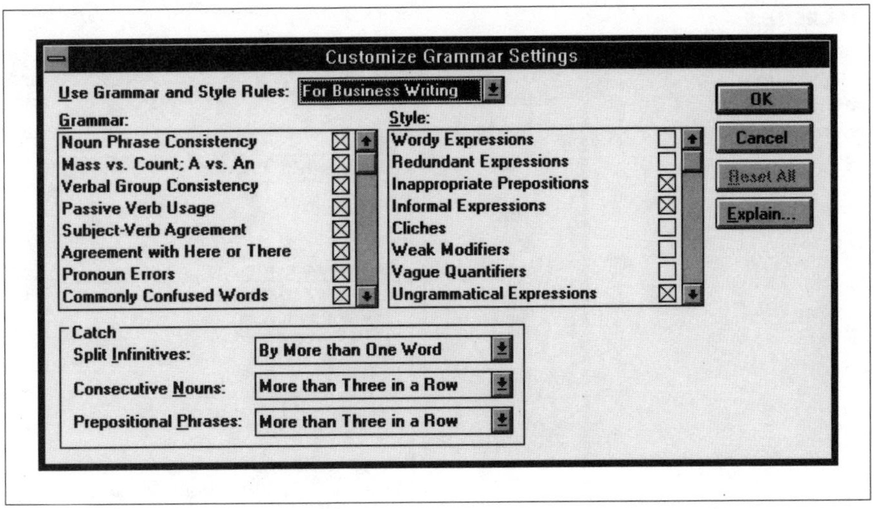

FIGURE 16.8: This is the Customize Grammar Settings dialog box. Obviously, you have nothing better to do.

button (then recheck or re-uncheck it if necessary, because it will change when you select it). From then on any rule you check will be explained in the Explain window.

You can also fine-tune the circumstances under which Word will catch split infinitives, consecutive nouns, or consecutive prepositional phrases by choosing among the range of options on the drop down list boxes at the bottom of the dialog boxes.

You can have the rules revert to the defaults for any of the three levels of strictness by selecting the level and then clicking the Reset All button.

Update or Change Your User Info

If you've moved or changed your name, or if you just want to mess up the person who owns the copy of Word you use, you can change all the basic User Info. Just select Tools ➺ Options and then choose the User Info category (see Figure 16.9). It's self-evident how to use this dialog box. Just type in any new information you want and then click OK.

FIGURE 16.9:

The Options dialog box with the User Info category selected. Invent your alter ego here.

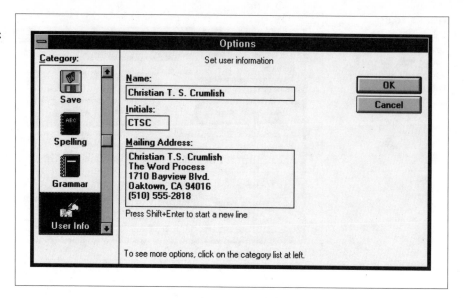

This won't change some of the information you may have typed into built-in templates that ask you for more information about yourself to fill in their forms.

Choose Groovy Colors for Your Screen

Normally, you should be able to forget about Windows. It should hang around in the background making everything work and making different programs consistent, but it shouldn't be a big part of your life. You'll run into it, though, if you try to change aspects of Word that are really controlled in Windows.

One easy thing to change is the color scheme. If you have a color monitor and you've never messed with the colors in Windows, then your Word screen is pretty boring—mostly gray and white with a touch of blue. To change it, go to the Program Manager, open the Main group and double-click on the Control Panel icon:

This will open the Control Panel window. Double-click the Color icon (three crayons). This will open the Color dialog box. Drop down the list box in the Color Schemes area and browse through the preset color schemes. If you click on a name, the sample area below will show you what active and inactive windows will look like in that scheme. If you feel like customizing your own color scheme, click the Color Palette>> button, and the dialog box will expand, allowing you to choose a color for each screen element.

When you have completed your color scheme, click the Save Scheme button and type a name for your scheme in the dialog box that appears. Click OK to save the scheme, and then click OK again to apply to color scheme to your current setup. Now, isn't that more interesting than blue and gray?

Chapter 17

PRINTING PROBLEMS AND SOLUTIONS

Curry's Law of Printers: If everything else is working correctly, your printer will start to malfunction

---

NO MURPHY'S LAW can do justice to the terrors and aggravation of printing. Every make of printer is different. Each individual printer has its own quirks and idiosyncrasies. So I'm not promising that I can get your printer working. No one could. But I can give you some advice that will help you avoid headaches, show you how to handle unique printing tasks, suggest things to check when you've got trouble, and give solutions to some of the most common problems.

Zen and the Art of Printing

Some problems can't be ducked. If you've pulled the plug on your printer with your foot, it won't print. But you can follow these rules of thumb to avoid some of the most frustrating make-you-feel-dumb kinds of problems.

Always save first, before you print

There's nothing quite like seeing you computer freeze up when you try to print your document, and realizing that you haven't saved and you're going to lose the last three hours' work.

A watched document never prints

Even laser printers can be slow, especially if they're printing graphics. So don't stand around grabbing each page as it comes out of your printer. Go stretch your legs, but remember the next rule.

Make sure everything's okay before you walk away

Stick around long enough to make sure the first page at least has printed all right (and not all down one side of the paper) and no smoke is coming out of anything. I've come back to a printer a half hour after I started it printing graphics and discovered it was out of paper. A half-hour of my life wasted! I've also seen reams of computer paper crumpled up around the mouth of a printer.

Don't forget to click OK

Wonder why nothing's printing? Check the screen. Did you select File ➥ Print and then walk away?

Use Print Preview

If you're printing anything at all complicated, look at it in Print Preview first to make sure everything's positioned right, there are page numbers where you want them, etc. Select File ➥ Print Preview, and then when you're ready to print, click the Print button.

Don't try to do other stuff while printing

Unless you've got a really fast machine, or you just *have* to work on something else, let the printing finish before you try to use the computer for anything else. Sure, with Windows you're supposed to be able to *multitask*, that is, do two (or more) things at once, but really the computer will do a little printing, then a little of your work, then a little printing, and it will take forever and annoy you.

Print draft output when you're printing a draft

People set up their printers and then forget all about them. Don't print a draft with the highest-quality output. It's a waste of time and supplies. If you're printing a draft, first select Tools ➠ Options, select the Print category, and then check off Draft Output and click OK. (You can also get there from the Print dialog box by clicking the Options button.)

Don't bother with printer control codes

Don't let anyone convince you it's worth learning to send Esc-ertio4t3 to your printer to get it to advance a whole page. Let Word control your printer for you.

Special Print Jobs

My general advice about printing is to click the Print button and leave it at that, but I realize sometimes you need to go via the dialog box and select a printing option that doesn't happen by default.

Print more than one copy of your document

Select File ➠ Print. The Print dialog box will appear (see Figure 17.1).

Type the number of copies you want to print into the Copies box. Then click OK.

Printing

FIGURE 17.1:
From the Print dialog box, you can print more than one copy of your document, print certain pages, print to a file instead of to the printer, or even select a different printer entirely.

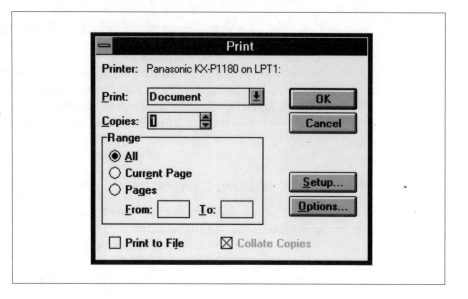

Print just the page you're on

If you've just edited a page and don't want to print the whole document again, just print the page you're on. To do so, select File ➤ Print and the Print dialog box shown in Figure 17.1 will appear. Click Current Page and then OK.

Print any range of pages

If you don't want to print your whole document, just some pages, select File ➤ Print. On the Print dialog box, select the From box and type the first page of the range you want to print. If you don't want to print the rest of the document from that page on, select the To box and type the last page of the range. Then click OK.

Print a bunch of documents at once

Printing a bunch of things at once is called *batch printing*. You can do this with a feature I've ignored until now because it's such a can of worms and it's only somewhat useful. Let's cut to the chase.

To print a bunch of files, select File ➤ Find File. The Find File dialog box appears (see Figure 17.2).

FIGURE 17.2:
The Find File dialog box. You could spend all day playing with these controls and not get any of your work done.

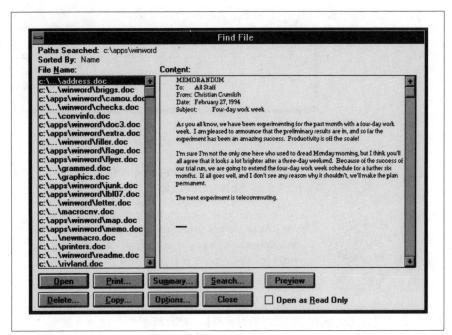

Select the files you want by holding Ctrl when you click each file name (so the names you've already selected aren't deselected), or Shift-clicking to select a list of consecutive file names. Then click the Print button. The Print dialog box will appear (see Figure 17.1). Click OK. Your documents will print one after another.

If the Find File dialog box is not showing you the files you wanted to print, click the Search button and play around with the options in the Location area on the box that appears. Then click the Start Search button. The files you're looking for should now appear in the Find File list.

Print your document to a file

If you have no printer or don't want to use the printer you're connected to, you can print to a file (sometimes called "printing to disk") and then print that file on someone else's setup. Select File ➤ Print. On the Print dialog box (shown above in Figure 17.1), check off Print to File and then click OK. The Print to File dialog box will appear:

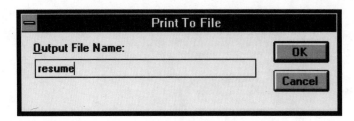

Type a file name for your print file (*not* the same name as the document) and click OK. Now you can copy your print file to a disk, take it to another computer and print it from DOS. Ask someone clever if you don't know how to do this.

Don't forget to uncheck Print to File the next time you print. If you do forget, just click Cancel when you're asked for a file name. Then uncheck Print to File and then click OK to print to the printer.

Choose a different printer

If you have a choice of printers to print, and you'd like to print to a different printer, first make sure the physical connection is made.

This may mean turning a knob on a switching box, or even pulling one end of the cable out of one printer and sticking it in another one, or you may have two printer ports (plugs) in your computer plugged into different printers. If you don't know how your setup works, ask whoever set it up or anyone else who can explain your connections to you.

Then select File ➤ Print Setup (or click the Setup button on the Print dialog box) and the Setup dialog box will appear (see Figure 17.3).

If you don't see the printer you want, you may have to install it or connect it, as explained later in this chapter in *Check the printer installation*.

Select the printer you want and then click OK.

FIGURE 17.3:
The Print Setup dialog box. Yours will undoubtedly have a different list of printers on it, or perhaps only one.

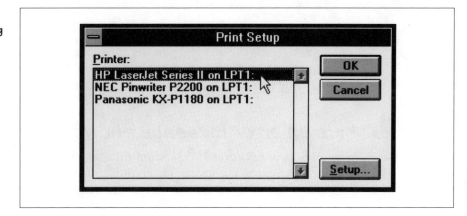

Things to Check
When You've Got a Printing Problem

A little later on in this chapter, I'll run through some common problems and things you can do to solve them, but first I want to give you a list of things to check whenever you have a printing problem. Many common situations involve simple errors that are easy to correct. Always check the easy stuff before getting involved in tricky solutions.

Is your printer plugged in?

It sounds dumb, but it's always the first thing you should check.

Is your printer turned on?

Don't laugh. This is probably the most common printing problem. It sometimes helps just to turn a printer off and then on again (geeks call this *power cycling* to mystify others).

Is your printer "on line"?

Some printers can be on and still not ready to print. See if there's an On Line or Set button on the front of your printer. If it's a laser printer, look for a message like READY or ON LINE. Then try again.

Is there paper in the printer?

Sometimes Word will tell you the paper's out. Sometimes it just knows something's wrong with the printer. A laser printer will tell you in its message area. With dot-matrix printers, you have to use your eyes.

Is there an error message showing?

Some printers can tell you when other problems are dogging them. A laser printer will tell you if it's out of toner or if the paper is jammed inside it. Look for a message on the front of the printer.

Are the cables all connected and tight?

Just like power cords, cables sometimes come unplugged, especially cables that people are always moving from one port to another. Make sure everything's nice and tight.

Is the correct printer selected?

You might be printing to the wrong printer, or one that isn't even there. *Choose a different printer* above tells you how to select the correct printer.

Is the printer installed?

Is the printer you want not on the Printer Setup list? You may have to install it. Read *Check the printer installation* below.

Is the printer connected to the right port?

You don't have to understand this, but your printer may be attached to LPT1 while Word thinks its attached to LPT2, or vice versa. *Check the printer connections* below explains how to change this.

Have you donated to a worthy charity lately?

It could just be bad karma. Have a lot of things been going wrong for you lately?

Solutions to Common Problems

Once you've asked yourself all those questions, it's time to do something about the problem. Here are some things you can try.

Jane, stop this crazy thing! Cancel disastrous print jobs

If you just sent a 100-page document to the printer and then realized there was a problem with it, you've got to stop the printing. First, turn the printer off line (or turn it off completely, as long as it's not on a network). Then click Cancel on the Printing dialog box that tells you how your printing's going. If that box has already disappeared, hold down Alt and press Tab until you get to the Print Manager, then highlight the print job in progress and click the Delete button. Then click Yes on the dialog box that appears asking you to confirm. Hit Alt-Tab again to return to Word.

Turn the printer off and then on again

That's easy enough, isn't it? This will often clear out whatever garbage is confusing the printer. Leave if off for a few seconds before turning it back on.

Check the printer installation

If your printer is not installed, or you think there's something wrong with the installation, get out your Windows installation disks. (If you stole Windows, you're burned now.) In the Program Manager, open the Main window and double-click the Control Panel icon to open the Control Panel (discussed in Chapter 16), then double-click the Printers icon to bring up the Printers dialog box. Click Add>> to expand the dialog box to include a printer list (see Figure 17.4). Then scroll through the enormous list of printers and look for yours.

If your printer isn't listed, read its documentation to see if it emulates (that means "behaves like") any other standard kind of printer. If it does, select that printer. If that still doesn't work, get in touch with the person you bought your printer from, or—failing all else—with Microsoft.

FIGURE 17.4:
Select the printer you want to install here in the Printers dialog box.

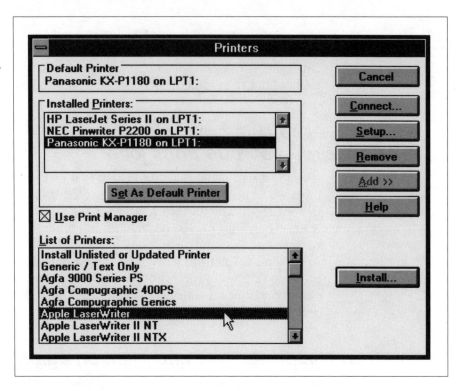

Select your printer and click Install. That will bring up the Install Printer dialog box:

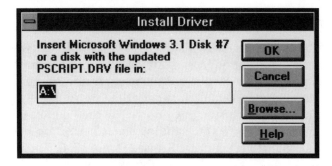

Put the disk you're asked for in drive A and then click OK. You may have to follow some more instructions, but they'll be straightforward.

Check the printer connections

If your printer is connected to the wrong port, that's easy enough to fix. (The question is, *why* is it connected to the wrong port?) From the Program Manager, open the Main group and double-click Control Panel, then double-click the Printers icon. In the Printers dialog box shown in Figure 17.4, make sure the proper printer is selected, and then click the Connect button. That will bring up the Connect dialog box, shown in Figure 17.5.

FIGURE 17.5:
In the Connect dialog box, select the port your printer is connected to.

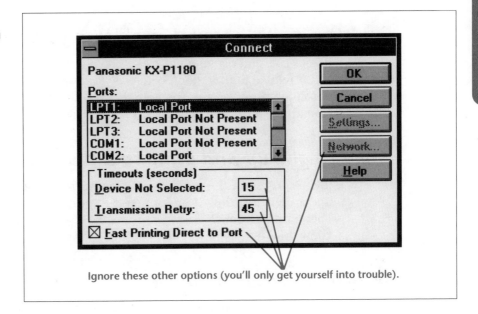

Ignore these other options (you'll only get yourself into trouble).

Select the correct port (if you don't know which one is right, you probably shouldn't be doing this), and then click OK. Then click Close.

Check the printer setup

There's probably nothing you can fix in the printer setup, but you can check it to see if there's anything screwy going on. Select File ➡ Print Setup, and then click the Setup button. Make sure the settings all look fine and then click OK twice.

Make your printer the default Windows printer

If you're always having to choose the same printer every time you print from Word, consider making that printer the default Windows printer (unless you share your computer with people who wouldn't like that).

From the Program Manager, open the Main group and double-click Control Panel, then double-click on the Printers icon. In the Printers dialog box shown in Figure 17.4 (above), make sure the proper printer is selected and then click the Set As Default Printer button. Then click Close.

Don't try to fix network problems yourself

If your computer is on a network and you suspect your printing problem is related to that, don't get in too far over your head. Talk to the system administrator or the friendly hallway guru and have someone who understands the network take a look at your setup.

When to give up and print to a file

If you can't solve the problem with your printer and you're working under pressure, hang it up for now and print your document to a file. Then print it from DOS or from someone else's machine. If you need to know how, read *Print your document to a file* above.

Restart a frozen machine

If your computer freezes up just as you start printing (or for that matter, at any point during printing), you're probably going to have to restart the program and you might have to reboot your machine (turn it off and then on again). I hope you saved. Read Chapter 20, *Disaster Recovery,* for more on this subject.

Advice for Specific Printing Problems

Finally, I'm going to run through some specific problems you might be having and things you can try to fix them.

My document is printing too faint

If your document is faint and hard to read, the problem could be one of several things. Most likely, your ribbon or toner needs replacing. Try to get someone else to change them unless you don't mind a little ink all over.

If it's not something mechanical, and your printer's the dot-matrix type, check to see if you're printing in Draft mode. First select Tools ⯈ Options and the Printer category. Uncheck Draft Output if it's checked, and click OK. Then select File ⯈ Print Setup. Click the Setup button, and then on the dialog box that appears, click the Options button. The Options dialog box that appears (see Figure 17.6) should include a Print Quality box.

FIGURE 17.6:

Your Options dialog box may look different from this, depending on your printer. What you're looking for is a Print Quality option.

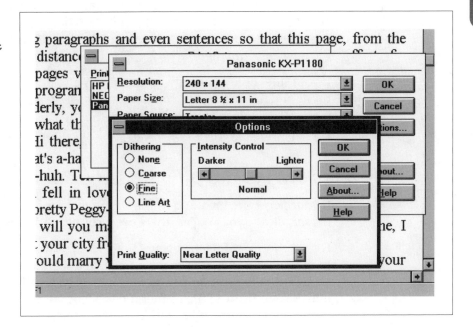

Make sure the Print Quality selection isn't Draft (try Near Letter Quality), and then click OK three times.

If your printer still prints too light, I hope it's still under warranty. If it's an emergency and you need your output sooner than you can get your printer fixed, in the Options dialog box pictured in Figure 17.6, slide the slider in the Intensity Control area all the way to the Darker side. Then try printing again.

Something's screwy with my fonts

Marketing hypesters make such a big deal about WYSIWYG ("What You See Is What You Get"), but you never really GWYS. Even if you stick with TrueType fonts, what you see on the screen will not match exactly what prints out. If your fonts look funny or if your lines are breaking differently from how they do on the screen, here are a few things you can check.

First of all, use TrueType fonts or printer fonts. Printer fonts won't look exactly right on the screen, but they'll print just fine. TrueType fonts should look about the same on the screen as they do when you print. For fonts you (or someone else) just installed, you may have to select File ➥ Print Setup and click Setup and then OK twice to let Word know the new fonts are there.

If your lines break one way on the screen and another way when you print, and this matters to you (for example, if you're desktop publishing), select Tools ➥ Option and select the View category. Then check off Line Breaks and Fonts as Printed in the *Show Text with* area and click OK.

My page breaks are all messed up

If your pages are breaking in the wrong place, or you get big gaps in the middles of your pages, there are a couple of things you can check.

For dot-matrix printers, because both Word and your printer may be trying to decide when to break a page, you want to make sure your printer is set up properly or the two approaches will conflict. Someone may have advanced the printer a bit to tear off a page. Turn off your printer and turn the roller until the top of the page is right above the print head. Then turn the printer back on. Now try to print again.

Make sure that hidden text isn't printing out. This is controlled separately from whether it appears on the screen. Select Tools ➥ Options and the select the Print category. Make sure Hidden Text in the Include with Document area is unchecked. Then click OK.

If you want page breaks updated constantly, so they're always correct, select Tools ➺ Options and select the General category. Make sure Background Pagination is checked off and then click OK. You can also turn off background repagination to save a little memory and speed, and then select Tools ➺ Repaginate Now whenever you want the pagination updated.

Finally, remember to trust the Print Preview, not how it looks on the screen, not even in Page Layout view.

My margins are all wrong

If you have a dot-matrix printer, the actual margins as printed may differ from the margin settings you have selected. This is because the *tractors* that pull the paper through the printer can be adjusted to the left or right. If the margins are off, you have two choices—you can fine-tune the positioning of the tractors, by trial and error, or you can set different margins to compensate for the offset of the tractors.

Just what I wanted, 400 pages of PostScript code

Sometimes you'll print to a laser printer and find, when you look to see what's coming out, page after page of computer programming language code. This means that you've got the wrong printer selected. Word is trying to print to a PostScript printer and the instructions are just being printed out verbatim on the non-PostScript printer you've actually printed to. Select the correct printer.

My frames don't look right

If your frame prints on the wrong page, it has probably moved along with the text during your editing. You can drag the name onto the correct page in Normal view, and then position it exactly in Page Layout view. If you select the frame and then select Format ➺ Frame, you can assign select Relative To in the Horizontal and Vertical areas and choose Page for each. Then the frame will be positioned relative to the page itself, not the text.

If you're not familiar with frames, you can learn all about them in Chapter 9, *The Wonderful World of Desktop Publishing*.

If text is or is not wrapping around the frame, contrary to your wishes, select the frame, select Format ➺ Frame, and then choose None or Around in the Text Wrapping area and click OK.

If you have text inside a frame and it's squeezed all over on the right side or it's just a long vertical string of a few letters at a time, click the text and then check the left indent on the ruler. Drag the split-triangle left-indent symbol on the ruler over to 0.

My tables don't look right

If the text in a table cell is squeezed into the right side of the cell or is a long vertical string of character, click in the cell and check the left indent on the ruler. Drag the split-triangle left-indent symbol on the ruler over to 0. (You can read all about tables in Chapter 8, *Organize Your Info.)*

Chapter 18

NO PROGRAM IS AN ISLAND

Lister's Law of Connectivity: Garbage from another program is no better than garbage you created yourself

BECAUSE WORD IS a Windows program, it has some built-in abilities to connect to other programs. And because Word exists in a world where there are other popular word-processing programs, its makers were smart enough to enable it to read documents produced by almost any other program. If you just use Word for simple word processing, and you never have to incorporate information that you or anyone else has produced with other programs, then don't read this chapter.

If you work with people who use other word processors, such as WordPerfect, or if you yourself formerly used another word processor, then you'll be happy to know that everything created in those other programs will be accessible to you through Word. If you regularly use spreadsheet or database software, then you might be interested to know that Word can incorporate data from those as well as other types of programs, including draw and paint packages.

On the other hand, this whole chapter may sound like technobabble to you. And nothing in here is essential. So if this all seems to be over your head or if you're not ready to take advantage of these features, skip it now and come back when you're ready, if ever.

Switch to Another Program

As I've mentioned in other places in this book, you can switch to other programs you're running by holding down Alt and pressing Tab repeatedly. The other running programs (including the Program Manager) will cycle through one by one up to Word for Windows again and then repeating in the same order. When the program you want to switch to comes up, release Alt and Tab and you're there.

Simple Copying from One Program to Another

If you just want to copy some material and you don't need what you copy to be *linked* or connected to the original program in any way, then just make your selection in the first program and copy it (most likely with Edit ➤ Copy in any Windows program). Then switch to the second program, position the insertion point (or other pointer) and then paste the copied material (most likely with Edit ➤ Paste). The pasted material will now be part of the document (or file) in the new program, with no connection to the old one.

Link Copied Material to Its Source

In Word, you have other, fancier, copying options available. Word makes use of a new Windows feature called *OLE*, which stands for *Object Linking and Embedding*. Now that's perfectly clear, isn't it?

DDE, OLE, and Doris Day, Nat Busby, Dig It, Dig It

Buzzword alert: You may hear any of the following terms bandied around and confused with each other: *DDE, Dynamic Data Exchange, OLE, object, linking, embedding, link, hot link,* and *paste-linking*. First of all, *DDE* (Dynamic Data Exchange) is an earlier way to link information inserted in one program to the program it was created in. There are still programs around that use DDE, but Word uses OLE, the new! improved! version.

Object is probably the most overused computer buzzword of the day, and it can mean many different things in different contexts. If you think about it at all, think of it as meaning a selection. *Linking* means copying material (an object) from one program to another (or from one document to another) and preserving the connection (the *link*) to the original (also called *source*) document so that changes made to the material in the source document will appear (be *updated*) in the *destination* document.

Embedding is a sort of weaker form of linking in which there is no link to the original material, but the destination document knows what program the object was created in and can open that program up when you want to edit the object. A *hot link* is a link that updates the object in the destination document whenever it changes in the source document. Finally, *paste-linking* refers to the way OLE links are created, with a variation on the simple copy-and-paste procedure. In Word, you use the Edit ➸ Paste Special command, and then choose Paste Link in a dialog box. In some other programs, there is an Edit ➸ Paste Link command that has the same effect.

When should I link and when should I embed?

That's a good question. Near as I can tell, you should almost always link. Simply embedding an object seems to have no real advantages over linking it, unless you know you won't want your embedded object updated if the source object changes.

An advantage of linking is that the object is actually stored in the source document, even though it appears in the destination document. An embedded object is stored in the destination document and therefore makes that document bigger. Anyway, let's concentrate on linking.

Paste-link an object into a Word document

To paste-link an object into Word from another program, first switch to that program, open the source document, and select the material you want to link, then switch back to Word and select Edit ➤ Paste Special. The Paste Special dialog box (shown in Figure 18.1) will appear.

FIGURE 18.1:
Select any data type that doesn't end with "Object" in the Paste Special dialog box to paste a link.

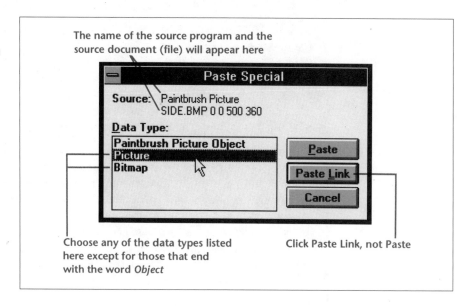

The name of the source program and the source document (file) will appear here

Choose any of the data types listed here except for those that end with the word *Object*

Click Paste Link, not Paste

The dialog box will show the source program and file and some code to indicate the portion of the file selected (if you've chosen just a range of cells in a spreadsheet document, for instance, it will give the cell range as well). Choose a data type from the list of options. Any of the choices that do not end in "Object" are okay. (The Object choices are for embedding, not linking). Then click the Paste Link button. The linked object will appear in your document, as in the example in Figure 18.2 (if the Paste Link button is grayed out, you're not going to be able to link to the source program).

FIGURE 18.2:
The Paintbrush picture is now pasted into the Word document.

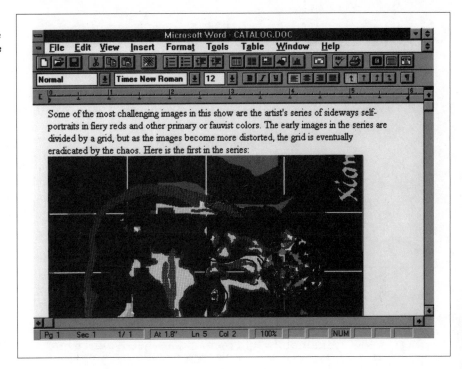

Paste-link a Word selection into another Word document

You can paste-link text, tables, graphics, or anything really from one Word document to another (or, for that matter, from one part of a Word document to another part of the same document) with exactly the same procedure outlined in the previous section (except you don't switch programs, of course, just windows, or not even that).

Paste-link a Word selection into a different program

To paste-link a Word selection into another program, just make the selection, choose Edit ➟ Copy, switch to the other program, place the insertion point (or whatever pointer there is) and select Edit ➟ Paste Link (if there is such a command) or Edit ➟ Paste Special, then select a data type that doesn't end in Object and click the Paste Link button.

Update a Linked Object

Now, the whole point of linking information is so that you can have it accurate and up-to-the-minute whenever anything changes in the source. Whenever you open a document with links to outside sources, you'll see a dialog box like the one shown below.

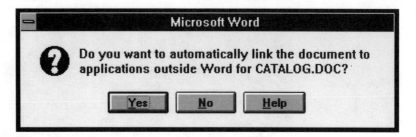

Click Yes. Unless you specify differently, all of your links will be updated automatically, whenever the source changes.

If you want more control over links, you can set them to be updated manually, and then update them yourself.

Any changes that you make in the destination document to linked material will be eradicated if the source changes and the link is updated. Instead, make your changes to the source, or if you don't want to change the source, lock the link or break it, both of which I will explain next.

If the Source Document No Longer Exists under Its Original File Name...

If the source document for a link no longer exists or has been renamed, you'll get an error dialog box when you open the document. It will tell you that Word cannot obtain the data. Click OK. If the source exists under another name, you can reconnect the link to its source. Select Edit ➤ Links, select the link you want to reconnect, and click the Change Link button. On the Change Link dialog box that appears, edit the information in the File Name box and then click OK. Click the Update Now button to update the link and then click OK.

Freeze a link

If you don't want a linked object to change any more, even if the source changes, you have several options. The safest is to lock it.

To lock a link, select Edit ➻ Links. In the Links dialog box, shown in Figure 18.3, select the link, check the Locked check box, and then click OK.

FIGURE 18.3:
Select the link you want to lock here in the Links dialog box.

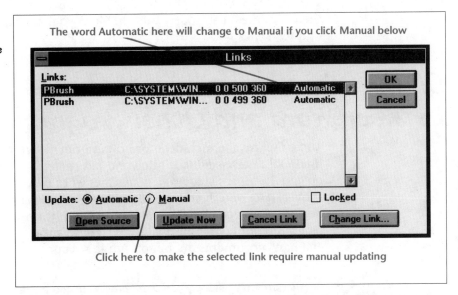

The word Automatic here will change to Manual if you click Manual below

Click here to make the selected link require manual updating

You Can Unlink a Link, but I Don't Recommend It

You can also prevent a link from being updated by unlinking it, but then there's no going back. To unlink a link, select File ➻ Links, select the link, and click the Cancel Link button. Click Yes to verify that you're really sure you want to do this. The link will disappear from the Links list. Click OK. Now you just have an embedded object.

Links & Converting

Edit a Linked Object at Its Source

If you want to change a linked object, edit it at the source, or the next time it's updated, your changes will disappear. The easiest way to do this is to double-click the object. The source program and document will open and you can make whatever changes you want. When you're done, be sure to save before quitting.

You can also select Edit ➺ Links, select the link you want to edit, and then click the Open source button. Make your changes, save, and quit, and then click OK.

Convert Documents between Word and Other Programs

There are ways to include information from different programs without linking it or embedding it into your document. Generally, you can just open a document created with another word processor, and Word will convert it for you. It can usually figure out for itself what program the document was created in. So if you work with people who use a different program or if you used to use a different program yourself, those "foreign" documents are not off-limits to you.

You can even open some non–word-processing documents in Word, such as Excel spreadsheets, although they'll be converted to Word documents when you open them. Spreadsheet information will appear in a table.

Open documents from other programs in Word

To open a document created in another program, select File ➺ Open. The familiar Open dialog box will appear. In the List Files area, select All Files (*.*), and then select the file name of the document you want to open and click OK.

The Convert File dialog box will appear (see Figure 18.4) with a guess (usually correct) about what program the document was created in.

FIGURE 18.4:
The Convert File dialog box. Word can usually tell which program the document was created in. If it's wrong, help it out.

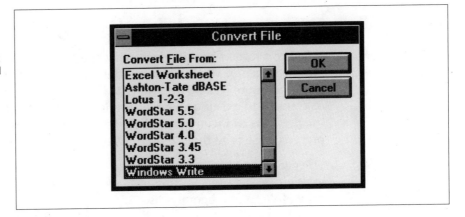

If it's wrong, select the correct program. Click OK. The document will open. When you next try to save it, Word will display a dialog box asking if you want to overwrite the original with Word for Windows format. Click Yes if you don't need the original saved in its original format, or click No and then use File ➺ Save As to save the Word document under a new name.

No conversion process is 100% perfect 100% of the time. There may be little things involving page setup or formatting that get screwed up in translation. That's life. Usually Word does a pretty good job of converting, though.

Save Word documents in other formats

If you want to give a document to someone else who doesn't have Word for Windows, you can save it in another format for them. Select File ➺ Save As. The familiar Save As dialog box will appear. In the Save File as Type list box, select the word processor whose format you want to save the document in. Then type a new file name and click OK.

If the word-processor format you want to save your document in is not one of the ones in the Save File as Type box, try one of the generic formats, such as Text Only, DOS Text, Rich Text Format, or one of the variations on these. You may have to experiment with a couple of copies to find the method that preserves the most formatting information.

Links & Converting

Word for Recovering WordPerfect Users

If you're a former WordPerfect user, then you may be finding a lot of Word confusing. The old key combinations you memorized just don't work any more. I hope this book has eased your transition a bit. As far as converting existing WordPerfect documents goes, the instructions in the previous two sections apply to WordPerfect as well as other word processors, so read them if you haven't yet.

The people at Microsoft (who make Word) are very keen on recruiting ex-WordPerfect users, as you may already know if you bought your copy of Word at a heavily-discounted upgrade price. To make you feel more at home, they have built in two special features. You can make the WordPerfect key combinations work in Word, and you can get special WordPerfect Help that explains the Word equivalent of every WordPerfect command.

Get around your documents the WordPerfect way

If you miss those old WordPerfect cursor-movement key combinations (such as Home Home ↑ to get to the top of a document, instead of Ctrl-Home), then you're in luck. You can install those key combinations as shortcuts instead of the standard Word key combinations. (The Word "navigation" keys are explained in Chapter 2, *Can't Get There from Here*.)

To do so, select Tools ➻ Options and choose the General category. Check off WordPerfect Document Navigation Keys and then click OK. There, does that feel better?

Use WordPerfect keys as shortcuts or for Help

You may have noticed another WordPerfect option on the General category Options dialog box (Tools ➻ Options, then General). If you check off WordPerfect Help and then click OK, you'll be able to press WordPerfect keys (besides the navigation keys) and either get immediate results or an explanation of the Word equivalent in WordPerfect Help.

So, for example, you can make a selection bold by pressing F6, the WordPerfect bold key, but if you press Shift-F7, the WordPerfect print key, the WordPerfect Help window will open up and explain the Word equivalents to the WordPerfect print commands, or even demonstrate the Word command for you. WordPerfect Help is explained further in the next section.

Get WordPerfect help

There are several different ways you can get WordPerfect help. At any time, you can select Help ➺ WordPerfect Help, and the WordPerfect Help window will appear (see Figure 18.5).

Now click the WordPerfect command you want the Word equivalent for (or press the WordPerfect key or key combination). An explanation will appear in the middle of the box. If the WordPerfect command has sub-options, double-click it to choose one. If you've got your answer, click Close.

If you want to refer to the help as you try out the Word command, select Help Text and then double-click the command you want to try. You'll return to Word with a little window to guide you through the procedure. Click Close when you're done.

If you'd like to see Word demonstrate the command you're interested in, select Demo and then double-click the command. Word will run through the procedure (just like a macro). If the demo was too fast to follow or annoyingly slow, select Help ➺ WordPerfect Help again and click Faster or Slower to choose a different speed.

If you'd like more explanation of the Word equivalent to the Word-Perfect command, click the Word Help button and the regular Help window will appear with the appropriate help text.

You can click the Automatic Keys to get the same effect as the Word-Perfect Help option on the General Options dialog box, explained in the previous section. If the WordPerfect Help window comes up when you don't want it, click the Disable Automatic button.

When you're done with WordPerfect Help, click Close.

Links & Converting

FIGURE 18.5:
The WordPerfect Help window explains the Word equivalents of WordPerfect commands.

Select a WordPerfect command here, or just hit the WordPerfect command key (or key sequence). Commands followed by ... have subcommands you can choose from

Select Help text and then double-click the command you want the equivalent for and a help window will guide you through the procedure

An explanation of the Word equivalent will appear here

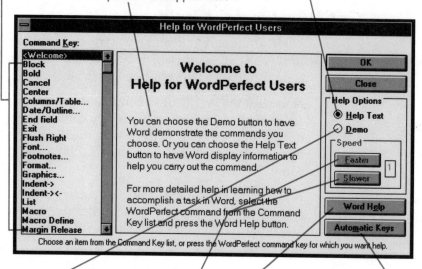

Select Demo and then double-click the command you want and Word will demonstrate the Word equivalent for you

Click Word Help to get more explanation of the Word equivalent from the regular help system

You can determine how fast the demo will run by clicking these buttons

Click Automatic Keys if you want this window to appear whenever you hit WordPerfect key combinations (this is the equivalent of the Word-Perfect Help option in the General category Options dialog box)

Chapter 19

LITTLE-KNOWN FEATURES TO MAKE YOUR LIFE EASIER

Crawford's Law of Expertise: As soon as you've mastered every trick in your program, a new version will come out

---

HERE IS A grab bag of features that might come in handy for you some time.

Make Icons for Your Documents, the Macintosh Way

If you ever wish Windows were more like the Macintosh interface, or envied Mac users, who can just click on a document icon to open up a document and its program at the same time, well, you can do the same thing.

First, switch to the Program Manager and open up the group you want to put your document icon in (or create a new Documents group). Then open the Main group and start the File Manager. Make sure the Program Manager group is still visible on the screen. Browse through the File Manager until you find the document you want to make an icon for. Then click it and drag it into the Program Manager group you want it in. An icon will appear. Figure 19.1 shows a document icon in a Program Manager group called Documents.

FIGURE 19.1:
I make icons for documents that I want to open frequently—you can too! Read on.

Now you can just click that icon to start Word and open that document.

If you didn't get a Microsoft Word icon for your document, it will still work. That means there's something screwy with your associations. That's a Windows thing I don't want to get into. If you know how to change the icon for a Program Manager item, then you can do it for your document icon.

You can also create document icons from scratch with the Program Manager's File ➤ New command. You just have to remember and include the entire path for the document.

Calculate Mathematical Problems Quickly

Sure, there's a calculator built into Windows and you may even have one on your desk, but you can also do math directly in Word. I'm not talking about spreadsheet-style table math (although that's possible too). All you have to do is type the equation you want to solve (use * for times and / for divide). Then select the mathematic expression and select Tools ➤ Calculate. Word will show you the result of the calculation in the status bar. Better yet, the solution is in the Clipboard, so you can just paste it over the selected expression.

Save Your Place
in a Long Document with a Bookmark

If you know you'll need to return to a spot in a document regularly, and you don't want to fumble around getting there, you can insert a bookmark to save the place for you. With the insertion point in place, select Insert ➤ Bookmark. The Bookmark dialog box will appear. Type a bookmark (and keep it short, because you might have to type it again later to get back here):

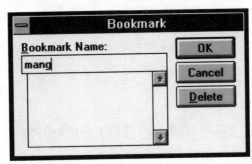

When you want to return to the marked place, select Edit ➤ Go To (remember, you can get to Go To by pressing F5 or double-clicking the status bar). Select the bookmark and click OK (or double-click the bookmark). You will be returned to the saved space.

Secrets

Collect a Bunch of Selections and Drop Them All in One Place

If you ever need to cut or copy more than one selection and then paste all your selections into one place, you can use the Spike. The Spike is named after the old-fashioned spike that office-workers used to impale receipts or invoices or whatever on. The Spike is a special breed of glossary entry. (Glossary entries are explained in Chapter 15, *Automatic for the People*.)

I use the Spike in a macro to create chapter outlines, by pulling out all the headings from my chapters one-by-one and then depositing them all in one place. *Voilà!* an outline.

To use the Spike, select the first item you want to put on the Spike, then press Ctrl-F3. The item will disappear from your document. Repeat this process as often as needed until you've cut everything you want. Then move the insertion point to the destination for all the Spiked items. To insert the contents of the Spike and empty it at the same time, press Ctrl-Shift-F3.

Bear in mind that the entries you store in the Spike are deleted from your document. Save it first, or save it as a new name, just to be sure you don't screw something up.

If you want to insert the contents more than once, you can treat the Spike like any other glossary entry. Type the word **spike** (case doesn't matter) and then press F3. The contents will be inserted in place of the word *spike* and the Spike will not be emptied.

Move the Ruler to a Pane for Close Measurements

If you're setting up a tricky header or footer and you'd like to have the ruler closer to your work, you can move it to the pane (you can move it to any pane, for that matter). First open the header or footer (or other) pane. Then click in the document area above the pane. Select View ➡ Ruler, so the ruler disappears. Then click anywhere in the pane and select View ➽ Ruler again. The ruler will appear in the pane. When you close the pane, the ruler will return to the main document window.

Make Cross-References That Update Themselves

One of the most difficult things in publishing is inserting references to exact page numbers into a document, because until the editing and formatting is absolutely finished, the pagination is constantly changing. With Word, however, you can insert cross-references that use fields to stay up to date (oh, no, not fields!). Here's how to use them.

First select the text you want the cross-reference to refer to. Now insert a bookmark. Select Insert ➽ Bookmark, type a name, and then click OK. (Bookmarks are explained a little more thoroughly above, in *Save Your Place in a Long Document with a Bookmark*.)

Now put the insertion point where you want the page-number reference to appear. Select Insert ➽ Field. The Field dialog box will appear. Select Page Ref. in the Insert Field Type box (you can hit *p* twice to get to it). Then select the bookmark name in the Instructions box. Click the Add button and then click OK. The page number will appear at the insertion point (or a field will, if you're displaying fields). Now, if the location of the relevant text changes, the page number will change with it, at least when you update the field. To update the field, select it and press F9.

Put a Precise Zoom Button on the Toolbar

If you often need to fine-tune your zoom percentage, you can put a button on the Toolbar that will let you click and drag to the right amount. To do so, select Tools ➽ Options and choose the Toolbar category. Make sure Commands is selected, not Macros. Then select ViewZoom100 in the Tool to Change box, and ViewZoom in the Commands box (you can use the same button). Click the Change button and then the Close button. Now you can click what was the Zoom 100% button and drag

Secrets

along a big cartoon arrow to the exact percentage you want, like this:

If you decide you don't like the Zoom button, select Tools ➤ Options and Toolbar, select ViewZoom in the Tool to Change box, and click the Reset Tool button. Then click Close.

Open Up the Style Area to Keep Track of Styles

If you're desktop publishing, or creating any kind of document that uses a lot of styles, you may want to be able to see which style applies to each document. You can do this by opening up the style area, an area of the screen you probably didn't know was there, because by default, its width is zero.

To open up the style area, select Tools ➤ Options and then the View category. Type a number of inches in the Style Area Width box (half an inch is usually okay), or click the little arrow buttons to select a width by .1-inch increments. Then click OK. The style of each paragraph will now appear down the left side of the screen in the style area (see Figure 19.2).

FIGURE 19.2:

This letter uses many
different styles, as you
can see in the style
area on the left.

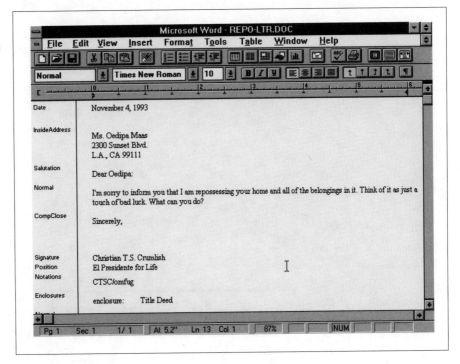

If you want to change the width of the style area, you can just click on
the line that divides it from the regular text and drag it as you would
drag a split bar. To reduce the style area width to zero again, just drag
the divider all the way to the left.

6

Tauber's Law: Preparing for a disaster only makes other disasters more likely to occur

This is the 911 section of the book. If something goes wrong (and, of course, it will), turn here for relief. If you want to make some preparations to avoid or minimize disasters, look no further.

In Case of Emergency, Break Glass

Chapter 20

DISASTER RECOVERY

Crumlish's Law of Irony: The closer a deadline comes, the more likely your computer is to crash

---

EVENTUALLY, SOMETHING'S GOING to go wrong. If you've been stuck working with a computer for any amount of time now, you've probably had a disaster or two already. Frankly, there's no avoiding it. Your computer is going to crash, your hard disk will die some day (as everything does), your copy of Word has bugs in it, you'll kick the plug out of the wall, there'll be a power outage (there was one here yesterday), and so on. All you can do is prepare yourself for the inevitable, and minimize the damage once it's done.

In this chapter, I'll tell you a few things you can do to avoid some disasters, I'll run through some typical calamities that may occur, and I'll give you a suggested course of action for when that bad day comes. This is the last chapter in this book, so I'm expecting all hell to break loose all around.

I Told You So

If there is one thing I've told you throughout this book, it's save your work regularly. I'll let you in on a little secret—I've broken probably every safety rule I know, so I'm in no position to lord it over anyone. Maybe that's the best way to learn these lessons. If nothing else, try to learn from your mistakes.

When something bad happens, don't just get upset or mad at yourself, ask yourself if you could have done anything different to avoid the disaster. If the answer is no, then just chalk it up to the hazards of the computer age. If it's yes, then ask yourself if you should add that safety measure to your regular routine. If it's a real hassle, maybe not. You have to weigh chronic inconvenience against one-shot big-time inconvenience.

An Ounce of Prevention

Here are some simple things you can do if you're disaster prone, to minimize the risk of disasters. I'm not going to tell you to save all the time again, but if you didn't read Chapter 1, *All You Really Really Need to Know about Word for Windows,* then you should know about autosave.

Start autosaving if you haven't yet

With autosave, Word saves your document in a temporary file at some regular interval. If Word, or Windows, or your computer, or the entire electrical system in your town crashes, there'll still be a fairly recent copy of your document there on your disk for you when you get things started again. To turn autosave on, select Tools ➺ Options and then select the Save category. Check off Automatic Save Every and enter a number of minutes you can live with. That's the number of minutes of work you're willing to lose in an emergency. Make it as small as you want. Then click OK.

Have Word make backups for you

You can make a backup copy of a document at any time by just selecting File ➺ Save As and saving it under another name. But you can set things up so Word makes a backup of the previously saved version of your document every time you save it. This may seem like overkill, but it just takes the safety procedure one step further. That way you'll always have the last two saved versions of your documents, and if you really screw things up and then accidentally save it, you're not screwed.

To have Word make backups for you, select Tools ➥ Options and select the Save category (see Figure 20.1). Then check off Always Create Backup Copy. (If you had Allow Fast Saves checked off, it gets unchecked. You can't have both.)

FIGURE 20.1:
The Save Options dialog box. Here's where you tell Word to make backup copies.

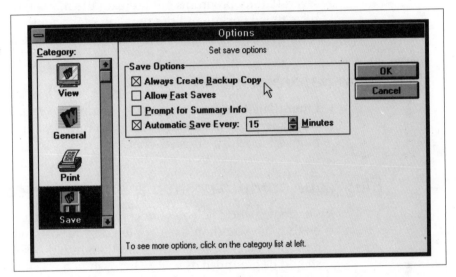

Now, every time you save your document, Word will first save the previous version of the document with the same name but the extension .BAK. These files don't pile up, though, because each time you save, the previous version of the document becomes the backup file, replacing the old one, and the new version of the document replaces the previous version. You *will* end up with two copies of every document, though, doubling your disk storage requirements.

Back up important documents to (floppy) disk

Hard disks are not immortal. They suffer from head crashes that basically ruin them, and a myriad of other ailments with a variety of results. You should always keep copies of important documents on floppy disks, and ideally, you should store those disks somewhere else than where your computer is, or in a fire-proof cabinet. What's an important document? One you might need in a hurry, or don't want to retype, or both.

If you've really got your act together, you should make a complete backup of your entire system at some regular interval, such as every week, or twice or month, or whatever works for you. You don't need to back up your applications, since you have the disks for them in case of emergency (assuming you didn't pirate them, of course). There are several utility programs out there on the market, such as Norton, that have timed backup utilities that can mostly automate the backup procedure for you. The new version of DOS, DOS 6, has such a utility.

Save before printing

I mentioned this in Chapter 17, *Printing Problems and Solutions*. Always save your document before you print it. Printing is a vulnerable moment in which disasters often occur.

Plug your computer into a surge protector

The dealer who sold you your computer probably already sold you on this, but you should really plug all your computer components into a surge protector power strip, and then into the wall. (The wall outlet should be grounded as well.) Then, when a spike of energy comes arcing toward your machine, your machine will be protected, instead of crisped inside.

Some Typical Disasters

Here are a few of the most common types of disasters, and some direction about how to recover from them.

My computer froze up (or broke down or died)

Sometimes computers just seize up from the digital equivalent of indigestion or muscle cramps. Sometimes your computer's fine, but Word

or Windows becomes catatonic. How you respond to this kind of problem, in which the screen is usually frozen, or partly missing, and the
keyboard has no effect, depends on whether you saved your document
recently or not. If you did, you can probably just restart your machine
and get on with things (unless the computer really is broken in some
serious way, in which case it might be a while or forever before you get
your document back). If you haven't saved recently, follow the advice
in the upcoming section, *First Aid*.

I can't believe I quit without saving

You exit Word so often that after a while it becomes a mindless routine,
which is okay. But then, for reasons no one understands, you inexpli-
cably click No when you're asked if you want to save changes. Or maybe
you didn't realize which document Word was asking you about. (I did
that just yesterday, and ended up having to retype two paragraphs.)

If you've got autosave going, you can probably resurrect a fairly recent
version of your document. But whatever you typed since the last
autosave (or since the last real save, if for some reason you don't have
autosave turned on) is blowin' in the wind. It was never stored on the
disk, just in the computer's memory, which is transient and now empty
for all intents and purposes.

I saved something bad over something good

I'm proud to say I've done this one too. I deleted over 90% of a document and then, intending to save it as a new name, I accidentally
selected File ➤ Save. So my 30-page document was replaced with one
paragraph. That's a tough one even if you have the capability of un-
deleting files, because your document isn't deleted, it's just gutted.
Again, autosave or a .bak version of your document would save
your neck.

Another fine mess—buggy problems

When using Word, you may well encounter apparently inexplicable
screwups, such as your document suddenly becoming a single vertical
column one character wide and hundreds of pages long, or something

somehow trashing the margins, headers, and footers you've carefully set in a template.

Some of these screwups are caused by bugs in Word—some of the commands don't yet work perfectly. Other screwups you may bring upon yourself by striking an esoteric key combination.

*If you do **hit some strange key combination**, and you're not sure what it was, Edit ➥ Undo might be able both to **tell you what you did** and **restore your document.** Even if you can't undo the problem, Repeat may tell you what you did.*

The only thing you can do to avoid glitches in the product is to make sure you have the most up-to-date version. From time to time, Microsoft quietly publishes updated versions of its programs (so-called *bug-fixes*). Last time I checked, they were up to version 2.0c of Word for Windows. They don't advertise these interim releases, so you have to write or call Microsoft and request them.

First Aid

Now I'm going to give you a suggested course of action for when something does go wrong. Different problems ultimately require different responses. But the moments immediately after disasters strike are remarkably similar, and it's a dangerous period, during which minor problems often become major ones.

Don't panic!

I know that's an easy one to say, but sometimes, the best thing you can do immediately after a bad thing happens is to get up and walk away from your machine. If you don't touch anything, nothing will get worse. (It's like the doctor's oath, "First of all, do no harm.") Also, you probably need to express your frustration in some safe way, not by pounding the keys or smashing your monitor.

Think the problem through. Figure out what the worst-case result will be and how you can live with that. Then figure out what the best possible resolution will be and think about how to achieve that result. (If you're worried that autosave will save a fouled-up version of your document over a good one, don't worry. If you don't touch anything and nothing changes, autosave takes a break.)

Quit without saving a fouled up document

If you've just replaced every letter in your document with # or deleted a huge selection by mistake or somehow fouled things up beyond belief *and* it's too late or otherwise impossible to undo your error *and* you've been saving regularly up to this point, consider quitting Word (or closing the document window) without saving the current screwed-up version of your document. You may lose a little work that way, but it may be better than losing a lot of work.

If you haven't been saving regularly, but you do have autosave turned on, then don't quit Word the normal way. Read the next section.

Shut down Word without quitting

If you've destroyed a document, but you've got autosave on, then there should be a fairly recent undestroyed version of the document in a temporary autosave file. The thing is, if you quit Word the normal way, it will delete all the autosave files as a matter of course, because autosave is designed to help you when the computer crashes and you don't have the opportunity to quit and save the normal way. In effect, you have to simulate a computer crash in this situation by shutting down Word.

Follow this same procedure if Word has frozen and you can't get it to respond to the keyboard or the mouse.

Press Ctrl-Alt-Delete (hold down Ctrl and Alt and press Delete). You will get a full-screen message from Windows with a list of options. To shut down Word, press Enter. This may return you to Windows, or Windows may also be frozen. If you still can't get any response from the computer, press Ctrl-Alt-Delete again and your computer will restart.

If Windows is working fine, you can start Word again from the icon. Word will automatically open up any autosave temporary files that it didn't have the chance to delete when you shut it down, and you will then have the most current available version of your document. A restored document will have "Recovered" after its title until you save it again. Save it immediately under a different name, then look to see what kind of shape it's in. Sometimes recovered documents are not fully recovered from what ailed them.

Bring a deleted file back to life

One of the advances of the last few years in the PC world is how easy it has become to bring a deleted file back to life. This is because when a file is deleted, it's not really erased from the disk—it's just marked as deleted and forgotten about. Now, it's true that eventually, newly-saved files will replace the deleted file, so you should generally try to restore a deleted file before doing anything else. The more water under the bridge, the longer the odds against resurrection.

The reason why I'm discussing deleted files at all is that autosave files are deleted when you quit Word and every time you save your document. Just like files you delete yourself, autosave temporary files can be undeleted with the DOS UNDELETE command or with Norton or other Unerase or SmartErase utilities.

If you know you'll need to resurrect deleted files, you should probably *reboot* the computer rather than exiting Windows the normal way, because Windows does a lot of saving (of temporary files that it uses) in the background, without telling you. If you quit the normal way, Windows may blunder into the remains of the file you want to undelete.

If you have a **boot disk** *(a floppy with a copy of DOS on it), put it in drive A before rebooting. Then press Ctrl-Alt-Delete and skip the next two paragraphs. If you don't know what I'm talking about, forget it.*

To reboot, press Ctrl-Alt-Delete, and if you get the full-screen message with options, press Ctrl-Alt-Delete again.

When your computer restarts, you might want to interrupt the autoexec procedure that begins happening automatically, to make sure it doesn't mess up any deleted files or put too much stuff into memory that might hinder the reconstruction of a badly destroyed file. To interrupt, press Ctrl-C repeatedly until you get the message

```
Terminate batch job (Y/N)?
```

Type **Y** and press Enter.

Then use UNDELETE or run your Norton Utility Unerase program off a disk. Temporary files will be in the directory your document was in, and there will probably be a number of ghosts (erased files) listed there. Their file names start with the tilde character (~) and end in .tmp and have gibberish in between. Look at the dates, times, and file sizes to see the most recent and biggest version of your file. After you undelete it, you'll have to rename it to open it in Word. Don't give it the same name as a file that already exists.

Reconstruct a badly damaged file

If you can't find an intact version of your document, you can use Norton's Unerase (if you have it—and if you don't and you're in this fix, consider running out and buying it) to search the entire disk for key text in the document and then piece the file together with the Manual Unerase feature. This method is not guaranteed to work and you might get a file that's missing some of its contents or even has other junk in it, but that may be better than nothing.

Give up and retype what you lost

Yes, sometimes you're better off just surrendering to fate and chalking it up to experience. I know it's no consolation, and whenever you have to write something again, it seems like it's not half as good as the vanished first draft, but you can also spend two or three times as long sifting through your computer's insides than it would take just to recreate the lost work. I understand that impulse, and on principle, I've sometimes spent a long time resurrecting deleted text when I knew it was possible, even longer than it would have taken to write it again from scratch.

If you've printed your document before it was destroyed, you can retype it from that hard copy, but somehow that rarely seems to be the case. Otherwise, you're stuck trying to step into the same stream of consciousness twice.

The Six Steps of Disaster Recovery

So what are the lessons of disaster recovery? I hope you take away with you these simple truths:

1. Take precautions.

2. Keep calm.

3. Do no additional harm.

4. Reconstruct as much as possible.

5. Recreate when necessary.

6. Learn from your mistakes.

Mega-Index

Are you ornery enough to take on The Murphy's Mega-Index?

There's a **MURPHY'S LAW OF INDEXES** too. It says that even if you list something in an index ten different ways, someone will always come along ornery enough to look for it an *eleventh* way!

If you look for some information in our index, and you do not find it listed the *first way you look it up*, let us know. We'll add your eleventh way of looking it up to future indexes AND you will earn yourself a place in Indexers' Heaven!

Throughout the index, we have used certain typographical conventions to help you find information. **Boldfaced** page numbers indicate primary explanations. *Italic* page numbers indicate illustrations.

Numbers and Symbols

Boldfaced page numbers indicate primary explanations.

Italic page numbers indicate illustrations.

Mega-Index

Boldfaced page numbers indicate primary explanations.

Italic page numbers indicate illustrations.

Boldfaced page numbers indicate primary explanations.

Italic page numbers indicate illustrations.

Italic page numbers indicate illustrations.

Boldfaced page numbers indicate primary explanations.

Italic page numbers indicate illustrations.

G

Boldfaced page numbers indicate primary explanations.

Italic page numbers indicate illustrations.

Boldfaced page numbers indicate primary explanations.

Italic page numbers indicate illustrations.

Mega-Index

Boldfaced page numbers indicate primary explanations.

Italic page numbers indicate illustrations.

Boldfaced page numbers indicate primary explanations.

Italic page numbers indicate illustrations.

Boldfaced page numbers indicate primary explanations.

Italic page numbers indicate illustrations.

Boldfaced page numbers indicate primary explanations.

Italic page numbers indicate illustrations.

Boldfaced page numbers indicate primary explanations.

Italic page numbers indicate illustrations.

Boldfaced page numbers indicate primary explanations.

Italic page numbers indicate illustrations.

Boldfaced page numbers indicate primary explanations.

Help Yourself with Another Quality Sybex Book

SYBEX

FREE BROCHURE!

Complete this form today, and we'll send you a full-color brochure of Sybex bestsellers.

Please supply the name of the Sybex book purchased.

_____

How would you rate it?

_____ Excellent   _____ Very Good   _____ Average   _____ Poor

Why did you select this particular book?

_____ Recommended to me by a friend

_____ Recommended to me by store personnel

_____ Saw an advertisement in _____

_____ Author's reputation

_____ Saw in Sybex catalog

_____ Required textbook

_____ Sybex reputation

_____ Read book review in _____

_____ In-store display

_____ Other _____

Where did you buy it?

_____ Bookstore

_____ Computer Store or Software Store

_____ Catalog (name: _____)

_____ Direct from Sybex

_____ Other: _____

Did you buy this book with your personal funds?

_____ Yes   _____ No

About how many computer books do you buy each year?

_____ 1-3   _____ 3-5   _____ 5-7   _____ 7-9   _____ 10+

About how many Sybex books do you own?

_____ 1-3   _____ 3-5   _____ 5-7   _____ 7-9   _____ 10+

Please indicate your level of experience with the software covered in this book:

_____ Beginner   _____ Intermediate   _____ Advanced

Which types of software packages do you use regularly?

_____ Accounting	_____ Databases	_____ Networks
_____ Amiga	_____ Desktop Publishing	_____ Operating Systems
_____ Apple/Mac	_____ File Utilities	_____ Spreadsheets
_____ CAD	_____ Money Management	_____ Word Processing
_____ Communications	_____ Languages	_____ Other _____
		(please specify)

Which of the following best describes your job title?

_____ Administrative/Secretarial _____ President/CEO

_____ Director _____ Manager/Supervisor

_____ Engineer/Technician _____ Other _____

(please specify)

Comments on the weaknesses/strengths of this book: _____

_____

_____

_____

_____

Name _____

Street _____

City/State/Zip _____

Phone _____

PLEASE FOLD, SEAL, AND MAIL TO SYBEX

SYBEX, INC.

Department M

2021 CHALLENGER DR.

ALAMEDA, CALIFORNIA USA

94501

SYBEX

SEAL

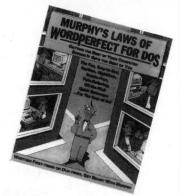

ALWAYS SMART, NEVER BORING.

THE MURPHY'S LAWS COMPUTER BOOK SERIES FOR EVERYONE

There's no law that says that learning about computer software has to be boring—except, of course, in the Republic of Freedonia. So Sybex is pleased to offer this new smart, simple, and wryly irreverent series—the Murphy's Laws Computer Book Series.

Written to entertain *and* inform, these books will help you to excel with Excel, dominate DOS, get the word on WordPerfect, do Windows, and more. They're packed with problem-solving, pain-relieving advice and step-by-step instructions in language even non-nerds can understand. (What a concept!)

So look for the Murphy's Laws Computer Book Series. As they say in the Saturday morning toy commercials, "Buy one or collect the set." Just visit your favorite bookstore or, if they're out, call Sybex at 1-800-227-2346.

Look for books in this series about DOS, WordPerfect for DOS, Word for Windows, Excel, Windows, and PCs.

SYBEX